DEVELOPING
GAME INTELLIGENCE
IN SOCCER

by Horst Wein

REEDSWAIN PUBLISHING

First published in Sevilla - Spain by CEDIFA (Centro de Estudios, Desarrollo e Investigacion del Futbol Andaluz), Sevilla 2000 under the title "Futbol a la medida del adolescente"

**Library of Congress
Cataloging - in - Publication Data**

Developing Game Intelligence in Soccer
Horst Wein
ISBN No. 1-59164-071-7
Lib. of Congress Catalog No. 2004092402
© 2004

Art Direction, Layout and Proofing
Bryan R. Beaver

Printed by
DATA REPRODUCTIONS
Auburn, Michigan

Reedswain Publishing
612 Pughtown Road
Spring City, PA 19475
800.331.5191
www.reedswain.com
info@reedswain.com

CONTENTS

PART TWO
DEVELOPING GAME INTELLIGENCE IN DEFENSE

PART THREE
THE INDIVIDUAL GAME

PART FOUR
ORGANIZING THE VICTORY

INTRODUCTION: THE DEVELOPMENT OF GAME INTELLIGENCE IN SOCCER

Each era is characterized by certain tendencies or fashions. This applies also to soccer. While teaching and coaching soccer was orientated in the early 50's and 60's mainly on improving technical skills, the following decade focused mainly on the physical preparation of soccer players, an aspect which up to then had been underestimated. The World Cup 1990 in Italy initiated a tendency in which individual, group and team tactics were considered fundamental for achieving good results, especially against stronger teams. And now in the first decade of a new century, where is soccer going? What will become a tendency in soccer teaching and coaching for the years to come? Certainly, there are different views and opinions about it around the globe but it could be of interest to know which of the various tendencies will finally come out.

Today, to make sure of frequent victories it is absolutely necessary to develop complete players with **excellent technical ability, physical fitness, tactical knowledge and mental capacity**. But is there still something to improve in their performance which has been left behind? Which aspects of the development of a complete soccer player has not been considered or stimulated sufficiently in training to bring the game to a superior level?

There is one aspect of the player's performance which needs more attention within the learning and teaching process which soon may become a tendency all over: **the development of game intelligence in soccer**, that quality which allows a player to recognize and adapt to situations on the soccer pitch quickly in the high pressure atmosphere of the match. Without a doubt, game intelligence is already an important criterion in evaluating the performance level of each player in many areas.

The development of the intellectual capacities of youth and adult soccer players is still in its infancy, largely due to the authoritarian teaching style preferred by the vast majority of trainers and coaches to shape and coach their players. The frequent instructions and hints that the players receive from the sideline before a game and during its development are not sufficient to take the game to a higher level.

The only way to improve the standard of play in the medium and long term is to, among other things, start a systematic development of thinking and tactical awareness from a very early age with the emphasis on a progressive stimulation of their perceptive and intellectual capacities. As the player's ball skills get better and better, he should also perfect his knowledge and thinking, **not only developing his muscles and tendons but also his brain**.

It is well known that practicing, experimenting and observing gives any child a wide variety of different experiences. Going one step further and using and interpreting these experiences leads to a correct behavior pattern when faced with different situations both in life and in soccer. But if nobody guides the child and helps him to interpret his experiences, he will never reach his full potential, either in life or in soccer. What he needs is the experience of an adult, to offer advice, to question almost everything and to give examples. This is not only true for everything the child experiences, for example in school or with the family, but also as far as the development of his overall performance is concerned.

As soon as possible, depending on the technical level of the player, all youngsters should be exposed during training to simplified games to gain first-hand knowledge and tactical experiences about the correct way to acquire tactical habits. **The more knowledge the youngster acquires, the better!** But subjective experiences alone are not enough! The acquisition of experiences and knowledge is much better when it is a result of a well-proven pedagogical process where the coach uses questions and demonstrations to unlock the development of experiences and knowledge so that they are clearly understood. Stimulation, encouragement or advice, an explanation or demonstration by the coach, together with the appropriate number of repetitions of the same game situation and subsequently the transfer of the solution to other similar situations that occur in the game forms a solid foundation in the young soccer player's mind for developing his game intelligence.

Intelligence must be developed mainly through the **global** and not the analytic method, exposing the players to a series of technical-tactical simplified games such as 3 v 1, 2 v 1 or 3 v 2. Depending on the simplified game, each player has to face and resolve a series of problems which should be shaped perfectly to his physical, technical and mental capacities. A great variety progressive exercises and games are proposed in this book which will help to develop step by step the youngster's tactical thinking and awareness until he has discovered himself, with the coach as a guide, a great variety of solutions for almost every situation that he may confront in a soccer game. It doesn't matter if the solution was discovered thanks to the frequent repetition of a similar situation in training or due to his imagination, creativity and spontaneity. The important thing is that the player has been able to understand and read the situation and resolve the problem successfully.

The ability to quickly and efficiently vary a previously learned skill is only possible when the player has been exposed to a systematic development of his intellectual capacity from a very early age right through to top performance level.

Good perception, a vital requirement for any player, followed by a correct interpretation of the game situation and the ability to make good decisions culminates in a good technical execution of the mentally prepared move. All these phases of the playing action must be coached over a period of years in order to be able to raise the performance level of any player.

What does game intelligence mean?

In soccer, every position in the team or task to perform requires a specific type of intelligence. The one required of a goalkeeper is totally different to that of a central defender or a front-line attacker as problems in attack are not resolved in the same way as they are in defense or in the middle of the field as in front of the goal.

The **intelligence** of a player should be considered as **the real driving force behind his performance**. Often, the difference between one soccer player and another is the level of intelligence he demonstrates in the game. His intelligence explains his success.

A high level in soccer is only possible when making constant use of game intelligence. Neither a player who is physically fit and technically proficient but without an alert mind or intelligence nor one who is capable of resolving problems mentally but is unable to transfer his brilliant ideas into actions which benefit his team can be considered a **complete player**.

Unlocking and developing systematically a soccer player's game intelligence is still beyond the knowledge of many coaches and teachers. Unfortunately there is no literature about developing this important aspect either in soccer or in other sports and few coaches are prepared to modify their coaching style (please consult the last chapter of the book "Stimulating game intelligence and understanding of soccer") which is an important prerequisite for being able to stimulate game intelligence. The continuous commands and instructions given by most coaches before, during and after the match prevent most of the players from using their intelligence. Instead of confronting the players in training with a great variety of problems to be resolved, they receive day by day the solutions to the problems from the coach which they have to obey. This rigid and authoritarian coaching style doesn't develop intelligent players with awareness and responsibility.

To get more intelligent players on the pitch in the future, coaches need to **stimulate more and instruct less**. Instead of being instructors on the soccer pitch, they should become consultants, guides or organizers of information, knowing how to complement the teaching of technical skills with the accumulation of game specific knowledge, thus achieving significant learning!

"There is no greater power on the field than the players' intelligence"

Developing game intelligence in any soccer player implies teaching him to:
• read the game and understand what is happening on the pitch (for which a certain level of perception, knowledge and experience is necessary),
• draw on past experiences when confronting any given situation to come to a correct decision,
• execute with an appropriate skill level, and quickly, the previously thought solution.

Apart from being able to **'read' the situation in the game**, an intelligent player can **anticipate** how the play is likely to develop thanks to the information previously processed. The ability to anticipate, which is always the result of good perception and decision making, is a significant tool for intelligent players.
To be able to focus maximum attention on his problem or task at hand and decide quickly and intelligently about his next move, his technical skills should have been consolidated and automated beforehand. Doing so, the quality of his game will be raised and the player will perform at a higher level. It is necessary to make intelligence work for soccer in order to achieve a better game!

Nobody is born with a high level of game intelligence in soccer, but to develop their innate potential, players must be exposed daily to a **varied and progressive training program with simplified games**. They are an ideal tool to unlock and not only develop game intelligence in any player, but also will hone his technical and tactical skills.

"A varied and progressive training program with simplified games is the best way to develop and improve intelligence in soccer step by step"

How does a soccer player's intelligence manifest itself on the field?

An intelligent player:
- generally chooses the best option in less time
- not only looks for the best solution to the problem he is confronted with on the pitch by quickly prioritizing all the various alternatives, but also calculates the risk factors involved. He rarely loses focus until he has resolved the situation.
- knows in any moment of the match how to give the adequate speed to the ball and to the rhythm of his team .
- is never rushed and feels secure and confident when performing a particular move anywhere on the pitch. He controls with his eyes all the space around him, in front, behind and to either side, taking full advantage of both very limited space and wide-open spaces! He always appears to have time. He knows that rushing and doing things too quickly tends to produce errors.
- always tries to achieve a balance between taking risks and safety. Too much risk could mean losing the ball or even the match, while playing without any risk rarely helps to turn the match to your favor. He is brave enough to take risks!
- stands out because he can adapt to the ever-changing situations in the game, to the referee, to his teammates , to his opponents and to the pitch and weather conditions.
- knows that things do not always come off. This is why his performance level rarely dips after making a mistake or two or three in a row.
- knows when and where to pass the ball or when it is better to keep possession.
- has good optical - motor assessment or spatial awareness. Assesses correctly the distances between him and his teammates and the opposition or to the lines of the pitch and the location of the goals, acquired through many years of practice with simplified games which also sharpened his decision making capacities.
- keeps it simple. Only a master, an outstanding player, can play simply.
- knows what he is going to do with the ball before he even receives and controls it.
- uses his creativity to the benefit of his team and teammates.
- knows how to play soccer, especially without the ball, constantly making himself available for his teammates to which he offers possible solutions to many situations that arise on the pitch.

"As soccer is largely a cognitive game it is advisable to focus learning on constructing a significant knowledge database, achieved by a balanced interaction between player, coach and situations in context"

Eduardo de la Torre (1998)

- is a player who contributes all his qualities for the good of his team. A soccer player who doesn't use his intelligence to serve his teammates around him will never succeed in the game because he will then tend to perceive only a portion of the whole game, seeing plays completely isolated and not in context with the whole. This type of player doesn't see everything that is taking place on the pitch.
- frequently asks questions and quickly learns from his mistakes. He is good at memorizing a great variety of plays and reproducing them.
- only does what is within his capabilities.
- knows how to pace himself throughout a game. His experience allows him to make appropriate decisions such as when to run or when it is a waste of energy.
- is not affected by stress, knowing that a high level of stress tends to narrow his focus and perception capacity and also influences his decision making negatively. This explains why sometimes key players do not make positive contributions in decisive matches. The pressure nullifies their usually intelligent play.

Communication and collaboration: requirements for optimal team performance

Playing soccer well not only demands the correct execution and application of different soccer techniques, tactical moves and physical and mental capacities, but also that the members of the team interpret the game the same way and achieve a mutual understanding which allows them to cooperate efficiently on the field.

To learn to pass the ball with different techniques, to run free from a marker, to channel an opponent, to tackle him, to shoot at goal or beat an opponent in 20 different ways is relatively easy. But to learn to play soccer is a different thing and much more difficult, because all of the above mentioned skills have to be melted together to form something superior: game playing in which intelligence plays a decisive role.

The first is an individual experience which many players dominate, but the second is a collective experience between various players who have to know and take into consideration the various principles of making collaboration and team work possible. Soccer is a team sport in which success depends on good communication and collaboration. Without them a well played game would not be possible.

The person responsible for achieving team play is the coach. He develops rules for his players to follow to allow optimal communication and collaboration between all team members. In the match, all the players must speak the same soccer language.

As the capacity to construct words and phrases is a requirement for lingual communication, the ability to execute the most characteristic soccer techniques and tactical moves could be considered as a base for a perfect mutual understanding in the game.

All actions on the field in which two or more players are involved have almost a lingual character. A player who, for instance, passes to the ball to a teammate after a mutual visual agreement with him, expresses with his attitude the following to the receiver: "Take the ball and do something valuable with it". That means that the pass should not be considered in soccer only as a technical-tactical ability but also as a social interaction and non verbal communication with a teammate.

"Without a common language it is difficult to decide the soccer match to our favor"

Playing soccer means looking out constantly for communication under pre-established norms. Before passing the ball, the player in possession has to evaluate the possible risks, considering the abilities and capacities of the ball receiver as well as his opponents in the vicinity. How he executes his pass and when he plays it depends on all these factors.

In the same way, a teammate who expects a pass has an expectation which has to be interpreted well by the ball carrier. Only when a player interprets the expectations of others and also anticipates his own play, will the next move on the field be a successful one.

Another example: When a player dribbles the ball diagonally close to the opposing penalty box toward a closely marked teammate, the latter has to perceive and interpret the intention of the ball carrier and act immediately as he expects the initiation of a through pass or a switch between both players involved.

To make sure that any play between two team members does not finish with a loss of possession, the expectations and the non verbal communication between both players should be interpreted and understood perfectly by both. The mutual understanding achieved in this way is different in soccer than in other team sports.

As a particular word may have different meanings in various contexts, a particular technique or move in soccer may give various kinds of information to the other players in the team, depending on the actual game situation. For instance, a run of one player into an open, uncontrolled space may mean to the ball carrier either: "Give me the ball" or "Here's a space for you to penetrate".

Consequently, all players of one team have to learn to interpret the actions of another teammate in relation to the actual game situation with the aim to achieve an optimal mutual game understanding. This must be taught from grassroots levels onwards and finally to coached at the professional level to perfection. But this requires a frequent participation of all components of the team in all training sessions as well as in the official competitions throughout various seasons.

"The way our players communicate between themselves and the way each individual communicates with himself often determines the quality of our team"

PART ONE

DEVELOPING
GAME INTELLIGENCE IN
ATTACK

THE POSITIONAL ATTACK:
ITS START AND PROGRESSION

"The three or four players of the last line of defense, when in possession of the ball, are the only ones who always play with a numerical superiority. Therefore it is their task to build up the attacks"

INTRODUCTION

When a team wins possession, but on starting the attack sees that the opposition are all back covering in defense and there is no possibility of springing a surprise, they should opt to play a planned and well-ordered positional attack, where there is little risk of losing the ball.

The objective of all positional attacking play, apart from keeping possession, is to make progress up the pitch where the final objective is to shoot at goal from the best possible position.

Positional attacks have a series of characteristics, or tactical rules, that allow the strikers to communicate and collaborate in the success of the move. The most important are as follows:

- **Risky passes should be avoided** in order to keep possession of the ball, even if this means passing it backwards as many times as necessary.

- Achieve **numerical superiority** near and around the ball as often as possible.

- **Reduce the number of runs with the ball and avoid 1v1 situations**; instead, pass the ball to a well-positioned teammate with better opportunities to continue the move.

- Develop **good play off the ball** (see "Keeping possession of the ball). It is particularly important for players to **support the man on the ball**. A player does 98% of his work during a game without the ball and this work is vital for success.

- Playing off the ball should be organized and meaningful. For example, if a player makes a forward run up field into the opponent's half, others should make themselves available for a side pass, through pass or back pass.

- Positional attacks require the collaboration of **all the players in the team**, regardless of which position they play.

- Once a team wins the ball, every player should quickly try to turn the defensive attitude into an offensive one as quickly as possible, looking to make the best pass or run to start the positional attack. Some go forward, while others move back, forming a **staggered formation**, and others make themselves available for attacking play down the wings. In this way, the principles of achieving **width and depth** are present in every positional attack.

- The player in possession has the option to pass the ball in several directions if his teammates know to spread out well on the pitch and take up good positions, allowing the build-up to continue and consequently making things more difficult for the defending team. It also helps to vary the main focus of the attack or switch the direction of an attack with a long ball played deep into the opposition's half. The latter should be played quickly and unexpectedly so that the ball arrives in space before the defenders have a chance to react and cover.

- When the attacking move involves three players they should always play in a **triangle**. If four players are involved, a **rhombus**, and if five, a **pentagonal** shape is the ideal formation.

- It is always best, if possible, to **pass the ball forwards** rather than to the side or backwards, but the golden rule, regardless of the type of pass played, is **never risk losing possession**.

- It is also very important that **eye contact and a visual agreement** is made between the player on the ball and the teammate he is about to pass to before he makes the pass.

- **Safety first** is always the most important thing when passing, receiving or controlling the ball.

"We should aim to avoid mistakes and the secret is to not be in a hurry"

Marie Curie (1898)

SIMPLIFIED GAMES

A PROGRESSIVE SERIES OF EXERCISES/GAMES TO PRACTICE THE START AND DEVELOPMENT OF THE POSITIONAL ATTACK

1. Learning to create space in a game of 4v2

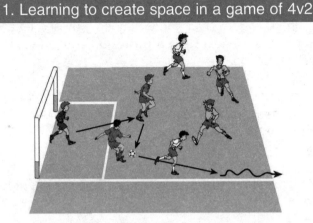

PITCH	One half of a full size pitch. Only 3/4 of the width of the full size pitch or the width of a 7 a-side pitch is used. Teams with lesser ability should use the whole width of the pitch.
PLAYERS	7 (2v2 with 2 neutral players on the wings and a neutral goalkeeper).
EXPLANATION	- After the goalkeeper passes the ball towards one of his 4 defenders (2 central defenders and 2 on wings) they develop a positional attack until they are able to cross the halfway line with the ball under control. The two opponents try to prevent this from happening. - Objective: 8 of 10 attacks should be successful.

LEARNING OBJECTIVES	- Knowing how to exploit the least defended areas by passing intelligently and by making effective runs off the ball, in order to take advantage of the space with good decision making and quick thinking.
	- Usually the best areas of the pitch to exploit are those opposite to where the ball is, whether that is lengthways or width ways.
	- In order to systematically create space for the attack, those doing the attacking (in this case 4 defenders) should:
	
	   - Secure possession of the ball without risking losing it. This is achieved by the excellent distribution of the 4 attackers throughout the pitch and by keeping the play simple.
	   - Keep changing positions to drag defenders out of the required zone.
	   - Play using one-touch soccer only when there is no risk of losing possession.
	   - Running with the ball should only be attempted under exceptional circumstances such as when there is no teammate available for a pass, but never in central areas of the pitch near the goal. However, further up-field, a successful dribble performed at the right time (when the defender is not covered by a teammate) gives the offense a numerical supremacy in attack.
	   - Study as many different offensive combinations as possible.

Note: See the chapter "Technical-tactical behavior before, during and after receiving and controlling the ball ", 2nd game, 3rd variation, in which the four defenders learn to pass and control the ball with an opposition.

Variation 1: Now, when the two opponents win the ball, they are joined by the two neutral players on the wings with the objective of scoring in the full size goal. Each goal is worth 1.5 points, each piece of control on the end line is worth 1 point, the first team to reach 9 points wins.

Variation 2: Two cone goals are set up in the wing position, placed 25 meters in front of the full size goal. The attacking defenders have to pass or run through one of these goals before controlling the ball on the center line.
This forces the players to use the space on the wings more, from where it is easier to penetrate and loss of possession is less likely.

Variation 3: Two cone goals are positioned on the center line. The 4 attacking defenders must dribble the ball through one of them. They have 10 attempts and should aim to achieve 8 controls.

> *"There is little to be gained, and much to be lost, by attempting to force young players into the full game before they are physiologically, biomechanically and cognitively ready for the activity. One of the fundamental goals of teaching is to ensure that every player has a high level of success. Therefore we need to assess the development readiness of the players in each age group"*
>
> *David Hemery in "The pursuit of sporting excellence"*

Variation 4: Apart from the two cone goals, one on the center line and another two (also 12 meters wide) are marked at 25 meters distance from the regulation goal. When the attackers score in either of the central goals they must finish the move in the opposite goal (2 points) or in the goal on the same side (1 point). In other words, if a player gets the ball through the goal on the right, he passes to his teammate on the other side, who controls the ball and goes through the goal on the left on the center line of the pitch.

Variation 5: To restrict running with a ball to a maximum, goals can be scored only with passes through the cone goals on the 25 meter -line or after on the center line.

THE FUNCTION OF THE 4 PLAYERS (DEFENDERS) AT THE START OF THE POSITIONAL ATTACK

WINGBACKS WITHOUT THE BALL:
They should take advantage of the width of the pitch making themselves available to receive a pass either inside the pitch some 4 meters away from the sideline or directly on the sideline, depending on whether or not an opponent is present. With no opponent in his channel, the wing back stays wide but if there is an opponent ahead of him he should come inside so that he has better passing options.

1 WINGBACKS WITH THE BALL:
The first option is to look to play a through pass parallel to the touchline to a teammate who makes a run into space in this channel. If this move is played in the opponent's half, make sure that the teammate is not offside.

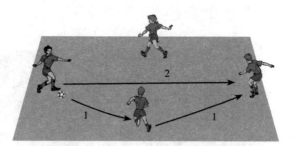

2 Play a powerful pass to the wingback on the opposite flank, disguising its direction. If the pass is too risky, the move is carried out in two stages: first the ball is passed backward to a central defender who, after one touch, passes the ball with a second to the other wingback. The quicker the change of direction in attack, the more likely it is to be successful.

3 If option 1 and 2 are not available, the wingback opts to take the ball inside towards the central areas of the pitch, away from where the opposition is pressing, and passes it to a teammate who made a switch with him (run behind him to fill his position).

CENTRAL DEFENDERS WITHOUT THE BALL:

1 When a wingback has possession of the ball, the central defender on the same side offers himself for a through pass, running diagonally into the depth of the field or for a back pass moving slightly backwards so that the 4 defenders do not attack too flat, which limits their attacking options and makes it easier for the opposition to defend against them. Under exceptional circumstances the wingback looks to make a run, preferably deep into the opposition's half, only if there is an uncovered space ahead of him and if his position is being covered by a central defender.

2 Move outside to cover the wing back if he makes a run inside towards the central areas of the pitch.

CENTRAL DEFENDERS WITH THE BALL:

1 If a central defender on the ball is put under pressure by an opponent he should play a diagonal pass back to the other central defender, who has dropped back to make himself available to receive the pass. Because of the low risk factor, this diagonal back pass is more desirable than a less safe side pass.

2 If the first and best move is not possible, the ball should be passed after a visual agreement with the wingback or winger on the same side, or with the winger on the opposite side of the pitch who is likely to have more space.

2. Making space in a game of 5v3

PITCH	One half of a full size pitch with its full width.
PLAYERS	9 (3v3 plus two neutral wingbacks and a neutral goalkeeper).
EXPLANATION	As Game #1. One of the three central defenders plays as a midfield player, always making himself available further up the field for a pass from any of the four defenders.

"We best learn to play soccer by playing simplified games "

3. Making space in a game of 4v3

PITCH	One half of a full size pitch. Initially, the full width is used, then ¾ width (40m).
PLAYERS	8 (2v2 plus two neutral wingbacks, a third neutral player and a neutral goalkeeper).
EXPLANATION	The third neutral player always helps the team not in possession of the ball. It is a good idea for this player to play in the middle so that he can easily swap teams.

4. Making space in a game of 5v4 (6v5)

The concepts and explanations of Game #1 have to be applied, including the variations 5v4 or 6v5.
>> See exercise #1 (Learning to create space in a game of 4v2)

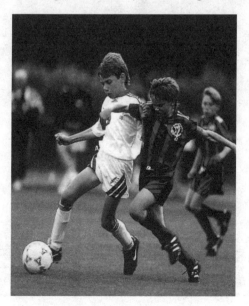

5. Playing 4v3 and 3v2 on different pitches

PITCH	One half of a full size pitch. Three zones are marked out using the width of a full size pitch: two zones of 22 meters separated by a 10-meter zone.
PLAYERS	13 (4v3 on the first 22-meter playing area plus a goalkeeper; 3v2 on the second 22-meter playing area.)
EXPLANATION	- First a 4v3 game is played with the ball being put in play by the goalkeeper (either with a throw or kick) towards one of his four attacking defenders. Although the three opponents do everything to stop them from progressing up field, they have to keep possession of the ball and mount a well-organized positional attack, until they are able to pass the ball without risk across the 10 meter-zone towards one of their three teammates in the second 22-meter playing area who have made themselves available for the pass despite the presence of two opponents. After the control of the ball they have to run with it across the center line. - On the first playing area, two of the three opponents play a two against one press against the ball carrier, while the third player covers. If the defending attackers manage to win the ball they mount a counterattack and try to score in the full size goal. No player is allowed to enter the central 10-meter zone. - Once an 80% success-rate has been achieved with the initial positional attacks in the first zone, the width of this area is reduced to 40 meters or two more players (an attacking and a defending midfielder) are introduced in the first playing area.

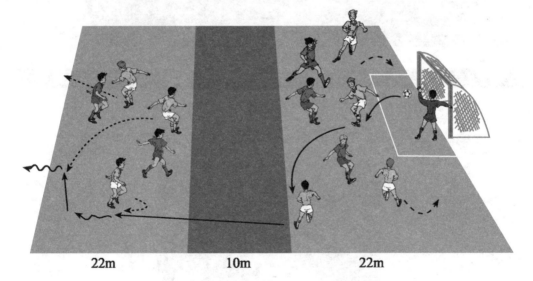

22m   10m   22m

"Passing the ball is easier than passing an opponent "

Variation 1: 4v3 and 2v2 on different pitches

PITCH	Two zones are marked using the width of a full size pitch: the first zone, where the attack starts, is 35 meters long and the other side expands from the theoretical 35 meter-line to the center line.
PLAYERS	12 (4v3 in the first zone plus a goalkeeper, 2v2 in the second zone).
EXPLANATION	- The goalkeeper initiates the 4v3 game in the first zone. His attacking defenders have to pass the ball at least 3 times to each other (for practice reasons) before they are allowed to play it with a through pass to one of their two teammates in the second zone. They learn to serve the ball into the space, particularly to the opposite space where the opponent is positioned. The objective of the two attacking teammates is to control the ball on the center line despite the pressure exerted by two opponents. - When, in the first zone, the ball goes to a wingback, his teammate in the second zone playing on the same side should make a run into the center of the pitch to create space for the wingback to play a long pass parallel to the touchline (a set move). This ball can be picked up by his teammate, who when the pass is made moves outside, completing a half circle run. - All the players must stay in their respective playing zone.

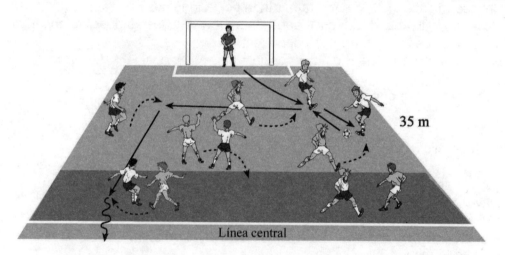

35 m

Línea central

Variation 2: Now one of the 4 attacking defenders can support his two teammates in the second zone if they are able to control the long pass.
It is important to learn which one of the four should do the supporting. They should finish the move by scoring in a full size goal that is 16.5 meters behind the halfway line after having managed to dribble the ball across the center line.

"Nothing can be understood completely as long as it wasn't experienced "

OBJECTIVES FOR PLAYERS INVOLVED IN A POSITIONAL ATTACK

The players who start the positional attack on the first pitch should:

- Observe and analyze the position of their teammates and of the opposition before playing a pass and running into space not defended by the opposition. It is imperative to know how and when to play the ball.
- Make eye contact with his teammate to indicate that he is about to pass the ball to him. He should always put enough pace on the ball.
- Choose to pass, instead of running with the ball, but if he runs, he should head towards an undefended area instead of trying to dribble through a crowded area.
- Avoid 1v1 situations and opt whenever possible for the numerical supremacy of 2v1.
- Always pass to the player who is in the best position and where there is less chance of losing the ball. If the only pass forward is a risky one, it is better to play the ball sideways or pass it back.
- Choose to pass the ball short rather than risk a long pass.
- Move the ball around with pace and with as few touches as possible, trying to conceal its destination from the opponent.
- Pass the ball along the ground if possible.
- After making a good pass, quickly run into space to an area of the pitch not defended by the opposition.

The three midfield players in the second area should:

- Lose their two defenders and make space ready to receive a pass from the player on the ball.
- Make eye contact with his teammate in possession of the ball on the first pitch and then quickly make a run into space so that when the pass is made he is favorite to receive it.
- Time their runs to perfection, not too soon or too late.
- Position themselves well tactically so that they have an advantage over the defenders and can continue the move.
- Control the ball on the move if possible and not from a static position.
- Make space for teammates by dragging their defenders to another area of the pitch.
- Change a 3v2 situation into a 2v1.

"Man must live in the middle of risk and safety.
Risk leads to self destruction, safety leads to stagnation.
Between both lies survival and progress."
Gunnar Breivik

6. 5v4 with a pass to a teammate on a different pitch

PITCH	One half of the full size pitch for the start of the attack and the other half for the finish
PLAYERS	13 (5v4 plus a goalkeeper in one half of the pitch; 1v1 plus a goalkeeper in the second half.)
EXPLANATION	- After the ball is put into play by the goalkeeper towards one of his five teammates in the first playing area, these players build up a positional attack with at least 4 passes (for practice reasons) before executing a through pass to their teammate in the second playing area. He is tightly marked and should try to control the ball and score in the full size goal defended by a goalkeeper. -The four defending attackers should play a press, making it difficult for the attacking defenders to mount a positional attack without risks. No player is allowed to leave his playing area.
LEARNING OBJECTIVES	- Knowing to occupy optimal positions in the width and depth of the field is fundamental for the success of the positional attack. The two wings make sure of the width in attack and the central defenders drop back and one midfield player pushes further forwards to give depth in attack. - Practice passing the ball around at speed with oriented controls, thus creating space. - Communicate as a ball carrier with the frontrunner to make sure that he receives the ball in the second playing area.

Variation 1: An extra player is added to each team (6v5 and 2v2).

Variation 2: 5v4 in each half of a full size pitch

PITCH	A full size pitch with a game of 5v4 in each half
PLAYERS	19 (5v4 plus a goalkeeper in the first playing area, 5v4 in the second)
EXPLANATION	- After the ball is put into play by the goalkeeper, the five attacking defenders should, for practice purposes, keep possession of the ball for at least 10 seconds until an opportunity arises to make an effective pass to one of their 5 teammates in the other half. These should control and keep the ball for at least 5 (10) seconds before passing the ball back to one of their 5 teammates in the first half. - The idea is to accomplish with 10 ball possessions (attacks) as many successful passes as possible from one area to the next.

Variation 3: 5v4 plus a goalkeeper and 4v5 plus a goalkeeper in the other playing area.

Each team is given possession of the ball 10 times to see how many successful passes they can achieve.

"A well played game of soccer generally starts from behind. When moving forward with the ball, it is often necessary to pass backward"

7. A game of 6v6 (7v7)

PITCH	One half of the full size pitch.
PLAYERS	13 (6 defenders plus a goalkeeper against 6 attackers).
EXPLANATION	The goalkeeper starts the positional attack by putting the ball in play. The team with 4 defenders, a goalkeeper and two midfield players should manage to control the ball on the center line of the pitch 4 times in 6 tries.

Variation 1:

In order to improve their play without the ball, the idea for both teams is to keep the ball as long as possible. The attacking defenders have the advantage of help from the goalkeeper, while the defending attackers are limited in their play because of the offside rule.

As a variation the coach can ask each team to play with one ball possession as many long passes as possible. A long pass should measure at least 20 meters.

Variation 2:

- 6v6 or 7v7 on 4 cone goals: Both teams try to dribble the ball across any of the two opposing cone goals(12 meters wide), placed in the wing positions on the center line and also on the end line of one half of the pitch.

Just as in previous games, the players should:

- ♦ Always support the player on the ball in attack or in defense. Cover the defender who tackles the ball carrier.
- ♦ Know when to pass the ball at the exact moment.
- ♦ Give width and depth to the positional attacks, looking to exploit the least defended areas in order to establish numerical superiority.
- ♦ Change the pace in order to surprise the opposition.

8. A positional attack carried out by one or two intelligent players

PITCH	One half of the full size pitch, or better still, a 7-a-side Soccer pitch, with two goals.
PLAYERS	14 (7v7 including a goalkeeper in each team).
EXPLANATION	- A team that wins possession of the ball in their own half cannot enter the opposition's half until their key player (indicated with a different shirt) has played the ball at least once. This player is tightly marked by an opponent and should therefore make himself available to get introduced in the build up of the positional attack. - Initially, it is a good idea to give the role of the distributor to the most skilful and intelligent player in the team. - If the ball is won in the opposition's half then a counterattack starts. - Later, each team plays with two key-players.
LEARNING OBJECTIVES	- Improve the way the distributor plays when not in possession of the ball. He should learn how to break free from his marker and play the ball under pressure. - His teammates learn to look for the best moment to pass the ball to him, despite being tightly marked

Variation 1: If the coach feels that the key players in each team are being put under too much pressure, he can change the rules, allowing the attacking team to cross into the opposition's half only after one of the two distributors has touched the ball.

Variation 2: The team is only allowed to cross into the opposition's half after each of the seven players in the side has touched the ball at least once.

TACTICAL RULES FOR THE DEVELOPMENT OF THE POSITIONAL ATTACK

- Support the player on the ball and always try to be in his field of vision, waiting for visual agreement before a pass is made.
- Don't wait for the ball to come to you, but go to it. This is especially true for long passes. Also decide on what you're going to do with it before you've even received it.
- Attempt to receive and control the ball technically perfect and with an optimal body orientation, always with your next move in mind!
- During the build-up look out constantly for areas of the pitch where there are few opponents or none.
- Put enough pace on the ball when passing, even if the pass is short.
- Passes should be well timed, accurate and not 'telegraphed'.
- Long passes should only be played when they are likely to be successful. If in doubt, play the ball short.
- If the circumstances allow, it is always preferable to play the ball forward rather than horizontally.
- When the attacking defenders are pressed, high or flat diagonal passes into uncovered areas of the pitch should be made.
- After making a pass, and depending on the outcome and how the rest of the team is situated, you should either support the player receiving the ball by quickly running into space or maintain your defensive position.
- Try to give width to the positional attack, whether you have the ball or not. This will create time and space to make the attack more effective.
- Change the pace of the attack when the moment is right, passing the ball into a teammate's path so that he can take it at full speed.
- Quickly change the direction of the attack or the focus of the attack
- Always seek to gain numerical superiority in attack, two against one.
- Force defenders to come out and challenge or drag them away from their defensive zone.
- Be aware of and adopt a variety of improvised attacking moves as they occur, making life more difficult for the defenders.
- It is better to counterattack if possible rather than play the positional attack.
- Keep it "simple".

"A player learns and grows by trial and error. The important thing is to learn from mistakes."

Moorhouse/Gross

KEEPING POSSESSION
OF THE BALL

"The most important thing is not having possession of the ball, but knowing what to do with it".

INTRODUCTION

REASONS FOR "FREEZING" THE GAME

Keeping possession of the ball for prolonged periods is a basic function for defenders and midfield players, as this allows the team with the ball to dictate the pace and rhythm of the game, develop and achieve numerical supremacy in attack, and ultimately, enjoy what is in essence the art of playing the game.

Other tactical reasons for "freezing" the game are:
- Playing in high temperatures.
- Being in numerical inferiority due to injury or a sending off.
- Playing specific critical moments during a game, such as the final couple of minutes at the end of each half, and the two minutes after having scored a goal.
- Being dominated by the opposition during a period of the game.
- Slowing down the game in order to organize the team or looking for a moment of reflection and calm.

In order to "freeze" the game it is imperative to know how **TO PLAY WITHOUT THE BALL** and to master certain technical skills such as passing, reception and ball control in all its forms.

KNOWING HOW TO PLAY WITHOUT THE BALL

Good positioning on the pitch makes it easier for the player in possession to play a safe pass to a teammate and makes it more difficult for the defending team to respond effectively.

As soon as a team wins possession of the ball all the players should **immediately look to take up a position on the pitch which will give them an advantage over their marker**. If, for example, a center forward drifts out to the wing, his marker has the option of holding his position, leaving the attacker in space ready to receive a pass, or following him, dragging the defender away from his defensive zone, thus leaving a space, which could be exploited with the incorporation of another attacker.

Well-organized and well-drilled movements off the ball by several attacking players at once demands a very high level of concentration in the defense, causing unease and uncertainty and producing a definite advantage for the offensive players.

A forward rarely plays in isolation as he should take into account where his teammates and his opponents are located, following and analyzing the play at all times, focusing on the movements of all the other players, calculating and imagining possible attacking options and their possible outcome. In other words, it is not just the position of the individual player, which is important, but especially his position in relation to the rest of his team.

Playing without the ball requires collaboration and understanding among all the members of the team. All the movements are compensatory, and so, while some players move forwards or to the wings seeking to exploit poorly defending areas, others move closer to the player on the ball. In this way, the player on the ball is given various passing possibilities. At the same time the movements without the ball produce a great physical exertion on the opposition's defense.

Some useful tips for good ball retention:
- It is **better to pass the ball** than run with it.
- Prefer **flat passes** to aerial passes because they are quicker.
- Passes along the ground are easier to **receive and control**.
- Keep the **goalkeeper involved** in the game.
- Take advantage of **the whole width** of the pitch.
- Develop moves **slowly and methodically** without rushing into things.
- **Avoid one-on-one situations**.
- Stick to the **tactical plan**.
- **Don't take risks** with moves which are not fully under control.

Other tips to counteract an opponent who plays a pressing game:
- Have plenty of **self-confidence**.
- Use your experience **(always be in the right place at the right time)** and don't lose patience.
- Make use of your **good perceptive skills** to **allow you to read the game correctly and produce a suitable solution to any problem or situation that arises**, like supporting a teammate or helping to give your side numerical superiority.
- **Keep it simple**, don't complicate things.

In conclusion, there is no doubt that if you follow this advice you will be able to keep possession of the ball with great success until the moment comes to accelerate the pace of the game by, for instance, playing a long accurate ball to a frontrunner.

In order to learn how to play the game by keeping possession of the ball it is important to practice a great variety of games and exercises.

"What every player should strive to achieve is, instead of worrying what your opposite number is doing, make him worry about what you're doing. How is this done? by having possession of the ball."

(Josep "Pep" Guardiola)

SIMPLIFIED GAMES

A PROGRESSIVE SERIES OF SIMPLIFIED EXERCISES/GAMES TO DEVELOP THE ABILITY TO KEEP POSSESSION OF THE BALL FROM UNDER 10s TO FULL INTERNATIONALS

1st TRAINING LEVEL - UNDER 10s

1. Keeping possession: Four static attackers outside against an active defender inside	
PITCH	A square of 6x6 meters
PLAYERS	5 (4 attackers and one defender).
EXPLANATION	-The 4 attackers stand at each corner but outside of the square. -They should pass the ball to each other outside the square, depending on where the defender is positioned inside, following the run of ball. The attacker on the ball should decide, without any rush, which of the two possible passes he should play (always parallel to one of the sides of the square and never diagonally). This of course depends on the position of the defender in relation to the possible receivers. The ball carrier learns to process all the information and chooses the safest pass which most likely guarantees the possession of the ball. - Before playing with the feet, it is a good idea to practice and gain experience in optimal passing by using the hands first.

"A simplified game is an integrated element of various dimensions (technique, tactics and physiques), which unfortunately are still taught and trained too often separately and without any context to the competition"

---

2. Keeping possession: Four semi-static attackers outside against an active defender inside

PITCH	A square marked by 4 cones with sides measuring 10 meters.
PLAYERS	5 (4 attackers and one defender).
EXPLANATION	- The 4 attackers form a rhombus. In other words, they are positioned at the central point of each sideline of the square but outside. They try to keep possession of the ball against a defender who is not allowed to venture out of the square. Without entering into the square, the 4 attackers should pass the ball, always without rushing, through the square across 2 sidelines. They are helped by the teammates without the ball who make themselves available for the pass, always with correct body positioning (orientation). - Again, before playing with the feet, it is a good idea to practice and gain experience in optimal passing by using the hands first.

Variation 1: The same as the first game but with two defenders in the square. Because there is more information to process, the task of the ball carrier is more difficult, but as he can now take as much time as he needs to read the game situation, he succeeds with the coach helping him to understand the key factors for passing to the best positioned teammate.

Variation 2: The same as the first game but with an additional attacker who is positioned inside the square in a 2x2 meter zone marked with cones in the middle of the playing area. He is the 3rd passing option for the 4 attackers. The defenders cannot enter the 5th defender's zone in the middle (see illustration on following page). When the attacker in the middle returns the ball to his teammate best positioned outside the square he has time to take into account the location of the two defenders. *(see the illustration on the next page)*

Variation 3: The same as above but now the player in the middle does not have to stay inside the 2-meter square, which has been removed. He can run to any spot of the playing area to receive and then return the ball.

3. Keeping possession: 4v1 in an unspecified area

PITCH	An unspecified area on the training field.
PLAYERS	5 (4 attackers and one defender).
EXPLANATION	- This game is played using hands. While the player with the ball looks for the best pass, the other 3 players offer themselves in correct positions to either side and in front of him (T-formation) in order to receive the ball. The direction of the ball depends mainly on the position of the approaching defender. - The ball cannot be thrown over the defender's head. The objective of the game is to keep possession of the ball for 20 seconds without letting it bounce and without giving the defender an opportunity to intercept it. - The defender wins the ball in two ways, either by intercepting a pass or by touching the player with the ball before he makes his pass. - After the practice with the hands the game is played with the feet.

Variation 1: The same as the original game but with three attackers against one defender. At first the players are shown how to make space and support each other without the ball. Then they practice in an unrestricted playing area, before finally playing in an area of 15x15 meters.

Variation 2: The same as the original game but now it is '5 against 2'. At first it is played in an unlimited playing area, which later becomes a square of 20 x20 meters.

Variation 3: The first two games are played with two defenders who, apart from intercepting passes, also win possession when they touch the player on the ball.

4. Keeping possession: 2v1 in an unspecified playing area

PITCH	Any area on the training field.
PLAYERS	3 (2 attackers and one defender).
EXPLANATION	- The player without the ball should support the player in possession, always breaking away from the defender in order to make himself available for a safe pass. The two attackers should either keep possession of the ball for 8 (10) seconds or make 6 (8) passes, but without kicking the ball over the defender's head. - The game is first played as handball and later is played with feet. - For a better understanding, initially the defender is not allowed to make challenges, thus allowing the second attacker time to seek the correct passing movement and his teammate to adopt the correct body position to receive the ball. - To win the ball the defender either has to touch the player in possession or intercept his pass.

2nd TRAINING LEVEL - UNDER 12s

5. Keeping possession: 3v1 without defense

PITCH	A square of 10x10-meters
PLAYERS	4 (3 attackers and one defender).
EXPLANATION	Three attackers positioned outside the square, each behind a different cone, pass the ball among themselves considering before each pass is made the position and body orientation of the defender inside the square. His movements and location determines the best pass to make.

6. Keeping possession: 3+1 against 1 inside the square

PITCH	A square 10x10 meters.
PLAYERS	5 (4 attackers and one defender).
EXPLANATION	The three attackers outside the square, with plenty time at their disposal, have to pass the ball correctly to the one who is best positioned to receive the ball as it was practiced in the game before. But now they also have the opportunity to pass the ball to a fourth attacker inside the square who shadowed by the defender. The defender conditions the movements of those outside, especially of the player in possession of the ball, and also of the attacker in the center of the square. It is recommended that first the three players practice the movements correctly playing handball in order to learn to make themselves available for a pass. This gives the player on the ball options for choosing the most intelligent pass.

Variation 1: After at least three passes outside the square the three attackers have only 5 seconds to serve the ball to their teammate inside the square. The latter is constantly making himself available for a pass, taking into account the position of the defender and the location of the ball. After receiving the ball he must return it immediately to one of the players outside, who should offer themselves for a pass.

Variation 2: 3+1 against 2 defenders inside the square

"The traditional coaching which was very much coach orientated concentrated merely on technical aspects, putting aside aspects related to motivation and knowledge."

Brenda Read

7. Keeping possession: 4+1 plus 2 neutral players against 2 defenders

PITCH	A square of 15x15 meters.
PLAYERS	9 (5 attackers, 2 defenders and 2 neutral players)
EXPLANATION	Each of the 4 attackers stands at a corner outside of the square. The fifth moves freely in the square supported by two neutral players. Two defenders inside the square try to stop one of the 4 static attackers outside from making a clear pass to the player in the middle or to one of the two neutral players. The neutral players in the middle try to make space and adopt a correct body position for making themselves available for a pass.

8. Keeping possession: 4v4 with a neutral player -Game of "prisoners"

PITCH	A square of 15x15 meters
PLAYERS	9 (4v4 plus a neutral player)
EXPLANATION	- This is played first as handball with the under 12s in their first year, and then as soccer in their second year. - The two "prisoners" in each team stand in diagonally opposed corners of the square. One of them starts the game by passing the ball to one of their teammates in the middle or to the neutral player. - The 5 players of one team should keep possession of the ball and look to make as many successive passes as they can to one another without losing the ball. Two defenders try to recover the ball and when they do they have the same objectives as the attackers had before. - The 4 static "prisoners" in the corners, not being allowed to be pressed by a defender, have a lot of time to choose the right pass and spot a player in the middle who is adopting a correct body position.

3rd TRAINING LEVEL - UNDER 14s

9. Keeping possession: 3v1 played on two playing areas next to each other

PITCH	Two contiguous 8-10 meter squares
PLAYERS	6 (3v1 on one area; two players stay on the second area)
EXPLANATION	-The three players on the ball try to keep possession as long as possible playing against one defender. If the latter wins the ball, or the attackers allow the ball to go out of their area, the defender kicks the ball to his two teammates on the other pitch, joins them and one of the three former attackers becomes the only defender on the other pitch in another 3:1 situation. -The team that keeps possession the longest is the winner.

8-10 m

8-10 m

"The natural order accounts for progressive development through time"

Variation 1: After each pass the player has to move at least 5 meters to another position. The ball is given to the opposing team when the passing player remains stationary.

Variation 2: Only high passes count (to improve receiving and controlling skills).

Variation 3: Only first-time passes count (to improve one-touch soccer).

Variation 4: Only passes made with the weaker foot count (to improve the weaker foot).

Variation 5: For older and more experienced players:Only headed passes count (to improve heading ability).

10. Keeping possession: 4v2 played on two playing areas next to each other

PITCH	15x30 meters, split in half lengthwise (15x15 m.).
PLAYERS	8 (4v2 in one area; the two teammates of the 2 defenders remain on the second pitch).
EXPLANATION	- As the previous game but now playing 4v2, after each pass the player must move to a different location in order to foster a dynamic game. - The team who keeps possession of the ball the longest is the winner. - For variations see the previous game.

11. Keeping possession: 4v2 (5v3) -Rescuing prisoners

PITCH	A square of 20x20 meters.
PLAYERS	8 players split into 2 teams of 4
EXPLANATION	- Two players of each team play in the center while the other two stand in diagonally opposed corners. Here they wait to be 'freed' by receiving a pass from one of their teammates. - Each team tries to keep possession for as long as possible without losing it to the opposition or allowing it to leave the playing area. Every time a player passes to one of his teammates in one of the corners (prisoners) he is 'freed' and the two players have to swap positions. - If the team with 4 players manages to keep possession of the ball for more than 15 seconds then they win a set. - To win the game a team has to win 3 sets

Variation 1: Instead of counting the time of ball possession, the number of long passes made during one ball possession is counted. Only passes of a minimum of 10 meters are valid. Short passes win no points for the team in possession. After each pass the player needs to move to another position. For an infringement of the rule, the attacking team loses the ball.

Variation 2: Only high passes count (to practice receiving and controlling a high ball correctly).

Variation 3: Only first-time passes count (to practice playing one-touch soccer).

Variation 4: Only passes made with the weaker foot count (to improve the weaker foot).

Variation 5: For older and more experienced players only the headed passes count (to improve heading ability).

Variation 6: Instead of just putting one cone at each corner, four cone goals 3 meters wide are established. Every pass made to the "prisoner" now has to be extremely accurate as it has to pass through the cone goal first. An inaccurate pass means that possession is lost.

Variation 7: Instead of being static behind his cone goal, each of the 4 'prisoners' actively looks to make himself available outside the square behind one sideline assigned to him. They constantly adapt to the play of the midfield players, offering themselves to receive passes from their two teammates inside the square.

Variation 8: Only one of the 'prisoners' in each team remains outside of the square where he moves constantly to offer himself for a pass from any of his three teammates inside. Once he receives a pass he switches positions with the passer.

Variation 9: The same game but this time with 2 teams of 5 players.

12. Keeping possession: "From 5v1 to 5v5"	
PITCH	Initially 1/8 of a full size pitch (5v1 and 5v2), later on 1/4 (5v3) and finally on half of the pitch (5v4 and 5v5).
PLAYERS	From 6 to 10 (a progressive sequence from 5v1 initially to a game of 5v5).
EXPLANATION	- 5 players try to keep possession of the ball against one defender in 1/8 of a full size pitch. 30 seconds later another defender joins the game and 30 seconds later a third etc. After 2 minutes the game converts to five against five, using half of the full size pitch. - The team that, despite the growing presence of the opposition, can keep possession of the ball the longest without making fouls or letting the ball leave the playing area, is the winner.

"The winner becomes generally the one who has given his very best"
Charles Buxton

13. Keeping possession: 2v1

PITCH	A square of 15x15 meters
PLAYERS	4 (2v1 plus a reserve who counts how many seconds the attackers keep possession of the ball).
EXPLANATION	- Two players try to keep possession of the ball for as long as possible against an opponent who tries to clear the ball out of the playing area. If he succeeds, the attackers infringe the rules or the ball runs out of the square, he swaps positions with his substitute. - The two attackers have 8 ball possessions to establish a time record, which subsequently the defenders try to beat when it is their turn.

4th TRAINING LEVEL - UNDER 16s

14. Keeping possession: Two games of 2v1

PITCH	There are 3 playing areas, two of 8 m. on the wings and a neutral zone of 12m in the middle, all 12m wide.
PLAYERS	6 (2v1 in each of the wing zones).
EXPLANATION	- Two attackers keep possession of the ball against one defender inside an established playing area with the additional possibility of playing long passes across the neutral zone to one of their two teammates in the opposite playing area where the ball must be received and then kept in possession until it can be returned the same way. - Every three minutes, one of the attacking pairs swaps positions and roles with the two defenders.
LEARNING OBJECTIVES	- Learning whether to run with the ball, pass it short or play a long pass. - Gaining experience in playing long passes (communicating with the player receiving the ball, hiding the intended direction of the ball and putting enough pace on the ball when passing).

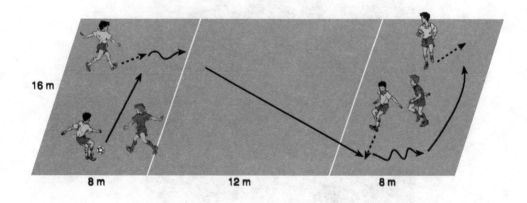

16 m   8 m   12 m   8 m

Variation 1: Game of 5v3 (2v1 +1v1+2v1)

Two additional players (an attacker and a defender) are introduced to the original game. They play in the neutral zone. The players in the outside playing areas can pass the ball directly to the players on the other side, or in stages, by passing it into the neutral zone where the attacker receives it then passes it to the other side, despite the presence of the defender.

Variation 2: Game of 4v4 (2v1+1v1+1v2)

- The 2 attackers in the first playing area try to get the ball to the teammate in the central zone or to the teammate in the other wing zone on the other side, despite the fact that the one in the middle is being marked by a defender and the one in the other wing zone is being marked by two defenders.

- The team of 4 players who keeps the ball the longest is the winner.
Note: This variation is for advanced players.

15. Keeping possession: 1v1

PITCH	A square of 10x10 meters.
PLAYERS	2 (1v1) and two other players for substitution
EXPLANATION	The game is started with a throw-in by a neutral and the idea is to keep possession of the ball for as long as possible.
LEARNING OBJECTIVES	- Learning to shield the ball, positioning the body in a side position between ball and defender which allows the ball carrier to read the game and watch the defender. - Learning to sell feints and dummies with the body and/or ball to gain valuable time and space. - Learning how to change pace and direction. - Learning to use the space behind when the opposition is blocking the way forward or to the sides.
CORRECTIVE GAME	Setting off from opposite corners, and with no ball, trying to tag the attacker as he escapes inside the playing area which should be increased to 15 x 15 meters. Clock the time.

10 m

10 m

16. Keeping possession: 3v2

PITCH	A square of 25x25 meters.
PLAYERS	6 (3v2 plus a substitute defender)
EXPLANATION	The 3 attackers should try to keep possession of the ball for as long as possible, while the two defenders do their best to see that this doesn't happen. After the ball has been won, or has gone out of the playing area, the substitute defender swaps with one of his fellow defenders. This way the defenders are always fresh. Attackers and defenders rotate and swap roles after every 10 "games".

"The only way to make strong people is through struggle. The best comes from difficulties"

Variation:

PITCH	An area 18 meters long and 15 meters wide divided into 3 equal zones
PLAYERS	6 (3v2 plus a reserve player who, from outside the playing area, times how long the three attackers manage to keep possession of the ball).
EXPLANATION	- Each one of the three attackers plays in a different area. They try to keep possession of the ball for as long as possible against two defenders who are free to challenge and pressure them in any zone. - At the start, no defender is allowed to enter the zone where the ball is located. Every time the defenders win the ball, or it goes out of play, the substitute defender swaps with one of the other two defenders. - With 5 attempts the team of three attackers tries to establish a new record of ball possession. - After, both teams swap positions and roles.
LEARNING OBJECTIVES	- Give depth to the attack and avoid playing on the same level. Instead, always adopt a staggered and triangular formation. - Hide the direction of passes and move the ball around at speed. - Systematically look to produce 2v1-situations to outnumber the opposition. - Learn to play the first-time pass when the opposition is pressing. - In defense, reduce the time and space available for the three attackers.

17. Keeping possession: 3v3 with a neutral player

PITCH	A square of 25x25 meters (the dimensions of the playing area have to be adapted to the standard of the players)
PLAYERS	7 (3v3 plus a neutral player who always acts as an attacker).
EXPLANATION	- Keep possession of the ball for as long as possible; when the ball is lost the defenders gain possession and attack supported by the neutral player. - No lifted passes are allowed, thus forcing the players to improve their play without the ball. After the pass has been made the player must move at least 5 meters.

18. Keeping possession: 4v4 with a neutral player

PITCH	A square of 30x30 meters (reduce or increase pitch size according to the standard of the players).
PLAYERS	9 (4v4 plus a neutral player who always acts as an attacker).
EXPLANATION	- Keep possession of the ball for as long as possible. When the ball is lost, the defenders attack, supported by the neutral player. - After the pass has been made the player must move away to offer himself again for a pass. - The player who loses the ball is deducted a point each time. - After 3 minutes of play, the scores of all players are compared.

"A player's performance level is not determined by comparing it with the other players. It should be related to his capacities"

5th TRAINING LEVEL - UNDER 18s

19. Keeping possession: 4v4	
PITCH	A square of 30x30 meters.
PLAYERS	8 (4v4).
EXPLANATION	- Keep possession of the ball for as long as possible. - For every 10 seconds they keep the ball the team gets a point. Losing the ball or if it goes out of play gives possession to the opposition. Each team has 6 ball possessions. - The team which scores the most points wins.

"The young soccer player should know that success is a stairway that he cannot climb with his hands in his pockets"

(American proverb)

20. Keeping possession: 5v5 (with and without a neutral player)

PITCH	A square 40x40 meters
PLAYERS	Initially 11 (6v5 with a neutral player); later 10 (5v5).
EXPLANATION	- Keep possession of the ball for as long as possible, first in a game of 6v5 (where one of the attackers is always the neutral player), and later in a game of 5v5 (with no neutral player). - For every successful pass longer than 10 meters a bonus of 3 points is won. - The coach may insist that the ball is to be played only along the ground.
LEARNING OBJECTIVES	- To learn, depending on how much pressure is being exerted by the defenders, whether it is best to keep the ball close to the feet or to play a short or long pass, while at the same time disguising the direction of the ball. - To learn how to play without the ball and play simple soccer to minimize risks.

40 m

40 m

Variation 1: Keeping possession with 3 teams of 5 players in two halves of the pitch

PITCH	A full size pitch split as shown in the illustration
PLAYERS	15 (3 teams of 5 playing a game of 5v5 in one half, passing to the other pitch where another 5v5 situation will arise)
EXPLANATION	- One of the two teams of 5 should keep possession of the ball, making at least 5 passes without leaving the playing area assigned to them. - After, they serve the ball to the third team of 5 players in the other half - Once the ball is with one of the 5 teammates in the other half, the team of 5 defenders from the first pitch tackles them to produce another 5v5 situation. The team that manages to play more through passes from one half to the other half wins.

"Don't look for guilty ones, look for remedies"

Henry Ford

Variation 2: 6v5 and 5v6 respectively played on two halves of a full size pitch

PITCH	A full size pitch
PLAYERS	22 (2 teams of 11, playing 6v5 on one half of the pitch and 5v6 on the other).
EXPLANATION	- After the goalkeeper puts the ball in play by passing to one of his five team-mates, they should try to keep possession for at least 6 seconds (1 point) before playing a long pass to one of their teammates on the other playing area, where they attempt to keep possession of the ball for another 6 seconds (1 point) despite being outnumbered by the defenders. The aim is to try to score as many points as possible. - Each team has ten ball possessions in a row with the goalkeeper starting the attack. - Instead of timing the game, the attackers could be asked to play at least 3 long passes of not less than 20 meters before passing it to their teammates on the other pitch.

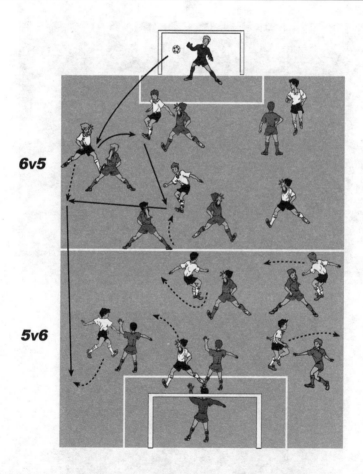

Variation 3: After passing the ball into the other half one player is allowed to go across and support his teammates, creating a 6v6-game.

21. Keeping possession: 7v6 to the center line

PITCH	Half of a full size pitch
PLAYERS	13 (7v6)
EXPLANATION	- The game starts with the goalkeeper putting the ball into play and the idea is to keep possession of the ball without taking any risks until the opportunity arises for the team to advance with it to the halfway line on the full size pitch. - Each team has 10 attacks. There is a one-minute break after every 5 attacks where the development and progress of the game is analyzed. - Depending on the performance level of the players, the game of 7v6 could be played with a goalkeeper who initiates the play with a throw-in (8v6).

22. Keep possession: "From one area to another"

PITCH	A square of 30x30 meters split into 4 equal sections of 15x15 (25 x 25) meters using cones.
PLAYERS	8 (4 games of 1v1) and later 16 (4 games of 2v2).
EXPLANATION	- One player from each team occupies one of the four areas (later on 2 players from each team). The team which conquers the through-ball in the first square tries to pass the ball from one area to the next without losing possession until they have completed a circuit, in other words, having controlled the ball in all 4 zones. - Once a pass has been made to another zone, the attacker (or later one of the two attackers) follows the ball to give the attacking team numerical superiority in the zone nearby, producing a 2 against 1 or 3 against 2 situation.
LEARNING OBJECTIVES	- Learning to pass to a teammate being marked, depending on how the opponent is marking him. - Learning to play without the ball. - Improving the perception and communication skills of the attackers. - Learning to use space effectively.

23. Keeping possession: 7v7

PITCH	Half or 3/4 of a full size pitch
PLAYERS	14 (7v7)
EXPLANATION	- The goalkeeper starts the game. Use a stopwatch to time how long a team of 7 players is able to keep possession of the ball or count the number of long passes they are able to produce (more than 20 meters) before the ball is lost. - The attacking defenders try to adopt a 'safety first' policy by supporting each other and creating 2v1 situations or passing the ball to the less marked teammate in space or back to the goalkeeper, always avoiding 1v1 situations.

Variation 1:
Depending on the performance level of the players, the above game of 7v7 is better played without the goalkeeper who initiates the play with a throw.

Variation 2:
- The goalkeeper is the neutral player who starts the game once for one team and then for the opposition. A player who loses the ball twice is eliminated from the game and the winner is the last player left on the playing field. Depending on the number of players, the coach may decide to change the dimensions of the playing area.
- To ensure that all players have the opportunity to practice and develop the techniques under pressure, the coach makes sure that a situation of an anomalous numerical superiority or inequality doesn't exist between the teams (for example 4v6, 7v5).
- Meanwhile, the players eliminated from the game practice keeping possession of the ball in a 2v1 situation.

Variation 3 (for less experienced players): Another two or three players make themselves available along any of the lines of the playing area but they are not allowed to go inside the playing area to play the ball.

24. Keeping possession: 8v8

PITCH	A full size pitch
PLAYERS	16 (8v8)
EXPLANATION	- The players are split into 8 pairs (attacker-defender). When one of the players has lost the ball twice the pair is eliminated (as worst attacker or best defender) and so on until only one pair remains with the player on the ball proclaimed the winner. - The playing area is made smaller and smaller relative to the number of pairs left in the game.

25. Keeping possession in 3 areas: 4v3, 5v5 and 3v4

PITCH	The full size pitch is split into 3 zones. The first two in one half of the pitch and the third taking up the other half.
PLAYERS	26 (4v3 in the first, 5v5 in the second, 3v4 in the third zone and two goalkeepers)
EXPLANATION	All players have to stick to the area assigned to them. The attackers in the opening zone are asked to pass the ball at least 3 times before playing it to the next area. The team that scores more goals during the 10 possessions wins. Goalkeepers should also take part in this game.
LEARNING OBJECTIVES	- Learning to communicate on the pitch and establish visual agreements between passer and receiver before passing the ball. - Learning to play without the ball. - Improving the perception skills of all the players. - Learning to manage time and space effectively.

26. Keeping possession in numerical inferiority: 4v5, 5v6, 6v7 and 6v8

PITCH	One half of the full size pitch
PLAYERS	9 (4v5); 11 (5v6); 13 (6v7); 14 (6v8)
EXPLANATION	- The attackers try to keep possession of the ball for as long as possible despite being outnumbered by the defenders. To achieve this they have to play well off the ball and support each other, looking to create 2v1 situations anywhere on the pitch. - This game works well when played as a competition on an individual basis, with the winner being the attacker who loses the ball the least.
LEARNING OBJECTIVES	- Learning to create situations of numerical superiority (2v1). - Learning to play slowly (to keep possession longer), shielding the ball using the body and forcing the opposition to commit fouls. - The defenders learn how to pressure and harass with order and discipline.

27. Keeping possession with two balls: 8v4 and 8v5

PITCH	One half of a full size pitch
PLAYERS	12 (8v4) or 13 (8v5)
EXPLANATION	The attackers try to keep possession of two balls for as long as possible without letting them go out of play.
LEARNING OBJECTIVES	- Learning to communicate on the pitch and establish visual agreements before passing the ball. - Learning to play without the ball. - Improving the perception skills of all the attackers. - Learning to manage space effectively.

"From the practice point of view every hour doesn't have 60 minutes: an hour only consists of so many minutes you are able to profit from"

COACHING MODEL: KEEPING POSSESSION

1st training level- Under 10s
Keeping possession: 4 static attackers outside vs 1 defender inside
Keeping possession: 4 semi-active attackers outside vs 1 defender inside
Keeping possession: 4 v1 in an unspecified area
Keeping possession: 2v1 in an unspecified area

2nd training level- Under 12s
Keeping possession: 3v1 without defense
Keeping possession: 3+1 outside against 1 inside
Keeping possession: 3+1 outside against 2 inside
Keeping possession: 4+1 plus 2 neutral players against 2 defenders
Keeping possession: 4v4 plus a neutral player-Game of "prisoners"

3rd training level- Under 14s
Keeping possession: 3v1 played on two areas next to each other
Keeping possession: 4v2 played in an area next to each other
Keeping possession: 4v2 (5v2) -Rescuing prisoners
Keeping possession: "From 5v1 to 5v5"
Keeping possession: 2v1

4th training level- Under 18s
Keeping possession: Two games of 2v1
Keeping possession: 1v1
Keeping possession: 2v2
Keeping possession: 3v2
Keeping possession: 3v3 with a neutral player
Keeping possession: 4v4 with a neutral player

5th training level- Under20s
Keeping possession: 4v4
Keeping possession: 5v5 with and without a neutral player
Keeping possession: 7v6 with progressing to the center line
Keeping possession: "From one area to another"
Keeping possession: 7v7
Keeping possession: 8v8
Keeping possession in three areas: 4v3,5v5 and 3v4
Keeping possession in numerical inferiority: 4v5,5v6,6v7 and 6v8
Keeping possession with two balls: 8v4 and 8v5

"Any change requires an initial period of discomfort, until the body and the mind adjust to the new demand."

ATTACKING FROM THE MIDFIELD

"It is generally assumed that the more you know about something, the better you will be at doing it. But a certain innocence will help you to perform better".

L.Moorhouse/L.Cross

INTRODUCTION

When the front-line attackers are being very closely marked and the ball is not getting to them easily, it is important to rely on players from the midfield (or even defenders) who know how to break forward from deep and surprise the opposition.

The players who attack from midfield will have more success if they do the following:

- Have a perfect understanding with the front-line attackers.
- Have a clear idea about what they are trying to achieve: whether it is to score or to distract their opponent. If they are looking to have a strike at goal they should take a good shot and be alert to any possible rebound off the goalkeeper.
- Make sure that their incursion does not affect the tactical balance of the team, that adequate cover is available and, if necessary, that the defenders move up to the midfield in order to set the offside trap in case possession is lost and the opposition mounts a counterattack.
- Quite often a good way to make attacks from the midfield more effective is for the front-line forwards not to spread out along the whole width of the pitch, but to occupy positions in the center or only on one flank. This forces the defender to go with them and concentrate on a very limited zone, where they mark their opponents, leaving space for an attack from the second (midfield) or third line (defense) through the wing channels or the opposite flank.

Numerous tactical variations of positional changes exist to create these spaces. It may also be worthwhile to practice a variety of different moves in which the players have to work together as a unit and synchronize their movements, both with the passing and ball reception, just as with the creation and use of space.

One of the important moves in this sense is what is known as the switch.
In a switch a player in possession of the ball drags his marker to one area of the pitch with a diagonal run, then pass the ball to a teammate who is coming from behind and offers himself in the former position of the ball carrier without any opposition.

Here is a series of progressive moves to practice attacking from the midfield.

Note: The majority of the proposed games also help to develop and improve cooperation skills and teamwork in defense, especially as far as interchanging with the attackers being marked is concerned.

"Small detail may dramatically change the outcome"

EXERCISE/GAMES

A SERIES OF PREPARATORY EXERCISES AND SIMPLIFIED GAMES TO PRACTICE ATTACKING FROM THE MIDFIELD

- **Preparatory Exercises 1 to 4**
- **Simplified Games 5 to 8**

1. Switching positions in the depth of the field

PITCH	A long rectangular playing area on the training pitch
PLAYERS	3 (2v1)
EXPLANATION	The player on the ball plays a long pass to his teammate who runs to meet the ball. As he controls and shields it from the defender, the passer runs behind the defender to support his teammate and make himself available to receive the ball in the depth of the field.

2. Triangular play with penetration

PITCH	A rectangular playing area anywhere on the training field
PLAYERS	4 (2v2) and 5 (3v2)
EXPLANATION	Two or three attackers practice triangular play with direct passes. The player who initiates the play from behind finally receives the ball as a front-line attacker in an uncovered space. As the combination progresses, the defenders become more active.

3. The 'switch' without opposition

PITCH	A rectangular playing area anywhere on the training field
PLAYERS	2
EXPLANATION	- The player on the ball dribbles the ball diagonally towards his teammate. When he is about 6 meters away, the latter suddenly runs behind the ball carrier, ready to receive a perfectly timed pass in the original position of the ball carrier. - The object of the 'switch' is: ◆ To break free from the tight marking from the opposition. ◆ To create space for a teammate to exploit. ◆ To hide real intentions and distract the opposition. ◆ To speed up the offensive move.

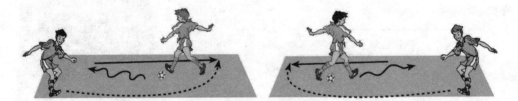

4. The 'switch' with passive opposition

PITCH	A rectangular area anywhere on the training field
PLAYERS	3 (2v1)
EXPLANATION	The ball carrier runs diagonally away from his defender into the channel of his teammate, encouraging his defender to follow him. When the teammate notices the intention of the ball carrier, he switches with him, ready to receive a pass in an open space before the defender can challenge the ball carrier.

Simplified Games:

5. 3v3 with two wide goals

PITCH	A square of 30x30 meters
PLAYERS	6 (3v3)
EXPLANATION	- The team in possession of the ball tries to cross the opposition's end line with the ball under control and after having executed at least one switch with or without a dummy pass. - During the diagonal run with the ball, before passing it in the opposite direction to his teammate, the ball carrier fakes the pass then suddenly changes speed and takes the ball out of the reach of the surprised defender into the depth of the field.

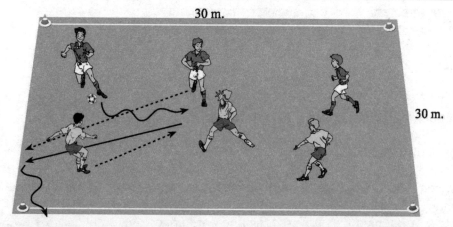

30 m.

30 m.

6. 4v4 with an attack from midfield

PITCH	An area of 30 x20 meters
PLAYERS	8 (3v3 with an outlet player on each team)
EXPLANATION	- A game of 3v3 is played in the designated playing area, plus an extra supporting player for each team stands behind their own goal-line. - The player with the ball can pass it to one of his two teammates within the playing area or to the one behind his own goal-line. The outlet player always makes himself available to receive the ball on the opposite side to where the ball is in order to open up the game and encourage the ball carrier to create space. If the ball is passed backwards to the player outside the field (attacker from the 2nd line), the passer swaps positions with him. After an oriented control of the ball the new ball carrier penetrates up-field to make optimal use of the space. His aim is to cross the opposition's goal-line with the ball, either individually or with the help of a 1-2 combination with one teammate. - To assist him in his advance, his teammates take their defenders with them to the opposite part of the playing field. - The decisive pass to open up the game, made to the player on the outside, needs to be played at pace, with accuracy and by surprise (so that he can take the ball in stride on the run), after having concentrated all defenders in a small area of the playing zone. - The three defenders, for their part, should regroup and reorganize when a run is made from deep, changing their marking but continuing to control their respective zones. The defending outlet player behind the goal-line is not allowed to enter the playing area without the ball.

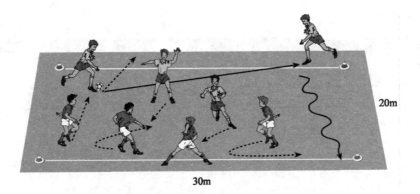

Variation 1:
Any of the 3 attackers can swap positions with the fourth player after the ball is played backwards across their own goal-line.

Variation 2:
The fourth defender can defend, but he cannot move off his goal-line.

Guidelines for attackers and defenders

FOR ATTACKERS:
- Create space systematically by running diagonally with the ball and executing switches with or without dummy passes, then penetrate by injecting a sudden change of pace.
- When a teammate is in possession, create space systematically by running towards the player on the ball, who, as he sees the defenders are being 'sucked' in, decides to pass back to the outlet, positioned behind the goal-line on the opposite side as far away as possible.
- Once an open space has been created, the player should take advantage by advancing with determination and speed.
- Don't risk losing possession of the ball by playing it within the defenders' reach.
- Packing all attackers in a small area of the field allows your midfielders or defenders to make use of the crated space by coming from behind with surprise.
- It is better to play the decisive pass into the run and not directly into the feet of the receiver. He should receive the ball at high speed to be able to make use of the open space.

FOR DEFENDERS:
- Concentrate and have a lot of defensive discipline.
- Communicate and support one another.
- Know when to hand an opponent to your teammate to mark in order to take care of another attacker, especially when the attack comes from deep..
- Make sure of a quick turn-over from defense into attack once the ball has been won.

7. 5v5 (6v6) with attacks from midfield

PITCH	An area of 30 x 20 meters
PLAYERS	10 or 12 (5v5 or 6v6)
EXPLANATION	See game 6

8. Support from the midfield after a successful long pass

PITCH	A 7-a-side Soccer pitch divided into 3 areas
PLAYERS	10 (5v5)
EXPLANATION	- The game starts with a thrown ball in the central area. A midfield player from either team can only enter the opposition's area after a long pass has been played out of the midfield to a single forward. Once the forward is ready to receive the ball, one of the three midfield players on the opposite side from where the ball is received advances up the field towards the opposition's area to support the player receiving the long pass. He then may receive the ball or the frontrunner scores himself with the midfield player going for the rebound. - A goal scored by an attacker is worth 1 point but a goal scored by a midfield player is worth 3 points.

>> SEE the chapter "The capacity to play through passes", variation of game #10

Important rules to attack from behind

- Create space systematically by making diagonal runs with the ball. Once the defender has been dragged out of his position, play a well-disguised surprise pass in the opposite direction (switch) to a teammate coming from behind.
- As frontrunners without the ball, create space systematically for the player on the ball and invite him to penetrate in the open channel.
- Make surprise attacks from deep, breaking from the defense or the midfield, with or without the ball.
- Always be alert, ready to take advantage of and exploit any space not being defended by your opponent.

-THE 2v1-SITUATION-
A BASIC ELEMENT OF THE
COLLECTIVE GAME

"The art of guiding players is nothing more than the art of associating their ideas"

INTRODUCTION

Winning or losing a match depends on a wide variety of factors, not just the technical ability of the players or their physical and mental preparation. That is why an optimal training program has to offer more than just these aspects of the game. Winning or losing depends on the grade of development of the game intelligence of all players, their capacity to use their knowledge, technique and physique in the precise moment on a determined spot on the field. Unfortunately this aspect of the performance of a soccer player doesn't receive at present the necessary emphasis and importance it deserves in soccer training programs, despite its fundamental impact on the final result.

Instead of offering solutions to specific problems during the match, the coach should give the players a series of problems appropriate for their level that they could and should solve for themselves during training. This coaching style can be used best by exposing the players to a series of progressive simplified games that stimulate the players' minds and conditions their tactical behavior. In other words, simplified games with increasing complexity, difficulty and demand help to develop each player's game intelligence in soccer. The end result is superior learning with a much better grasp of tactical concepts, which will allow the player to make good use of his enhanced tactical awareness when he is faced with the many varied and different situations in a match.

The 2v1 situation, the "atom" of the tactical game

The 2v1-situation has to be considered the "atom" of the tactical game. This situation occurs on numerous occasions during a match but never in exactly the same way. Dealing with it effectively is a decisive factor in determining the result of any match. Consequently, it is very important for every player to know how to deal with 2v1 situations in attack and defense as they arise in a match and of course to know how to create this situation systematically to his benefit.

COOPERATION

Reference: C. Govaerts Deurne

A MODEL TO HELP DEVELOP A CORRECT TECHNICAL-TACTICAL RESPONSE WHEN IN A 2V1 SITUATION

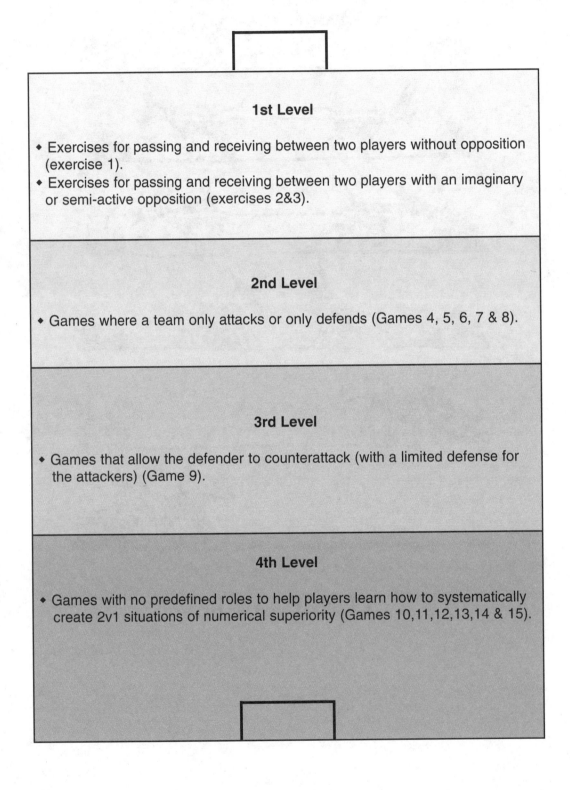

1st Level

• Exercises for passing and receiving between two players without opposition (exercise 1).
• Exercises for passing and receiving between two players with an imaginary or semi-active opposition (exercises 2&3).

2nd Level

• Games where a team only attacks or only defends (Games 4, 5, 6, 7 & 8).

3rd Level

• Games that allow the defender to counterattack (with a limited defense for the attackers) (Game 9).

4th Level

• Games with no predefined roles to help players learn how to systematically create 2v1 situations of numerical superiority (Games 10,11,12,13,14 & 15).

A QUESTIONNAIRE TO HELP YOU REFLECT UPON AND LEARN HOW TO RESOLVE 2V1 SITUATIONS BOTH IN ATTACK AND IN DEFENSE

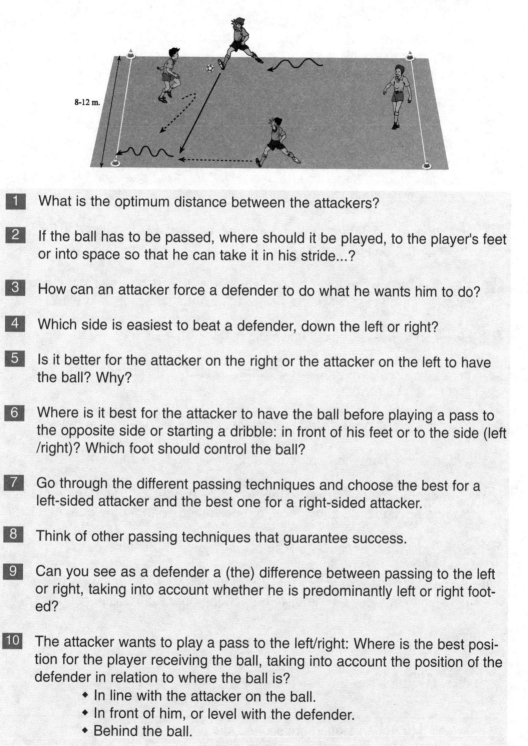

8-12 m.

1 What is the optimum distance between the attackers?

2 If the ball has to be passed, where should it be played, to the player's feet or into space so that he can take it in his stride...?

3 How can an attacker force a defender to do what he wants him to do?

4 Which side is easiest to beat a defender, down the left or right?

5 Is it better for the attacker on the right or the attacker on the left to have the ball? Why?

6 Where is it best for the attacker to have the ball before playing a pass to the opposite side or starting a dribble: in front of his feet or to the side (left /right)? Which foot should control the ball?

7 Go through the different passing techniques and choose the best for a left-sided attacker and the best one for a right-sided attacker.

8 Think of other passing techniques that guarantee success.

9 Can you see as a defender a (the) difference between passing to the left or right, taking into account whether he is predominantly left or right footed?

10 The attacker wants to play a pass to the left/right: Where is the best position for the player receiving the ball, taking into account the position of the defender in relation to where the ball is?
- In line with the attacker on the ball.
- In front of him, or level with the defender.
- Behind the ball.

11 Generally, which is the best way to beat a defender: dribbling or passing the ball?

12 Does a defender prefer an attacker to dribble or pass the ball?

13 Does a defender prefer an attacker to have the ball to his left or to his right?

14 Does a defender prefer an attacker to beat him outside or down the inside?

15 How can a defender force an attacker (left/right) to pass the ball to another attacker (left/right)?

16 How should a defender position himself in relation to the two attackers: head-on (frontal) or to the side?

17 Which is best, depending on the situation in the game, to challenge an attacker in possession of the ball, wait or run backwards with him?

18 How can a defender slow down an attack?

19 How can a defender convert an unfavorable (1v2) situation into a more favorable one for him?

20 How can a defender distract an attacker in possession of the ball?

21 When is the ideal moment to pass to a teammate in support?

22 How can an attacker be sure that when he passes to a teammate the latter has enough time and space to receive and control the ball?

23 When is it most effective to play a 'one-two' or a first-time pass?

24 Suggest a series of factors that could force an attacking team to play more than one pass in order to breach the opposition's defense.

---

*"Telling or asking closed questions save people from having to think.
Asking open questions causes them to think for themselves."*
John Whitmore

SIMPLIFIED EXERCISES/GAMES

A SERIES OF PROGRESSIVE SIMPLIFIED EXERCISES/GAMES TO PRACTICE THE 2v1 GAME SITUATION

1st Level:
Passing exercises between two players, with or without the intervention of an imaginary or semi-active opposition.

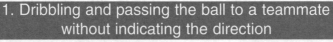

1. Dribbling and passing the ball to a teammate without indicating the direction

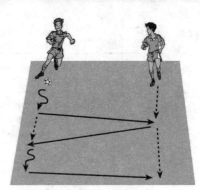

PITCH	Any open area on the training pitch
PLAYERS	2
EXPLANATION	- The two players advance parallel to each other 6-8 meters apart; the player on the ball should pass it to the other, who should always receive it on the run and return it first-time. - The passes should be played using both feet and with the outside of one and/or the inside of the other foot. - Various pairs practice at the same time and also in opposite directions.

Variation with cones: The passes should be played well away from the cones, thinking of these as imaginary defenders.

2. Square passes in the presence of semi-active defenders

PITCH	Any open area on the training pitch
PLAYERS	5
EXPLANATION	With the players (2 attackers and 3 defenders) positioned as in the illustration, the attackers should pass the ball beyond the reach of the defenders. The defenders try to intercept the passes but while doing so they have to touch the cone with one heel.

3. Square passes using two balls

PITCH	Any open area on the training pitch
PLAYERS	2
EXPLANATION	Same as the previous exercise but without defenders. Now both the attackers, with a ball each, run down the playing field and have to pass at the same time (without talking), making sure that the two balls do not collide.

2nd Level:
Games where one team only attacks and the other only defends

4. 2v1 with a wide goal

PITCH	Any open area on the training pitch
PLAYERS	3 (2v1) Two pairs of attackers are competing at each cone goal.
EXPLANATION	An attacker scores a goal when he runs with the ball under control across the goal line. During each attempt, each pair tries to get past the defender in a different way each time and run across the goal line marked with cones (8-12 meters wide, depending on the performance level of the players) by doing the following: • Playing a sideways/diagonal pass into his teammate's path and beyond the reach of the defender. • Dummying the pass and dribbling down the outside, accelerating immediately after the feint. • Making a diagonal run towards his teammate, who runs into space either behind the defender or the player in possession of the ball. Depending on what the defenders does, the attacker either plays a pass sideways or exploits the space and takes advantage of the distraction by going on an individual run.

12 m

"Knowing when to move is as important as knowing which move to make"

---

5. 2v1 with two wide goals

PITCH	An open area of the pitch with two cone goals 8-12 meters wide and 15 meters apart.
PLAYERS	4 (2 attackers in the middle of the pitch and a defender in each goal)
EXPLANATION	- The two attackers take on one opponent in one cone goal and after having scored or failed in their attempt they turn around to face the opposite goal defended by the second opponent. - Attackers and defenders swap roles after the first 10 attacks. - When an attacker manages to dribble the ball over a goal line his team earns one point. - However, if a defender claims the ball and manages to touch it three times in a row then the defense earns a point. - The target is to score at least 7 goals in 10 attacks.

Variation: Please consult a proposal of 10 more variations in "Developing Youth Soccer Players" by Horst Wein, Human Kinetics, 2000, pages 75-99

6. Two 2v1 situations (or more) with two wide goals

PITCH	A rectangle of 20x10m with two cone goals (10 m), one in the middle and another 20m away from the two attackers. Various channels are set up in front of both penalty boxes to keep all players active.
PLAYERS	4 (2v1+1)

EXPLANATION	- Two attackers should first beat the defender in the first goal and then the second, controlling the ball on the second goal line.
	- The defenders can only play in front of their goals. They are not allowed to run behind them yet.
	- Every 10 attacks the pairs swap roles.
	- The game ends:
	   ◆ When a goal is scored in the second goal.
	   ◆ When a defender wins the ball.
	   ◆ When the attackers commit a foul or lose control of the ball.

(see illustration on the next page)

Variation 1: Race between several attacking pairs in different channels at the same time. The pair that scores first in the second goal (with or without playing the offside rule) wins.

Variation 2: 4 goals are positioned one behind the other, with two defenders covering the first and second respectively. Each time a defender is beaten, he should run to cover behind his teammate in the next empty goal. So, the first player will cover the third goal and the second player the fourth.

Variation 3: In this variation the teammate of the ball carrier makes himself available for a through pass in an area between the first two goals, which means he offers himself behind the first defender. The second defender is not allowed to mark him here and can only come off his line when the ball enters his zone. The ball carrier starts the game with a pass or a dribble across the first goal line

Variation 4 (starting with a pass): Three or more 2v1 confrontations with wide goals. The game starts with a pass from a third attacker to one of his two team-mates in the best position to receive the ball. Their objective is to beat the defenders one after another in each cone goal and then score in the 7-a-side Goal (6 x 2 meters). (See the illustration on following page)

Variation 5 (with goals in a zigzag formation):

PITCH	Half of the 7-a-side Soccer pitch. Three cone goals are positioned in a zigzag formation between the center line and the penalty box line.
PLAYERS	6 (2v1+1+1 plus a goalkeeper).
EXPLANATION	- The attacking pair should manage to run with the ball through each of the three goals being covered by a defender. After having taken the ball across last goal-line a goal shot has to be executed within 2 seconds at the 7-a-side goal. - A competition is organized among the pairs. Each pair has 10 attacks.

"If at first you don't succeed you are doing about average"

Variation 6 (with a defender covering two goals at the same time):

PITCH	A channel with 3 cone goals
PLAYERS	4 (2v1+1) or 3 (2v1 in each of the three goals).
EXPLANATION	- The first defender covers the first two goals without having any restrictions, and the second defender covers the other one. The attackers try to beat the two defenders and control the ball in the last cone goal. - At the end this game should be played with one defender covering all three goals.

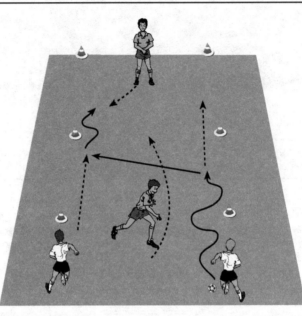

7. 2v1 with three teams

PITCH	An area of 25x10 meters
PLAYERS	6 (3 teams of two players)
EXPLANATION	- Two teams defend their own goals (10 meters wide), opposite each other, against a third team starting from the center of the pitch to attack the two goals alternately. - One of the players in each defensive team stands beside his goal, not taking part. He only joins in once his teammate has won the ball and the two players then become the attackers, while the player who lost the ball goes in goal and his teammate waits for his turn. - After scoring, the same team continues attacking. The team who scores the most goals wins.

Variation: For effective learning purposes each pair carries out 10 consecutive attacks. Instead of waiting for his turn the second defender plays as a goalkeeper in a 7-a-side goal 10 meters behind the cone goal.

"The player who doesn't learn from mistakes will always be a beginner"

8. A fast attack 2v1 with a shot on goal

PITCH	Any area on the training field
PLAYERS	5 (2v1 plus a supporting defender and a goalkeeper)
EXPLANATION	Setting off from the halfway line of a 7-a-side pitch, the two attackers try to beat a defender who is located between them and the goal and score. A second defender, who starts from 6 meters behind the attackers, joins once the ball is played by the one attacker.

30m

3rd Level:
Games that allow the defender to counterattack (with a limited defense for the attackers)

9. 2v1 with counterattack	

PITCH	A rectangular playing area 15 meters long divided into two zones separated by a halfway line and with a cone goal 6-8 meters wide at each end.	
PLAYERS	4 (2 attackers and 2 defenders).	
EXPLANATION	Each defender covers his goal against 2 attackers. When he wins possession of the ball he immediately starts a counterattack with a long pass to his teammate in the opposite goal while the attackers try to avoid it, but only in the upper part of the playing area.	

Variation: 2v1 with an accurate pass for counterattacking

PITCH	A rectangular playing area 8-12 meters wide. A cone goal covers the whole width of one end of the pitch and on the opposite side there are two other goals, 2 meters wide.	
PLAYERS	3 (2v1) With two other pairs waiting their turn.	
EXPLANATION	- The attackers try to control the ball in the wide goal (1 point), but if the defender wins the ball, he quickly tries to score with a accurate pass through one of the 2-meter wide cone goals (2 points). To avoid this, the attackers need to transition quickly from attack to defense. - The first to achieve 10 points wins.	

4th Level:
Games with no pre-established roles to learn how to take advantage of 2v1 situations in attack

10. 2v1 with two goals 3 meters wide	
PITCH	An area of 20x15 meters, with a cone goal 3 meters wide at each end .
PLAYERS	3 (2v1) Rotations
EXPLANATION	- The attacking pair tries to score from close-range in the goal defended by an opponent. But if the opponent wins the ball he can counterattack with a shot from anywhere on the pitch at the goal at the other end. - Rotations are made every minute until all three players have played as a defender. - The defender who achieves the best results wins.

20 m.

11. 1v1 plus a neutral player played on a Mini-Soccer pitch	
PITCH	A Mini-Soccer pitch, with two cone goals at each end
PLAYERS	3 (1v1 with a neutral player)
EXPLANATION	- After the ball is put into play by a neutral, the player who wins the ball forms an attacking partnership with the neutral player as they head for the goal at the far end now defended by the third player. - If the defender wins the ball, he immediately mounts an attack with the neutral player on the goal at the opposite end of the pitch, which is now being defended by the player who lost possession.

12. 2v2 or 3v3 with four crosswise goals

PITCH	A square of 15x15 (20x20) meters, with a cone goal (7.5m) on each side of the pitch
PLAYERS	4 (2v2) or 6 (3v3)
EXPLANATION	- Each team attacks and defends respectively two opposite goals. The aim is to score as many goals as possible in the opposition's goals. A goal is scored by running through a goal with the ball under control. - The game starts with a thrown ball. - The game last 12 minutes, divided into 4 periods of 3 minutes.

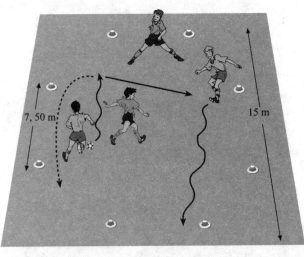

Variation: The same as the previous game but each team now attacks or defends two goals next to each other rather than opposite each other.

13. 2v2 or 3v3 with two wide goals

PITCH	A playing area of 20 x 15(20)m or 30 x 25m with a cone goal at each end
PLAYERS	4 (2v2) or 6 (3v3)
EXPLANATION	- A goal is scored by running with the ball through the opposition's cone goal. - The game lasts 12 minutes: 4 periods of 3 minutes.

14. Keeping possession of the ball in a 2v1 situation

PITCH	A square of 12x12meters ,depending on the level of the players
PLAYERS	3 (2v1)
EXPLANATION	- The aim of the game is to keep possession of the ball for as long as possible, not letting the defender win or the ball go out of play. The second defender outside the square counts the seconds the possession lasts. - After every trial to establish a record time in ball possession the two defenders swap roles, thus staying fresh and energetic to press the attackers. After 6 attempts, attackers and defenders switch functions.

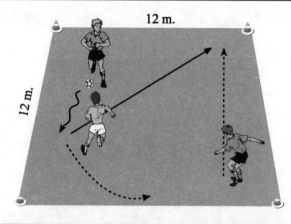

15. 2v2 and 3v3 using 4 goals, as in Mini-Soccer

Perform all the games 2v2 and 3v3 proposed in this chapter using 4 goals, as in Mini-Soccer (See "Developing Youth Soccer Players" by Horst Wein, Human Kinetics, 2000).

"Coaching is a tool for optimizing people's potential and performance. Commanding, demanding, instructing cannot produce sustainable optimum performance."

John Whitmore

FIRST TIME PLAY

"A fast player is one who finds solutions quickly, and besides runs the fastest"

Cesar Luis Menotti

INTRODUCTION

The capacity to play the ball one-touch or first-time in the precise moment on an adequate place on the field has to be considered an important attacking weapon. First-time play is used by attackers to get, in limited spaces, an advantage against the opposition. Especially close to and inside the opposing penalty area where generally limited space and time are available, it helps to get the ball behind the crowded defense. First-time or one-touch play creates space, often surprises the opposition and thereby generates goal-scoring opportunities.

Basic requirements for playing one-touch
- High level of individual technique (ball sense).
- Knowing when best to play it and when not.
- Understanding the game situation and the need to communicate first and then cooperate with a teammate in this set move along the lines established in practice.

An example of a first-time play
- The attacker dribbles the ball towards a defender to commit him. Before getting close (but not too close) to him, he establishes a mutual agreement with his teammate, passes the ball with accuracy and speed at exactly the right moment. The ball receiver, closely marked, gets away from his opponent with a sudden change of speed to play a first-time or a direct wall pass diagonally into the run of the passer who appeared suddenly in the uncovered space behind the first defender.
- It is important for the player receiving the ball to time his move perfectly, not showing too soon (which would give away his intentions to the defender) or too late (which would give his teammate fewer passing options).

Alternatives

If the defenders seem to have anticipated the attackers' intentions, the latter can choose an alternative to surprise them in one of the following ways:

 * The player in possession of the ball dummies a pass in one direction and dribbles down the opposite side.
 * The receiving attacker does not return the ball, instead he lets the ball go by, turns quickly and penetrates with it or passes it to another teammate.
 * The receiving attacker, instead of playing a first-time triangle pass to the passer, returns the ball first time to him and then gets beyond his defender in order to receive the ball behind him (the double one-two).

Ways of playing a first-time pass

Depending on the position of the defenders and the support available from teammates, the first-time pass can be played diagonally, forwards, backwards or sideways.

Experiences gained when practicing the following exercises and games for first-time play:

 * The initial pass from the attacker should be unexpected for both defenders, taking them by surprise.
 * The initial pass should not be too strong and preferably along the ground as this helps the man receiving it play it first-time.
 * The player who makes the initial pass should immediately make himself available to get it back by moving quickly into space, taking into account the movements of the opposition's defense so as not to run into offside.
 * The return pass should be played accurately, first time and into the path of the player, so that he can collect the ball at full speed.

"The difference between good and excellent is a little more effort"

EXERCISES/GAMES

A SERIES OF PROGRESSIVE EXERCISES/GAMES TO GAIN EXPERIENCE IN FIRST-TIME PLAY

1. First-time passes in a stationary position in a circle	
PLAYERS	5, standing in a circle (diameter 6-10m)
EXPLANATION	- The five players should make a minimum of 20 consecutive first-time passes without committing mistakes. Before passing, a good balance is acquired with both legs slightly bent. - At first the passes are played along the ground and later at different heights, but they should always be played first-time.

Variation 1: After playing the pass, the player should immediately move 5 meters away from his original location in order to occupy another position in the circle.

Variation 2: Practice with two balls in a larger circle where the players are consequently further apart from each other. Then reduce the diameter of the circle.

Variation 3: The original game is played, but this time with a defender.

2. First-time passes with a partner while running

PITCH	A channel 10-12 meters wide (marked with cones) between the center line and the penalty area, or between the two penalty areas of a 7-a-side Soccer pitch
PLAYERS	3 (2 attackers and a goalkeeper)
EXPLANATION	Both attackers advance in the channel passing the ball to each other first-time and without making any mistakes until they come level with the last cone. From there a first-time shot has to be taken towards the goal defended by a goal-keeper.

Variation 1: The pair of attackers who scores first after having made at least 4 first-time passes wins. To make the practice more difficult one or two high passes have to be played before executing the first-time shot.

Variation 2: The presence of two or three static defenders in the channel makes the function of the attackers a little bit more difficult. The defenders have to position themselves in front of a cone which they must touch with one heel when trying to intercept the first-time passes.

Variation 3: Three pairs compete in a first-time passing practice at full speed. Two pairs start the exercise, one from each end of the channel, attacking in opposite directions. The third pair starts from the center. The aim is to see which pair finishes the circuit first (once or twice).

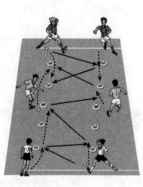

Variation 4: The same. One player always passes along the ground and the other gives aerial passes.

3. Keeping possession in a 2v1 situation

PITCH	Square of 10x10 or 15x15 meters (depending on the level of the players)
PLAYERS	4 (2v1 plus a reserve)
EXPLANATION	- The aim of the game is for the attacking pair to keep possession of the ball for as long as they can and play as many first-time passes as possible. - The players should decide at all times, depending on the circumstances, whether to pass first time or control and dribble it. - After a mistake from the attackers or a ball loss, the only defender swaps with his recovered substitute who counted the first-time passes executed by the 2 attackers with one ball possession.. - The pair which, with 6 ball possessions, executes the most first-time passes is the winner.
LEARNING OBJECTIVES	The players learn and appreciate when and when not to play first time in a 2v1 situation.

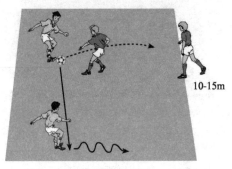

10-15m

10-15m

Variation: Keeping possession in a 3v2 situation

PITCH	Square of 15x15 or 20x20 meters (depending on the level of the players)
PLAYERS	6 (3v2 plus a reserve defender)
EXPLANATION	- Again, the number of first-time passes made by the attacking trio during a possession are counted. - When the attackers make a mistake or one of the defenders wins the ball, the substitute defender swaps with one of the defenders and the game resumes. - A competition can be organized to see which team is able to carry out the highest number of first-time passes with one ball possession.

4. Keeping possession in a 4v2 or 5v3 situation

PITCH	Square of 15x15 or 20x20 meters
PLAYERS	6 (4v2) or 8 (5v3)
EXPLANATION	- The aim of the game is to play as many first-time passes as possible without losing possession of the ball or letting it go out of play. - Initially, it is a good idea for one or two attackers to make themselves available only at internal boundaries of the playing area, which will prevent a congestion of players around the ball and give the rest of the attackers more time and space in which to play it. - Later, three and finally all four attackers play inside the square.
LEARNING OBJECTIVES	- Only play the ball first-time if the circumstances allow it. - The first aim is to keep the ball in possession and the second is to play as many first-time passes as possible without committing any mistakes.

5. 1v1 plus a neutral player

PITCH	12x20 (rectangle), with two cone goals, one at each end the width of the whole side
PLAYERS	3 (1v1 plus a neutral player)
EXPLANATION	- The game starts with a thrown ball between two players. The player who wins the ball attacks with the help of a third neutral player, who always supports the attacker with the ball. - The attacker on the ball should get the better of the defender by beating him individually, or better by playing a one-two with him, using the teammate as a wall. - Every three minutes a different player becomes the neutral player.
LEARNING OBJECTIVES	- Always look out for the least defended areas. - After a pass, immediately run into a space which is not defended by the opposition. - Don't play the ball first-time if there is a risk of losing possession. - Before passing to a teammate, take into account his position and that of the defender.

"Awareness of errors is essential to improvement."

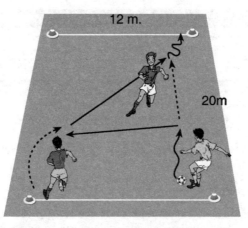

Variation: A goal scored after having played a first-time pass (one-two) is worth 3 points, while with any other passing combinations only 1 point is won.

Corrective Exercise: 2v1 practicing playing the one-two
The defender stands with both feet on the center line to let the attackers gain experience in playing the one-two. The timing and trajectory of the initial side pass, the return first-time pass and the run into space made by the player who started the move are all evaluated.

6. Quick passing between four defenders in the width of the field

PITCH	1/3 of a full size pitch with four cones positioned as in the illustration
PLAYERS	4
EXPLANATION	- The players (2 central defenders and 2 wingbacks) each stand behind a cone. - The aim of the game is to pass the ball as quickly as possible from one side to the other until one circuit of 6 passes has been completed (pass and return) around the outside of the cones. - A stopwatch is used to time how long it takes to complete one circuit.
LEARNING OBJECTIVES	- The players learn to play speedy passes, always along the ground and towards the outside foot of the receiver. The receiver either controls and passes the ball with his inside foot or passes it first-time (one touch) with the outside foot to the next teammate if there is no risk. - Players learn that playing first-time passes with either foot may increase the speed of the ball circulation.

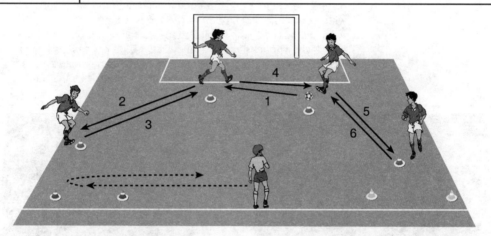

Variation: The same exercise as before. Now an opponent joins the game to cover two cone goals (12 meters wide) situated a few meters in front of the wingbacks close to the sidelines. The four attacking defenders should pass the ball in the same way as in the previous exercise to allow a wingback to receive the ball on the run in front of the cone goal ahead of him and then dribble it across the goal line before the defender, who can move across to cover either goal, has the chance to tackle the wingback.

"A mainly technique orientated training cuts out a lot of fun and enjoyment which generally is generated by game playing. Too much drill is kill"

7. Examples of attacking moves with one-touch deflection or double one-two

PLAYERS	5 (3v2)
EXPLANATION	The players are positioned as in the illustration. A player starts the move by passing the ball to a teammate close to the center line just as the latter moves away from his marker to make himself available. From this point there are three possibilities to continue the play: A. Deflecting the ball first-time towards a third attacker, who has just moved goal side of his defender, ready to receive the ball in his stride (1st illustration). B. The double one-two. The ball is returned first-time to the player who made the initial pass. Immediately after his return pass the attacker gets behind his defender, ready to receive the ball again from the first attacker in an advanced offensive position. The one-two can be played along the ground or can be lifted over the defender's head with the second first-time pass (2nd. illustration). C. A double one-two with a third attacker. Return the ball first-time to the player who made the initial pass. This player passes first-time, along the ground, to the second attacker, who has made a run to lose his defender and get goal-side of him to receive the ball in an advanced offensive position (3rd. illustration).

A

B

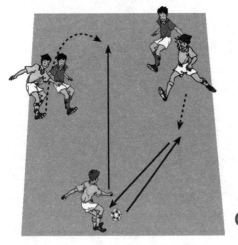

C

ADVANTAGES AND DISADVANTAGES OF PLAYING THE BALL FIRST-TIME

Advantages:

- In today's modern game, speed is an ever increasingly important 'weapon'. Passing the ball frequently first-time does not give the opposition enough time to analyze the game situation and respond effectively.
- Playing the ball first time is an effective way to overcome a zonal defense, which often moves up to catch the opposition in an offside position.
- Experience and statistical information proves that controlling and distributing balls in restricted and crowed areas (like close to the penalty area) leads to many ball losses. However, surprising first-time passes, despite the difficulty and complexity in executing them correctly, avoid the risks that go with executing the sequence: reception of the ball, control and the following pass or dribble.

When being pressed, the first-time play may be an ideal solution.

Disadvantages:

- Passing the ball first-time with any part of the body can create many mistakes.
- It requires a perfect understanding between the players, an excellent reading of the game situation and quick reflexes.
- Playing the ball first-time in the first third of the pitch should be strictly forbidden. Due to the difficulty of the technique, there always exists the possibility of losing the ball, in which case the goal is under serious threat.

THE COUNTERATTACK

> *"The more you increase the speed, the more it becomes difficult to assure accuracy"*
>
> *Cesar Luis Menotti*

INTRODUCTION

The counterattack has to be seen as an ambivalent concept or principle of play. It consists first of the collective effort of a team to recover the possession of the ball in a determined part of the field followed by a quick offensive response of a few players who surprise the opposition, which has difficulties in regrouping defensively. A counterattack starts because the attackers, besides having space in front of them, are not in a numerical inferiority.

In today's soccer, where well organized defenses with numerical superiority don't allow the attackers time and space to develop their play, the art of counter-attacking after a quick turn-over from defense to attack is an important tool which decides many matches, and indeed more goals then ever result nowadays from counterattacks.

Fundamental requirements for good counterattacking play:
- **Planning.** All tactics need to be well planned and the counterattack is no exception, as it needs to be studied previously and practiced sufficiently, so that it can be applied in a well-coordinated and effective manner in a match.
- **Study your opponent.** A team must study and be familiar with the defensive tactics of the opposition, which will allow them to anticipate their moves and win the ball anywhere they decide.
- **A counterattacking mentality.** Any counterattack is always preceded by a mistake made by the opposition. So even before making such a mistake happen through successful tackling, each and every one of the defenders should be thinking about a possible counterattack. That means while defending they should observe, apart from the ball and the opposition, the position of their teammates to turn quickly over into attack as soon as the ball is recovered.

- **Technical and tactical ability**: The success of a counterattack often depends on the technical ability of the players, and this is particularly true for those techniques which are especially relevant for the counterattack (quick, powerful and accurate passing, controlling the ball on the run, running with the ball at speed...), combined with a thorough knowledge and tactical awareness. (See the table with the characteristics of the counterattack).

The importance of training for the counterattack

Having good technical ability, tactical awareness and a thorough knowledge of all the factors involved in a counterattack is the product of an intense and methodically well planned training. Once the technical-tactical skills and capacities to launch counterattacks have been understood and experienced in training their use in the match becomes much more effective. For this reason the adequate preparation of the counterattack in training is to be considered essential.

The main characteristics of a counterattack:

Before it begins, without the ball	During its development, with the ball	When finished, depending on the outcome
- Look out to achieve numerical superiority in defense in the area where the ball is located. - Channel the opposition's attack towards an area on the pitch, which is more easily controlled by the defense, such as near the sidelines of the pitch. - Position and distribute the team effectively with two players up front (in different channels) ready to mount a counterattack at any moment. - Before, during and after the defense have a counterattack mentality. This is also true for the goalkeeper ! - Have a series of signals (visual and audio) that facilitate better communication and understanding during the game. - Use set plays or dead ball situations (corners, free kicks) as a platform for launching counterattacks.	- Quick turnover from defense into attack or vice versa as quickly as possible. - Change pace and speed (surprise effect). - Make good decisions fast and execute techniques quickly. - Be aggressive. - Be creative, imaginative and improvise. - Surprise and anticipate. - Take risks when trying to make optimal use of the uncovered areas of the pitch. - Don't give the opposition's defense time to reorganize. - Look for parity or better still, numerical superiority in attack. - Play as a team although only one or two defenders (midfield players) and two attackers are involved in a staggered formation. - Use always orientated controls of the ball for saving costly time - Play few passes. - Play especially vertical or through passes, if possible behind the defenders. - Pass first time. - Make sure sufficient speed of the ball - Pass the ball with accuracy mainly into the teammates' run to be picked up at high speed. - Pass along the ground, if possible. - Switch play not more than once from one wing to the other. - Make well timed, fast, surprise penetration runs into space up front (but not in off-side), for supporting the ball carrier giving him several passing options. - Keep your team compact, what allows the player involved in the counterattack to return in time for their defensive duties -Look out for first -time shots on goal to surprise the goalkeeper. -Take systematically rebounds.	- Depending on how the counterattack finished the team has to be prepared to quickly form again an compact defensive unit, with all players being able to assist each other in order to block the opponent's attack or launch another counterattack. - The attackers closest to the ball should slowdown the opponent's attack in order to gain time to form a compact defensive unit, necessary to avoid a counterattack from the opponent. - During their defensive task they should contemplate the possibility to slightly infringe the rules (tactical foul), but without risking a warning from the referee. - In case a defender took part in the counterattack his position or zone should be "filled" for some seconds by a teammate not involved in the last attack. No rushing back is necessary, as this would be an unnecessary waste of energy.

EXERCISES/GAMES

A PROGRESSIVE SERIES OF EXERCISES/GAMES TO LEARN AND IMPROVE COUNTERATTACKING

1. Individual counterattack from the center line	
PLAYERS	2 (an attacker and a goalkeeper)
EXPLANATION	- An attacker sets off from the center line (or any other location on the pitch), dribbling the ball as fast as he can towards the goal. Before he shoots at goal from inside the penalty area, he has touch the ball at least three times during his run. - A stopwatch is used to time how long each player takes to successfully complete the exercise. Time starts as soon as the player sets off and finishes when the ball hits the net of the goal.
LEARNING OBJECTIVES	- Learning to always take the shortest and most direct route to goal in a counterattack. - Developing the technique of running with the ball under control at maximum speed. - Minimizing the time to prepare and execute the goal shot.

Variation: Two attackers compete against each other, both setting off from the center line or from anywhere on the pitch, running towards the same goal to see which one scores first. Only shots from inside the penalty area are allowed. Both players could also head for a different goal, which means that they dribble in opposite directions.

"An individual who is forced to proceed too soon may lose the prerequisite self confidence that is essential for success at subsequent levels"

Ric Purser

2. Individual counterattack with pressure from a defender

PLAYERS	3 (an attacker, a defender and a goalkeeper).
EXPLANATION	- The attacker sets off with a ball from the halfway line and runs as fast as he can inside the penalty area from where he has to shoot. - The defender, who starts 3 meters (later only 1 meter) behind him tries to tackle and prevent him from scoring.
LEARNING OBJECTIVES	- Gaining experience in running at full speed with the ball under control and when being put under pressure from a defender. - Learning to shield the ball, keeping it on the opposite side to where the defender is pressing. - Learning to execute a body charge against the opponent (as ball carrier but also as defender) at the right time, respecting the rules of the game - Learn to choose the best suitable moment for moving the ball aside and step or cross into the path of the defender, thus preventing him from tackling.

Variation: The defender starts the game next to the attacker.

3. Collect a through pass, run and shoot

PLAYERS	3 (1 attacker, 1 passer and a goalkeeper).
EXPLANATION	- An attacker positioned on the halfway line picks up the ball from a through pass given by teammate behind him. He must collect the ball before he enters the penalty area and shoot without any wasted time. - The individual attack with the control of flat and high passes which come from all possible angles should be practiced from different locations on the pitch.
LEARNING OBJECTIVES	- Serve a well timed and accurate pass. - Conclude the fast run with a powerful shot with no previous preparation.

Variation:

PITCH	One half of a full size pitch.
PLAYERS	4 (a passer, 2 attackers and a goalkeeper).
EXPLANATION	The feeder passes the ball (along the ground or in the air) from the center line into the run of two attackers (one each side of the feeder). The winner becomes the attacker and tries to carry the ball under pressure from the defender (the player who didn't touch the ball first) towards the penalty area, where he shoots and looks out for any rebound.
LEARNING OBJECTIVES	Gaining position in relation to an opponent at one side by running across into his path and/or playing a 'legal' charge.

"The performance of a soccer player is only limited by the rules of the game and his own capacity"

4. A fast attack by two players

PLAYERS	3 (2 attackers and one goalkeeper).
EXPLANATION	- Two attackers, 10 meters apart, set off from anywhere along the center line heading for the goal defended by a goalkeeper. At least two passes have to be made in the quick attack before the ball can be shot from inside the penalty area towards the goal. Later on the coach, for practice reasons, may increase the number of passes to be played. - When the opposite goal is used a competition between pairs can be organized with the winner being the pair that completes the attack with a goal the quickest.

Variation (2v1): There are no more restrictions concerning the number of passes. There are no more restrictions concerning the number of passes.

5. Fast attack 2v1 + 1 from the center line

PLAYERS	5 (2 attackers, 2 defenders and a goalkeeper)
EXPLANATION	- Two attackers (10 meters apart) start the game from the center line. The aim of the game is to advance towards the goal and score in less than 6 seconds. - Both attackers are tackled by one defender who sets off 5 meters behind them (later this is reduced to 3 and then 1 meter) and a second who meets them halfway. - After 5 attacks the players swap roles. - The coach is asked to change the starting position of the first defender in relation to the attackers, putting him on either sideline as a wingback far way from the ball.
LEARNING OBJECTIVES	The players learn how to solve the problems caused by the different positioning of the first defender and find the most effective combination in attack, an example of which can be seen in the illustration.

6. Counterattack by a midfield player or a winger

PITCH	One half of the pitch with a full size goal at one end and an 8 meter wide cone goal positioned in either wing position on the center line
PLAYERS	4 (1v2 plus a goalkeeper)

EXPLANATION	- A wingback tries to dribble the ball across the opposing cone goal on the center line defended by the opponent's wing and center forward.
	- If the defenders win the ball, they should mount a counterattack as quickly as possible, trying to score in the full size goal defended by a goalkeeper.
	    The two counter-attackers have two options:
	    1. Mount an individual counterattack down the wing or through the middle in case the teammate remains behind.
	    2. Built up a quick combination when the tackling back defender can position himself between the ball and the ball carrier. Care has to be taken not to run offside.
	- The wingback, on the other hand, has to tackle back after his ball loss.
	- The counterattacking pair which needed less time between the start and the conclusion of the counterattack wins.

Variation (2v1+1and a goalkeeper):
A second defender is introduced into the game. He waits for the two attackers near the penalty area, forcing them to get past him before they can score a goal.

7. Counterattack: 3v1 + 1

PITCH	On half of a full size pitch
PLAYERS	6 (3 attackers, 2 defenders and a goalkeeper).

EXPLANATION	- Three forwards start a counterattack from the center line against a defender who starts 4 (3) meters behind them. When reaching the penalty area they have to face a second defender. Then the ball carrier has two options:
	    1. Pass the ball diagonally into the space to the better positioned supporting teammate to run onto and score.
	    2. Depending on what the defender does, sell a dummy pass and try to beat him and score.
	- The game should start from all possible attacking positions (center forward or left/right wing)
	- The offside rule is applied.

8. Counterattack: 3v1+2

PITCH	One half of a full size pitch
PLAYERS	7 (3 attackers, 3 defenders and a goalkeeper)
EXPLANATION	- Three forwards counterattack with the ball anywhere on the center line with 2 defenders tackling from behind at an initial distance of 5(8) meters. A third defender (sweeper) confronts the forwards before they come close to the penalty box. He faces them early in order to slow down their fast attack and thus gives more time for his two defenders to interfere. - The coach simulates attacking moves from anywhere on the pitch with the three defenders in different positions in order to force the attackers as well as the defenders to read and adapt to the ever-changing situations. The offside rule is always in force. - The coach can also give the signal for initiating the counterattack by passing the ball out of defense to one of the attackers. From that moment the game is on.

"Techniques and tactics in soccer are like two wheels of a bike which move simultaneously. But to progress more quickly and safely it's better use a car with 4 well balanced wheels to carry you to your destination (techniques, tactics, physical and mental fitness and game intelligence)"

Variation 1: In this version of the game the two defenders are positioned near the penalty area while the third starts from the center line with the attackers. The counterattack should be completed in a record time with the fewest number of passes and runs possible. The attacks start from the three possible attacking positions (center forward or wing positions).

Variation 2: Now all three defenders expect the attackers somewhere near the penalty box.

"The good coach doesn't instruct anything to anybody, he only helps his pupils to discover and to think"

9. From 7v7 to 7v5 (5v5 to 5vs3)

PITCH	7-a-side Soccer pitch.
PLAYERS	14 (3 attackers, 3 defenders and a goalkeeper in each team) or 10 (two teams of 5 players)
EXPLANATION	- When a team manages to score a goal, two of their members have to leave the field and celebrate it with a run around the outside of the pitch. Meanwhile, the team with 2 more players, after winning the ball, mount a swift counter-attack against the five remaining players of the goal-scoring team. - But if the remaining 5 players win the ball, they try to keep possession and slow the game, thus giving their two players outside time to complete their run around the field and rejoin the team. From that moment on they change their pattern of play and attack. - The winner is the team that scores more goals during the three periods of five minutes.

Variation 1: The game is played with goalkeepers.

Variation 2: Two teams of 4 players compete against each other on a smaller pitch.

Variation 3: Instead of two players leaving the pitch after a goal, one has to leave or even three have to go outside the field for a run. This way the players are exposed to almost all possible counterattacking situations.

"When a simplified game is introduced, more than one variation must be offered with different grades of difficulty and complexity in order to achieve effective learning"

---

10. Counterattack: 4v4

PITCH	One half of a full size pitch
PLAYERS	9 (4v4 plus a goalkeeper).
EXPLANATION	A wingback intentionally makes a mistake by passing the ball to the opposing inside-right, who, without wasting time, mounts a swift counterattack, supported by his three teammates (two wingers and a center forward). The four defenders spread out across the width of the field quickly have to change their attitude from attack to defense, try to regroup their defense and force the attackers to play more in the width and not in the depth of the playing field, thus slowing down their fast attack.

11. "Kick and Rush" 5v0

PITCH	3/4 of the full size pitch.
PLAYERS	11 or 13 (5v5 or 6v6 plus a goalkeeper)

EXPLANATION	- The five defenders are placed in their penalty area and the attackers line up behind the center line.
	- The game starts with one of the five defenders kicking the ball in the other half.
	    1. The attacking team positions itself intelligently (giving width and depth) behind the center line where any of the 5 picks up the long clearance and mounts a fast attack. This is best done by playing, after the orientated control of the ball, a long pass into the run of a teammate close to the goal, who collects the ball and scores from inside the penalty area. Any of his teammates should support him in the counterattack.
	    2. As soon as the ball is cleared up-field, all defenders rush into the center circle (or to the center line, depending on the performance level of the players involved) without worrying about defense, touch the area or the line and try to return to their penalty box before the opposition has had a chance to score.
	- A point is awarded for every "defender" who manages to get back to his penalty area before a goal has been scored. If the initial kick is poor or goes out of play the clearance has to be repeated
	- If one defender tackles an attacker in his counterattack, five penalty points are awarded to the defenders.
	- The two teams swap roles when all "defenders" have had their turn.

Variation 1: Counterattack 5v1

The player who starts the game becomes the only defender. He tries to anticipate and intercept the long passes from the attackers and slow down the counterattack, thus gaining time for his teammates to reach the penalty area before
the ball is in the goal. The more defenders who manage to return before a goal
is scored by the attackers, the more points the defenders will collect.

Variation 2: Counterattack 5v2

Instead of clearing the ball field-up the defender now passes it sideways to a
teammate inside the penalty area. The latter starts the game with a long clearance across the center line. Both players who touched the ball become the two
defenders. Once the ball is out of the box, the attackers in the other half of the
field may move into the defenders' half to mount a counterattack 5v2.

Variation 3: Counterattack 5v2

Similar to variation 2, but with a neutral goalkeeper and the application of the
offside rule.

Variation 4: Counterattack 5v3

One defender starts the game with a square pass to a teammate (as in variation
2) who then kicks the ball up-field. Both players who touched the ball have to
run into the center circle or to the center line and then back to the penalty area
before the opposition scores. The remaining three defenders who didn't participate in the clearance of the ball have to stop the counterattack. The defenders
can now win a maximum of only 2 points.

Variation 5: Counterattack 5v4

Now any one of the five defenders has to run and the rest do their best to thwart the counterattack.

12. A fast attack 4v4, 5v5 or 6v6 from the middle of the pitch

PITCH	A full size pitch, with a central area 35 meters long and the whole width of the pitch (35x55 m.).
PLAYERS	4v4, 5v5 or 6v6 plus the goalkeeper in either of the two full size goals.
EXPLANATION	- Without leaving the marked playing area in the center of the pitch, the team with the ball tries to keep possession despite the pressure from the opposition, until the coach signals the start of their fast attack with everybody being allowed to leave the central area. It should be launched preferably with a long through pass out of the playing area into the run of a teammate who offers himself up-field and then tries to score. - Shots at goal, depending on what the coach decides, can be taken from any where on the pitch or only from inside the penalty areas. - Initially, the offside rule is not applied, but later this rule comes in force when a sweeper is positioned in front of each penalty area.

13. Quick and accurate passing played on a 7-a-side pitch

PITCH	A 7-a-side pitch
PLAYERS	8 (2 teams of 4)
EXPLANATION	Various balls are placed next to each goal. On a signal from the coach, both goalkeepers pass their ball to one of their two midfield players, who after an orientated control plays a long pass to his attacker. The team who's attacker scores first is the winner.

14. Counterattacking after corner kicks

PITCH	A 7-a-side pitch or full size pitch
PLAYERS	14 (7v7)
EXPLANATION	- The attacking team takes a corner, which has to be directed into the goalkeeper's area. This way it is relatively easy for the goalkeeper to collect the ball and immediately start a swift counterattack by throwing the ball to one of his teammates outside the penalty area without any opposition. Generally, in a corner defense two defenders watch the area between the 11 meter-line and the 16.5 meter-line. When the trajectory of the corner kick tells them that the goalkeeper will collect the ball, they decide to forget about their defensive functions and rush up-field, both heading in different directions to give the goalkeeper an option. That means that the counterattack from the goalkeeper starts well before the ball is recovered. - A goal scored from a corner is worth 3 points and a goal scored with a counterattack is only worth 1 point. Each team has 10 corners (5 from each side). The team with the most points wins.

Variation: Use additional players in the rest of the field, for instance one forward far up with an opponent and one or two midfield players half way and also shadowed by one or two defenders, thus creating 2v1, 2v2, 3v2 and 3v3 situations.

"The step to step approach for the task at hand (for instance the development of counterattacking skills and capacities) is a key to success. Each accomplishment is broken down into a series of small steps, gradually and methodically leading to the final goal"

15. Counterattack: 5v3 plus a goalkeeper

PITCH	One half of the full size pitch, with a line of cones 25-meters from the goal
PLAYERS	9 (5v3 plus a goalkeeper)
EXPLANATION	The game starts when the goalkeeper throws the ball to one of the three defenders. From this moment on the five attackers, who are positioned 25 meters away, start their full press to try to win the ball. If they do, they mount a swift counterattack in a maximum time of 5 seconds. On the other hand, the three defenders try to keep possession and control the ball on the 25-meter line.

16. Counterattack: 5v5 plus a goalkeeper

PITCH	One half of the full size pitch, with a line of cones 25-meters from the goal
PLAYERS	11 (5v5 plus a goalkeeper)
EXPLANATION	- As in the previous game the goalkeeper starts it with a pass to one of his defenders. The opposition, situated on the 25 meter-line, move forward and play a full press in an attempt to win the ball, especially close to the sidelines, and then mount a swift counterattack. The defenders, on the other hand, try to progress in the field with the aim of controlling the ball on the center line. - After 10 ball possessions the teams change positions and functions. - After each counterattack the coach analyzes together with his players their positive and negative contribution in the different phases of the counterattack, in defense as well as in attack. In the same way the defenders have to work out how to best avoid the full press of the attackers.

17. Counterattack: 9v6

PITCH	First only one half of a full size pitch and then all of it. Two cone goals (4 meters) are positioned on the center line and one full size goal on the end line
PLAYERS	16 (8 plus a goalkeeper against 6 plus a goalkeeper)
EXPLANATION	- In the first part of the game, played on half of the full size pitch, six attackers try to score in the full size goal against six defenders and a goalkeeper. - When a defender wins the ball he should pass it, with or without the help of a teammate, to one of his two stationary midfield players behind each of the cone goals on the center line. These players finish the counterattack initiated by the defense with a shot.on goal at the other end of the field. The full size goal is defended by a goalkeeper. - The time for this counterattack should be clocked.

Variation: An additional attacker is positioned close to the center line to intercept the passes of the attacking defenders to one of the two static midfield players who, when they receive the ball, play a 2v1-counterattack against him.

"Training is a development through gradually increasing demands (Moorehouse/Gross) within the capacity level of the players involved. First the player may not be aware what he has done wrong and therefore relies on the coach's feedback and questioning which should help him to grip the problem. After more attempts the players knows what he hasn't done well after having made the error and finally his awareness is integrated with his mind and body before he acts and the errors are corrected before they are made"

INTELLIGENT PASSING

"It's easier to pass the ball to a teammate than to pass by an opponent"

The tactics to be adapted by a team must always proceed from the capabilities of that team as well as from their opponent's style of play. Where possible, therefore, tactics should be planned so as to surprise the other side. Quite independent of team formations or strategies in attack, this principle is also generally valid for tactics in passing.

Even if an individual player succeeds, especially in winning a personal duel against a defender, a combined movement between two or more players is the safest procedure to get close to the opposition's goal and into a position for a shot at goal. In a match, therefore, and for energy saving reasons, **passing should be more frequently used than dribbling**. The pass is the **'soul' of soccer** and to master it is a pre-requisite for carrying out any tactical plan.

In order to ensure successful passing, all players must understand and learn the **language of passing and receiving**. Before passing the ball the passer should know when, how and where the receiver wishes to receive the ball. It is absolutely fruitless for the passer to indicate when, how-or where the ball will be passed if the receiver is not ready for the pass. The receiver should communicate with the passer with a visual agreement or eye-contact, through body movements and the position of his head. The majority of the mistakes in passing are caused, apart from lack of skill, because the passer rather than the receiver has instigated the pass.

The higher the level of communication between two players, the more chances exist of **retaining possession**, of making **goal scoring passes** and of **deceiving the defenders**. The fast, mobile and skilful play of the modern defender who allows little space and time to his opponent will be less successful when the attackers have achieved an excellent level of mutual understanding. The potential receiver is the player to ask for a certain type of pass. Provided the technical ability and tactical knowledge of the ball carrier is highly developed, he should be able to pass the ball exactly where the receiver wants it.

What makes passing more difficult is the requirement that the ball carrier is **disciplined enough** to look for and carry out those passes demanded by the team tactics. He generally should prefer to pass instead of attempting to beat his opponent, especially when his aim is to:
- 'pass by' an opponent (generally a through pass)
- allow a better positioned teammate to attack with less risk or to score (constructive pass or assist)
- relieve pressure from his own defense (clearance)
- initiate an attacking move (build-up pass)
- progress in the field (pass into the run of the teammate)
- retain possession (with a back pass or possession pass)

"Look at your pass from the receiver's point of view"

A good pass is characterized by:

* its necessity (very often players pass the ball when there is absolutely no reason for passing)
* its accuracy
* the exactness of the timing
* the speed and the disguise of direction.

The team whose players do not possess these abilities (which can be remarkably improved by intensive training) will hardly meet with success, however much dribbling ability their players do have. **Poor passing is a failing which cannot be offset by other abilities**.

Accuracy in direction

Accuracy in passing is without doubt one of a team's most powerful weapons for overcoming an opponent. It depends not only on the technical ability of the passer but, to a certain degree, on the skilful movement towards the ball and away from the defender by the receiver, **who should instigate the pass instead of reacting to it!**

The **short pass is the easiest**, for the shorter the distance the ball has to travel, the less is the danger that a ball will not reach the receiver. A player who cannot pass accurately over 15 meters will most certainly not be able to do so over 30 meters. Executing long passes is a very difficult technical-tactical maneuver, yet when it is used accurately and at the right moment, it is also the most effective (see the chapter about through passes).

The times when defenders used to clear their lines by long, hard up-field clearances are well past. In fact, there is little sense in simply clearing the ball as far up-field as possible. The ball will more easily fall into the possession of the opponents, who can then immediately mount a new attack. The modern defender clears up the situation, and at the same time, initiates an attack. To do this, he does not always use the long pass, but, more frequently, a short one. But his job is not finished with the clearance pass alone. The defender must immediately run into position again to make himself available for a return pass. The short pass, reaching only the nearest player, must also be part of the modern defender's stock-in-trade.

In a match, passes are made in all directions, to the front (through passes), to the side (square or diagonal passes) and backwards (back passes). The tactical aim in passing is to **keep possession**, which means that every pass that is intercepted by the other side not only gives away the chance of a shot at goal but also nullifies all the efforts of the individual player and of his team.

In order to be able to give an accurate pass, the passer must have checked up previously on the position of his teammates in relation to himself. The "ready position" of the receiver (side-on or frontal with the legs sufficiently bent) or his disposition (to be seen by his head orientation and the direction in which he looks) serve as important indicators to the passer regarding the direction, timing and speed of the pass. For example, if a frontrunner is expecting a pass from behind in the side-on position, with his left shoulder pointing towards the passer, the latter should always pass the ball to the inside left and not in his back. The passer must always play the ball to the side indicated by the receiver.

The shorter the distance of the pass, the more accurate its direction must be, for a long pass gives the receiver more time to get into position, even if the direction of the pass is inaccurate. However, in that case the opponent has more time to intercept the ball.

A common mistake is **lack of responsibility** when passing. Players often kick the ball in any direction without looking first, only then to realize that the player for whom the pass was intended has no chance of reaching it.

Before the pass takes place, both players must make certain that no opponent is standing along the line of the pass, that no opponent can reach the line of the pass in time to intercept it and that no opponent can tackle the player receiving the ball from behind. These conditions must be observed all the more the longer the pass is. The direction of the pass is determined by the position of its target. A teammate's feet are often not the target, however the ball is often played through the gap between two players or between an opponent and the sideline. In these cases, the exact direction of the pass is determined by the size of the gap, the speed of the player running onto the pass and the ground conditions.

The larger the gap, the more possibilities there are for the accuracy of the pass. If the gap is very small, then the ball has to be lifted along a clearly defined line or else it will be intercepted.

The timing of the pass

The best moment to give a pass is when the opponent makes an attempt to tackle the player with the ball. Naturally the moment for giving the pass will be determined not only by the conduct of one's opponent but also by the build-up of one's own team attack. Every good player should learn to feel (with the help of numerous little games of 2v1, 3v2 and 4v3 shown in "Developing Youth Soccer Players"by Horst Wein in Human Kinetics 2000) when the precise moment arrives to pass the ball!

The pass should take place at the moment the receiver is ready to run to it and is not yet in an off-side position.

The speed (force) of the pass

The speed of the pass is decisive for the swift flow in combined movements. The players must have fixed in their minds the need to lose as little time as possible in passing. Each pass must have a definite speed. Any substantial variation in that necessary speed may well result in the ball being lost. The ball should reach the gap between the two players in the shortest amount of time, taking into consideration the individual ability of the player receiving the ball. The mistake is frequently made of playing short passes too weakly. Slow passing allows the opponent time to run into the line to intercept. For example, if a player, after a brief look around, sees a teammate standing unmarked 15 meters away, he must count on the fact that the covering defender is lying in wait in the immediate vicinity of the other player, probably just behind him. If the ball arrives very slowly, this generally gives the opponent sufficient time to run forward and reach the ball first. This example shows very c1early how important it is to run to meet an approaching ball. If the pass, and with it a combined move, is to proceed smoothly, then no player can afford to wait passively for the ball to come to him (see the chapter about receiving and controlling the ball).

Passing reaches its highest tempo when players pass first-time to each other, from which very rapid combination play results. However the first-time pass is not always possible, so the ball has to be controlled for a short while before the pass can be served. The player who wants to be able to move the ball quickly, at least at certain stages of the game, must understand quite clearly that the fastest dribbler can never compare with the speed of a ball when passed.

Disguising the direction of the pass

The player must learn to disguise the direction of his pass (see exercises in "The principle of anticipation") but to avoid misunderstandings, he must practice so thoroughly together with his teammates that they get to know the characteristics of the passer.

The direction of the pass can be disguised, when for instance the player does not look in the direction in which he intends to play the ball or if the player does not dribble it in the direction in which he is going to pass. A further method of disguising the direction of the pass is the dummy pass executed at the same time as a body swerve.

All actions occurring in the game, including dummy maneuvers, must be practiced so thoroughly that they can stem almost **automatically** from the course of the game. When the principles outlined above are heeded when passing, the ball will certainly reach the player to whom it is destined.

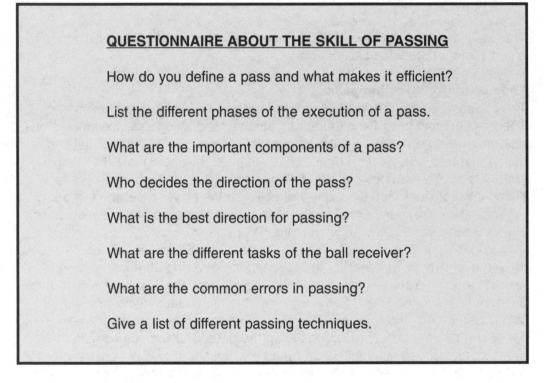

QUESTIONNAIRE ABOUT THE SKILL OF PASSING

How do you define a pass and what makes it efficient?

List the different phases of the execution of a pass.

What are the important components of a pass?

Who decides the direction of the pass?

What is the best direction for passing?

What are the different tasks of the ball receiver?

What are the common errors in passing?

Give a list of different passing techniques.

"A good (bad) pass can become a bad (good) one through the quality of the reception and control of the ball"

CORRECT TECHNIQUES AND TACTICS IN RECEIVING AND CONTROLLING THE BALL

"A good control is able to turn a bad pass into a good pass "

INTRODUCTION

Mastering the reception and control of the ball is of paramount importance as it provides the team the opportunity to maintain or instigate their attacking moves. The high percentage of failure in this aspect of the game (between 15% to 20%) is due not only to technical deficiencies and lack of knowledge (intelligence) but also because of **poor concentration**. That is why more attention has to be focused in training on improving the player's performance in this important aspect of the game.

At the moment a player receives and controls the ball, and even immediately prior to and after it, he should not only know how to 'absorb' the oncoming ball using any part of his body but also what to do, considering a wide range of technical-tactical and perceptive-cognitive aspects such as:

The importance of running towards the oncoming ball

The run into space making himself available to receive the ball should only be made after a visual agreement with the passer and just as he is about to play the pass.

Instead of waiting for the ball and giving the opponent an opportunity to intercept the pass with anticipation, the receiver has to go for it, doing everything to lose his marker, assuming an optimal position which allows him to shield the ball by putting his body between it and the opponent.

The better he masters this skill, the more he provokes a psychological reaction in the defender (loss of self-confidence and frustration) while the attacker becomes more confident in his play.

"Attacking" the ball at the precise moment the pass is made is particularly important for weak passes. Passive behavior of the attacker, before, during and after the pass is made should be considered as a serious tactical mistake. The only time this is remotely acceptable is when the attacker knows how to shield and maintain his position well, not allowing the defender to anticipate and get to the ball.

Orientated control and making use of the speed of the oncoming ball

Through varied and repetitive training all players have to learn not only the wide range of techniques for receiving and controlling the ball but also the capacity to choose between them the ones to master. Selecting the most effective technique to solve the game problem and to get away from his defender is one of several capacities of an intelligent player.

In an **orientated control** the receiver more or less already knows what he is going to do with the ball before he touches it. Often he only deflects or lets the ball bounce off either foot in the desired direction out of his opponent's reach and picks it up behind the beaten opponent. In a well executed orientated control of the ball, the receiver knows how to make optimal use of its speed, allowing him to resolve often difficult situations.

On the other hand, the technique and tactics applied to receive and control the ball depends also on the position of the player involved. This is why many coaches frequently demand that their forwards receive the ball with their back to the goal, as this is more secure and while he is protecting the ball from the opponent a teammate can overlap by surprise and receive a **penetrating pass**. Although this technique can prove effective in certain situations (for instance in the last few minutes of the game when your team is winning), controlling the ball with your back to the goal is usually a disadvantage, especially when counterattacking, as it gives the defense more time to re-organize and the attacker does not have the goal in his sight.

That is why it is better to receive the ball in a **side-on position**, which allows you to continue the attack without any loss of time. A player who masters this technique will become more dangerous and incisive. Even though there is more risk of losing possession of the ball, when it works, an orientated control of the ball often produces goal-scoring opportunities.

The different stages involved in coaching the capacity of receiving and controlling the ball:
1. The preparation stage
- Focus on the ball and correctly calculate its trajectory, height and speed and the distance between the passer and the receiver, as all these factors influence the player's line of approach and the choice of the most effective technique to receive it. - Anticipate where you are going to make contact with the ball. - Get in line with the trajectory of the ball. - Choose the most appropriate part of the body with which to control the ball. - Anticipate and choose the best body position (side-on, head-on or with the body and feet pointing towards the goal but looking over the shoulder to the oncoming ball) to allow a quicker and more fluid attacking move while receiving the ball. - Take your eyes off the trajectory of the ball as soon as you receive it in order to be able to scan and see different options of play. - Stay well balanced.
2. The main (principal) stage
- Know how to relax the muscles in order to soften the impact of the ball as it hits a part of the body. - Know how to make full use of your arms when executing the control. - Know how to "sell" a dummy as you receive the ball. - Know whether to control the ball close to your body or further away, depending on the distance to the next defender. - Know how to select appropriate techniques which facilitate the reception and control of balls arriving along the ground, in the air or bouncing. - Know how to get aerial passes down to the ground as quickly as possible. - Know how to receive the ball depending on what you want to do with it next: keep possession of the ball, play a pass, run with it or shoot at goal. - Know how adapt to poor passes and make sure to keep the ball in possession.

The importance of training

As previously stated, a high percentage (15-20%) of ball losses are not only a result of technical flaws or the inability to correctly calculate the trajectory of the ball, its speed, spin and bounce, but are also due to a lapse in concentration with the consequence of poorly executed passes.

The exercises and games proposed here are directed to develop this facet of the game on an individual and team basis and they specifically deal with how to practice the technical and tactical aspects of receiving and controlling a pass with or without opposition.

EXERCISES/GAMES

A SERIES OF PROGRESSIVE EXERCISES/GAMES TO PRACTICE AND IMPROVE RECEIVING AND CONTROLLING THE BALL

1. Run towards the ball before receiving it	
PITCH	A 20 meter-wide channel is marked with parallel lines, 3 meters apart, at each side
PLAYERS	2
EXPLANATION	- The players should pass the ball only after a visual agreement has been made. The player in possession passes the ball from the inside line of his side to his teammate on the opposite outside line, who at the moment the pass is made runs to the ball before it crosses the inside line. The latter returns the ball to his teammate who, after passing, had moved back to the outside line. - The ball should always move between the two internal lines. - Practice different ways of controlling the balls that arrive at different heights and speeds. That is why controlling the ball on the move will be practiced with different parts of the body (thigh, chest, inside and outside of the foot, head), always trying to make a cushion for the ball, relaxing and inclining the playing knee or the body slightly forward. - The control should be executed preferably in a side-on position, as this allows the player to perceive the situation in the game better and make his next move quickly without losing any time on post-control analysis.

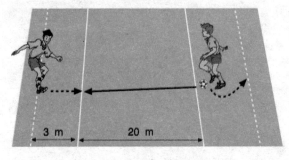

Variation 1: Various pairs compete against each other. The first team that manages to make ten correct passes (on the ground or in the air, according to the demand of the coach) wins.

"To rationalize the teaching and learning process, the number of exercises or simplified games has to be reduced and the number of repetitions has to be increased"

Variation 2:

PITCH	See the main exercises. Two cone goals, 5 meters wide, are placed opposite each other on the two exterior lines.
PLAYERS	Various pairs
EXPLANATION	- At the start of the game all the players are in their own cone goal. - On a visual signal from the coach the player with the ball passes it to his teammate in front who, at this moment (and not before), runs out of his cone goal to receive the ball beyond the 3 meter-line in front of him. Then he turns more or less than 180 degrees and dribbles the ball through the cone goal ahead of him. - The team that scores first with a dribble wins. - The coach, apart from demanding different types of control, insists on the importance of the orientated control for flat and aerial passes.

2. Orientated control of the ball around a square

PITCH	A square 15 x 15 meters marked by cones
PLAYERS	5
EXPLANATION	- All cones of the square are occupied with by player who has to position himself slightly outside the square. - The player with the ball, with a fifth player waiting behind him, passes the ball to the next player and follows his pass. The next player, after an oriented control, does the same until two laps of passing around the square have been completed in the quickest possible time, with neither the players nor the ball entering into the square at all. Again, immediately after playing a pass the player has to follow the ball until he reaches the next cone, and so on. - The players should look for the best control technique that allows them to play the ball as quickly as possible. For example: receiving with the exterior foot (orientated control) and passing with the inside foot, being in a balanced position, never touching the ball more than twice and playing it when possible first-time. If the players don't discover the correct way to pass the ball around quickly, the coach asks questions and also demonstrates how to do it best. - A competition can be organized in various squares between various teams of 5 players (perhaps insisting on passes in the air).

"It is not correct to help the players a lot and to do for them the things that they should and can do on their own"

Variation 1: Instead of passing the ball in a clockwise direction, it should now go counter-clockwise, which forces the players to control the ball with the right (outside) foot and pass it with the left (inside) foot.

Variation 2: A sixth player is introduced into the game. His mission is to run without the ball twice around the square, trying to beat the ball passed by the 5 players. If the runner wins, all possible mistakes by the 5 players have to be analyzed in detail.

Variation 3:

PITCH	4 zones 25x55 m. (1/4 of a full size pitch). The 4 cones are positioned as in the illustration with 4 teams made up by 4 players, each team forming a trapezoid shape within the playing zone.
PLAYERS	4 teams of 4 players, that means 2 wingbacks (playing in a slightly advanced position) and two central defenders on a different level as shown in the illustration. Each team occupies one of the 4 zones.
EXPLANATION	- Each team has to circulate the ball from one player to the next until the ball has crossed the whole width of the field. A circuit there and back (outside of the cones and as quickly as possible) has to be completed. - The team that finishes the 6 passes and receptions first wins. - The coach asks thought-provoking questions to elicit ideas as to how to complete the exercise more quickly.

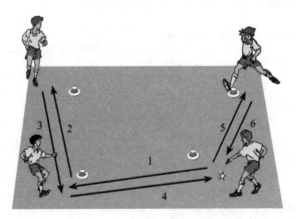

"A good reception of the ball turns a bad pass into a reasonably good one"

3. Reception and control of the ball when fatigued

PITCH	Two cone goals opposite each other 20 meters apart with a center line.
PLAYERS	2
EXPLANATION	- An attacker stands beside a cone positioned 3meters behind one of the goals. The player in the opposite goal passes to him and he runs to control the ball before it reaches the center line and passes it back. He immediately turns and heads back to his cone. As soon as he reaches his cone, the other player makes the next pass and so on until the time is up (30 or 45 sec.) - After a few minutes of practice a competition can be organized. A tally is made of the number of correct controls the player achieves in the allotted time of 30 seconds (45). Pairs can also compete against one another, practicing several different types of control.

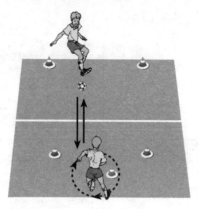

Variation: The player who receives the ball beyond the goal line should run back with it to the cone before passing it back. To not lose too much time, the orientated control is used in this variation.

4. Making use of the pace of the ball

PITCH	A cone goal 10 (12) meters wide
PLAYERS	2
EXPLANATION	- The player 8-12 meters in front of the cone goal plays a hard pass to the opponent who from a position 1 meter behind the 10-12 meter-wide cone goal runs to the ball, absorbs its speed and takes it with an orientated control towards one of the 2 cones. - Before the ball is received, the opponent looks up to observe to which cone the passer is heading. He then adjusts his orientated control and dribbles the ball towards the opposite cone before the passer can touch the cone he is headed for. - The passer of the ball is not allowed to change his mind once he is running towards one of the two cones which mark the goal.

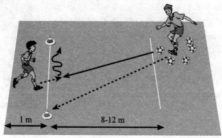

1 m   8-12 m

Variation 1: The same as the original game but this time with aerial passes.

Variation 2:

PITCH	Two cone goals are positioned on an imaginary line on the training pitch some 8 meters apart. One player (passer) is 8 meters in front of the goal and the other (receiver) is 3 meters behind it and opposite him.
PLAYERS	2
EXPLANATION	- The game starts with a hard 8m pass to the receiver, who goes towards the ball to take advantage of its speed, executes an orientated control and, with as few touches as possible, takes it through either cone goal, as the passer follows the ball and tries to stop him. - The ball receiver should use either foot when executing an orientated control or dribble in order to shield the ball.

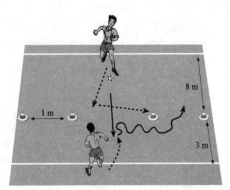

5. Control of inaccurate passes

PITCH	A channel 12x30 meters, with a 10-12 meter wide cone goal at each end
PLAYERS	2
EXPLANATION	- A player starts the game 8 meters in front of his cone goal inside the practice area. The aim of the game is to score with a powerful shot in the opposite goal. The shot is always taken from a spot where the player intercepts the ball. So as soon as the kick is taken the opponent should run to get closer to the ball so that he can control it closer to the opposite goal and thus have a better chance of scoring with the next shot. The game requires plenty of courage, aggressiveness, mobility in the joints and flexibility apart from reaction speed. - All shots should not be at or below waist-height. The defending player is not allowed to save the ball with his hands. - If the ball runs across any sideline of the playing area, the game is restarted with a kick-in from the spot where it went out of play. - For a shot above waist-height the opponent is awarded 1 point and scoring a legal goal earns a point for the attacker. - The winner is the first to 6 points.

6. Controlling the ball against opposition

a)	Controlling the ball and then taking on an opponent
PITCH	Two goals (12 m) are positioned opposite each other 20 meters apart. A line is drawn 3 meters behind each goal parallel to the goal line.
PLAYERS	4
EXPLANATION	- An attacker, looking up with the ball at his feet, is in one of the goals, while his teammate is in the other waiting for a pass, with a defender standing on the line 3 meters behind him. - As soon as it is played, the teammate runs at least 3 meters towards the ball, while the defender chases him trying to win the ball. The rules of this game are such that the defender is not allowed to chase the receiver beyond the 3-meter line. - Once the attacker manages to control the ball beyond the reach of the defender, he should turn and face the defender in the 3-meter zone where he tries to dribble past him and control the ball on the second goal-line (12 meters wide). - When the defender manages to win the ball inside his 3-meter zone three times in a row, he and his teammate behind the other goal become the attacking pair. - The team that scores 10 goals first wins. The coach should organize a competition between various pairs once all players understand their function.
LEARNING OBJECTIVES	- Improve mutual understanding between the passer and the receiver. - Don't wait for the ball, go for it with acceleration to avoid the anticipation of the opponent. - Control the ball in such way that the next move is successful. Perform orientated controls, especially when the defender is nearby. - As an attacker, know how to lose your marker in the 1v1-situation, shielding the ball with your body when changing direction and speed. - When the attacker manages to control the ball and shield it with his body, the defender should retreat a few steps and wait to make the challenge. Patience is necessary for the defender to find the right moment for tackling the attacker. - As a defender you should try to anticipate what the attacker is going to do as he is controlling the ball, especially if the pass is poor or weak.

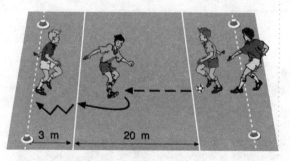

3 m   20 m

"A continued participation in an activity is directly related to the amount of success attained by the individual."

D. Millmann

b)	Controlling and passing the ball when being marked
PITCH	A square of 10 x 10 meters with 6 meter channel around it
PLAYERS	4 , two in the square and two outside, on opposite sides
EXPLANATION	- One of the players on the outside is in possession of the ball. He should pass it to his teammate inside the square who is being very tightly marked by the defender from any side or from behind (but in this exercise never from in front). - If the attacker is being marked from behind, he should move towards the ball, shielding it with his body during the control, turn and pass it out to the third player waiting on the opposite side 6 meters outside the square. As a variation the attacker can also deflect the oncoming ball straight to his teammate behind him. It is recommended to demand passes with plenty of pace. - If the attacker is being marked from the side, the pass should be played to the opposite side and if he finds himself being marked from in front, he should make himself available behind the defender, indicating to his teammate through cues where he wants the ball to be passed. - Initially the attacker is not allowed to return the ball to his teammate. He must shield it and take it to spaces not controlled by the defender. - Each control with a subsequent pass earns a point for the attacker. A defender who wins the ball and passes it back to the passer also earns a point - After a foul the player who received it earns a point. - After 5 minutes the attacker who played the initial pass can support his teammate, thus creating a 2v1 situation.
LEARNING OBJECTIVES	- Improve the establishment of visual agreements between the passer and the player receiving the ball. This is why it is important to look up. - Learn to pass the ball to the appropriate area, depending on how the attacker is being marked. - Pass at exactly the right time and with appropriate speed. - Learn to play a controlled and accurate pass. - In order to receive the ball with an advantage over a defender who is marking tightly, the attacker has to get away from him. - While controlling the ball take into account the next attacking move - If the attacker is unable to play the subsequent pass immediately because he is under pressure, for whatever reason, he should take the ball towards a zone not controlled by the defense, always shielding it with his body. This will give him the necessary time to think and play an effective pass.

c)	Control of the ball when being marked
PITCH	1/3 of a full size pitch with a full size goal
PLAYERS	4 (2v1 plus a goalkeeper)
EXPLANATION	- A midfielder, positioned 15-20 meters outside the penalty area, should pass to his closely marked frontrunner on the edge of the area. Despite being marked by a defender, he should control the ball, beat him and then score. - The orientated control should be performed preferably in a side-on position using a variety of different techniques and shielding the ball from the opponent. - If there is enough space to one side the ball should be played into this area so that the receiver does not have to try to beat the defender. Instead he lets the ball do the work and allows it to pass by as he turns, chases after it into the area, shields it with his body from the defender and shoots at goal with the ball on the opposite side from where the defender presses.
LEARNING OBJECTIVES	The attackers learn to sell dummies before they control the ball, to use changes of speed to get away from the defender and try to combine the reception of the ball with beating the man, shielding the ball always with their body. That is why while receiving the ball it is important to know exactly where your opponent is before, during and after you control the ball.

Variation 1: Now we have two receiving frontrunners with their respective markers. They should control the ball despite the pressure being imposed by the defenders. On their way towards the goal the attackers should create situations of numerical superiority (2v1, 1v0) that will give them a greater chance of finishing the move with a shot on goal.

Variation 2: In a square of 25 x 25 meters, four attackers have to make themselves available to receive a pass from their teammate 15-20 meters outside the square despite tight marking from four defenders. Any attacker who manages to receive, control and return the ball to the passer outside the square earns 1 point. All the players take turns playing each role (passer, attacker and defender), which they swap after every 10 passes.

As the exercise progresses the attackers learn how to play feints and dummies before controlling the ball, re-directing the ball around the defender, performing both control and dribble in the same move (taking the defender by surprise). Here is the move performed by the attacker broken down into the three main parts:

Run to the ball as quickly as possible to prevent the defender from anticipating the move.	At the same time get a positional advantage over the defender pressurizing you by getting in front of him, blocking his path to the ball with your body, leg or your nearest arm if he is approaching you from the side.	At the precise moment you receive the ball, helped by a good body position and angle of your foot, let the ball rebound off your foot towards an area difficult for the defender to get to, preferably behind him if possible.

7. Control of the ball by a midfielder under pressure from three defenders

PITCH	A square 20x20 meters
PLAYERS	8 (5v3)
EXPLANATION	- The attacking team positions four attackers around the outside of the square and one inside who is competing against three defenders. The aim of the game is to pass the ball to the player inside and he tries to play a return pass to one of his teammates outside despite the pressure being exerted by the defenders. - Each pass made along the ground that goes through the square from one attacker to another is worth 1 point, while a pass of at least 5 meters to the player in the center with his return pass to any of the teammates outside the square is worth 3 points. - It is a good idea to start with two defenders at first and then, after some practice, include a third one. - The first team to 15 points wins.

8. Control of the ball by a central defender

PITCH	A full size pitch
PLAYERS	8 (2 neutral wingers, a central defender and 5 pressing defenders)
EXPLANATION	- The two neutral wingers center the ball (preferably not higher than shoulder-height) to the central defender in the penalty area, where he should control the ball and clear it with no more than two touches towards the sidelines. He has to achieve it despite the fact that at the moment the cross is made, five opposing forwards are moving from different positions on the edge of the penalty area to put him under pressure, trying to win the ball and score. - After a few minutes practice, the central defender learns to use an effective orientated control in which he lets the ball bounce towards the end line of the pitch where there are no opponents at all. With his second touch he kicks the ball clear up-field. - The players rotate positions every 10 crosses.

9. Control of the ball by a midfield player

PITCH	A rectangular playing area with a width of 20 meters is established in one half of the full field, divided into 3 zones 16 meters long (so each of the three areas is 20x16 meters)
PLAYERS	8 (5v3)
EXPLANATION	- The attacking team positions two players in each of the outside zones and one midfield player in the central zone, while the defending team has one player in each of the three zones. - The game starts with a 2v1 situation in the first zone, from where the attackers have to pass the ball to the midfield player in the central zone who, despite the pressure from one defender, controls the ball and passes it on to the teammate in the third zone who is less marked by the defender. - A points system can be established for successful moves and for winning the ball. - The midfield player should practice controlling and passing the ball with two touches and playing the ball first-time as well as receiving the ball in a side-on position, using preferably the orientated control.

10. Control of the ball by a frontrunner

PITCH	A square of 6x6 meters marked by cones in front of the penalty area
PLAYERS	7 (4v3)
EXPLANATION	- A center forward, inside a 6m square, expects together with two inside forwards, each positioned on a different side of the square, a pass from his midfield player who is 15 meters from the square. - Three defenders, one behind the center forward and the other two on each side of the square but all outside of it, start to press the center forward the moment the latter receives the 15m pass from the midfield. As soon as the ball enters the square all three defenders may enter as well to press the receiver. - The striker needs to decide whether to play the ball himself or pass it first-time to one of his teammates so that they can finish the move with a shot on goal. - If one of the defenders wins the ball he has to return it to the initial passer who repeats the exercises until all attackers have played 6 times in each attacking position.

11. Control of through passes

PITCH	One half of the full size pitch
PLAYERS	5 (3v2)
EXPLANATION	- From close to the center line a midfield player passes the ball in the air to one of his teammates about 15 meters away. They are each closely marked by a goal-side defender. Despite the presence of the two defenders either of the two strikers should be able to gain an optimal position which allows him to collect the ball with one touch in the space behind the defense and with a second touch execute a shot at an empty goal. - Any goal scored after more than two touches does not count.

12. Control of the ball by an attacker in the penalty area

PITCH	One half of a full size pitch is divided into 3 equal zones, 16.5 meters each. None of the players can enter the middle zone.
PLAYERS	12 (6v6)
EXPLANATION	- The two teams are distributed as in the illustration. One team made of four midfield players in the zone of initiation and two attackers inside the penalty area is opposed by another with 2 midfield players in the zone of initiation and 4 defenders inside the penalty box.. One of the defenders acts as sweeper starting from the penalty spot. This way the two frontrunners have some space to offer themselves without running offside. - One of the four midfield players passes through the neutral zone about 10 meters "deep" towards one of the attackers in the box. Despite the numerical supremacy in defense he should gain position in relation to the defenders first, then receive or deviate the ball and finally shoot at goal or pass it to his teammate close to him if he is in a better position to score.

33 m

13. Orientated control of the ball by wingers or wingbacks

PITCH	An 8 meter wide cone goal is established on either sideline and 10 meters further up-field there is another cone goal 10 meters wide but parallel to the end or center line.
PLAYERS	2
EXPLANATION	- Out of the center of the pitch a midfielder tries to score with powerful passes in a cone goal 25 meters away. A wing or wingback inside the cone goal defends it and collects the accurate or inaccurate pass (lower than shoulder height) with an orientated control in a head-on position without stopping it. Whether the pass was played along the ground or in the air, he lets it rebound with any surface of his body into the direction of his run towards a cone goal 10 meters ahead. The receiver who needs less time for receiving the pass and then controlling the ball in the cone goal ahead of him is the winner. - The receiver performs different techniques of the reception and control of the ball, depending on how it arrives. Ideally he combines the techniques of receiving/controlling and dribbling into one in order to save time. - Every 3 minutes the two players swap roles, practicing on both sidelines.

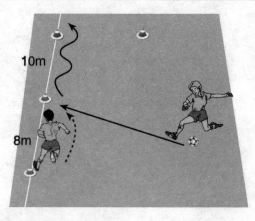

Variation 1: Passer and wing attacker are from the same side. Two pairs are competing making use of both sidelines. After a visual signal, both midfield players from different teams start the exercise at the same time with a pass directed towards the cone goal on the sideline. The winner is the pair that scores first by controlling the ball on the 10m wide goal line.

Variation 2: Two pairs of opponents face each other at the same time in both wing positions. The passer and the receivers are always from different sides. Now the passer, after his powerful pass, has to defend the second cone goal to which the wing is heading to not allow him to score with a dribble before he arrives to prevent it.

"The player or coach who doesn't learn from mistakes or a defeat will always be a beginner"

Variation 3:

- A third player, a defender with the function to intercept the initial pass to the wing, places himself between passer and receiver which now form a team. He employs a zonal marking, which means he tries to cover as much space as possible and also disallows a direct or a diagonal pass to the winger.
- The receiver learns to show for a pass in different ways. For example, when the defender is close to him, he sprints diagonally towards the center to get in front of the defender and receive the pass. He could also make a surprise run down the wing, forcing the defender to go with him, only to turn suddenly and go back to receive the pass behind the defender.
- This game can also be played with the passer supporting the winger or wing back.

"Tasks that are too difficult result in frustrations and anxiety, whereas those not challenging enough result in boredom."

Harter

THE CAPACITY TO PLAY THROUGH PASSES

"When the soccer coaches of today tend to teach and coach the way they were taught in the past, how can we expect progress?"

EXERCISES/GAMES

A SERIES OF PROGRESSIVE EXERCISES/SIMPLIFIED GAMES FOR IMPROVING THE CAPACITY TO PLAY THROUGH PASSES

1. 3v1 with a through pass to one of the three attackers

PITCH	3 playing areas 15x20 meters separated by a neutral zone in the middle 15-20 meters long
PLAYERS	8 (2 x 3v1)
EXPLANATION	The game starts in either of the two outside areas with three attackers facing one defender who exerts constant pressure on them to prevent them from passing the ball out of their zone towards one of three teammates who are offering themselves in the opposite zone. There a second defender tries to read the intention of the passer and do everything to intercept the long through pass through the midfield inside the second playing area. The six attackers should manage to play four through passes without losing possession of the ball. The coaches are asked to adapt the dimensions of the playing areas to the performance levels of his players.

Variation: 2v1 with a through pass to one of the attackers in the opposite area

PITCH	Two playing areas of 10x16 meters separated by a neutral zone of 10(20)x16 meters
PLAYERS	6 (2 x 2v1)
EXPLANATION	See the main game with the exception that there is one attacker less in each zone to make the game more difficult.

"Coaches should make sure that their players learn in an atmosphere of success. They should only expose them to the next exercise or game when they have mastered the previous one."

2. 2v2 with a through pass to one of the two attackers

PITCH	Mini-Soccer with 2 goals at each end
PLAYERS	8 (2v2 in the midfield area plus 2 players from each team in each penalty box)
EXPLANATION	- After the initial thrown ball, two midfield players, despite the pressure from two opponents, try to play a through pass to either of their two frontrunners in the shooting zone. The forwards have to control the ball and score in either of the two goals. - Every 3 minutes the attackers and midfield players swap roles

Variation 1: 2v2 with a through pass to the attacker

PITCH	Mini-Soccer with 2 goals at each end
PLAYERS	6 (2v2 plus an attacker in each team)
EXPLANATION	- The two midfield players of each team as well as the outlet player of each team cannot leave the zone assigned to them. - After the thrown ball in the center of the Mini pitch the team that wins the ball looks for a through pass to the frontrunner. Running into an uncovered area is as important as establishing a visual agreement with the passer. - Once the ball is in the upper zone of the pitch, any teammate or opponent from the midfield may support the receiver in attack for scoring in either goal or in defense. - All players should practice as midfield players and attackers. - As a variation the attacker is not allowed to score. He has to wait for a support from one of the two midfield players in his team.

"Poor performance in the short term doesn't mean that the long term objectives cannot be accomplished"

Variation 2: 3v3 with a through pass to one of the two attackers

PITCH	Mini-Soccer with 2 goals at each end
PLAYERS	10 (3v3 in the midfield area with two players from each team in both penalty areas)
EXPLANATION	- After the ball is played in by a neutral, a 3v3 game takes place in the midfield area of the pitch until they are able to feed one of the two attackers with a through pass, preferably the one who is in the best position to receive the ball. - A competition can be organized played in a fixed time-period.

Variation 3: Same as variation 2 but with only 1 attacker in each end zone.

3. 2v2 with a through pass to a marked attacker	
PITCH	Mini-Soccer with 2 goals at each end
PLAYERS	8 (2v2 in the midfield and one attacker/team marked closely by a defender in each shooting zone)
EXPLANATION	- See illustration. The attacker offers himself up front, covered by a fifth player in each team who always has to remain on the shooting zone line to intercept through passes to the frontrunner behind him. - Two goalkeepers can also be introduced into the game, one for each pair of goals.

"You can help a player a lot by correcting him, but more by encouraging him"

Variation 1: 3v3 with a through pass to one of the two attackers being marked

PITCH	Mini-Soccer with 2 goals at each end
PLAYERS	12 (3v3 in the middle plus two attackers up front in each team and another defending only on the line of the 6 meter-shooting zone)
EXPLANATION	- After a thrown ball the three players from each team try to gain possession and keep it in the midfield area until they see the opportunity to serve a through pass to the shooting zone. - In each of the two shooting zones, two attackers offer themselves up front, covered by a sixth player in each team who always has to remain on the shooting zone line to intercept through passes to the frontrunners behind him. - The attackers should adapt their play and move into space to be available for a through pass. Besides agreeing visually with the ball carrier, they should give cues to understand each other better and improve the effectiveness of the through passes. - Every five minutes the players in both teams swap roles until all have experienced each role (the 3 positions: midfield player, defender on the shooting zone line and attacker in the shooting zone).

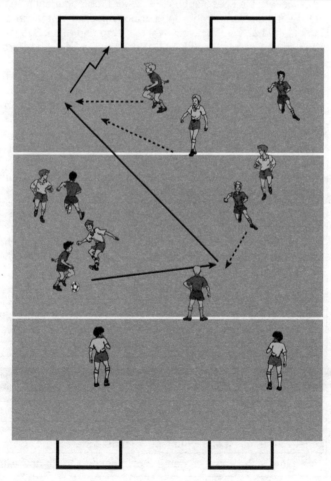

Variation 2: 3v3 with a through pass to the only attacker being closely marked

PITCH	Mini-Soccer with 2 goals at each end
PLAYERS	10 (12) (3v3 in the midfield area plus an attacker up front for each team and another defending along the shooting zone line)
EXPLANATION	There is only one attacker in each team in this variation who is also being defended by a defender moving along the 6m line.

4. Through pass to an attacker being tightly marked

PITCH	A square 10x10 meters marked by cones and another area 6-10 meters away.
PLAYERS	4 (2v2). A game of 1v1 in the central square and another player in each team 6-10 meters away one on either side.
EXPLANATION	- The player in the attacking team outside the square plays a through pass to his teammate inside who is being very tightly marked from behind or to the side. For learning purposes, initially the attacker should never position himself in front of the defender. - The attacker tightly marked to one side should always expect the ball being passed into the space opposite to where the opponent is marking. First, the receiver indicates with his hand or body position to the ball carrier where he wants the ball to be passed. While turning and running to the oncoming ball he should always place his body between the ball and his opponent, thus shielding the ball. - His aim is to pick up the through pass and serve the ball to his teammate outside the square 10 meters away. - After 5 minutes the four players should swap positions and roles until all the players have experienced each one. - A competition can be organized between different pairs to encourage more repetitions of the capacity to pass and control the ball despite severe marking. - As a variation the passer can enter the square after he has made the pass to establish a numerical superiority 2v1.
LEARNING OBJECTIVES	- This game helps to improve understanding between the passer and the receiver of the ball. The passer learns to play well-timed passes into the space or directly into the feet of the receiver depending on how he is marked and what the receiver demands. The idea is to always receive the ball with an advantage. - The receiver should always try to place himself in such a way to the defender that he can control and observe him in order to later make optimal use of the space behind him. It is fundamental for the attacker to have mutual agreements with the passer concerning the meaning of his body feints. This will help him to get away from his opponent.

5. 2v2 with a through pass to the attacker being tightly marked

PITCH	Mini-Soccer with 2 goals at each end
PLAYERS	8 (2v2 in the midfield area plus a front-line attacker in each team, one in each penalty area, being tightly marked by a defender)
EXPLANATION	This game is the same as game 2 of variation #1, but now with a defender

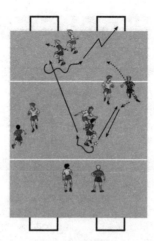

Variation 1: 3v3 with a through pass to the attacker being tightly marked

PITCH	Played in the midfield area of a Mini-Soccer, 7-a-side Soccer or full size pitch. The dimensions of the playing area depend on the performance level of the players. At each side of the central playing area are two adjacent zones.
PLAYERS	10, 6 of whom dispute the ball in the central area of the pitch (3 against 3) and one front runner with a marker each is in each of the outside zones
EXPLANATION	- As soon as the game situation allows it, one of the 3 attacking players in the midfield area should play a through-pass to his teammate in the opposition's area, the latter being tightly marked by a defender from behind or to the side. - The frontrunner should make himself available to the ball carrier in the midfield in order to receive the ball, control it and swivel to get the better of the defender and go on to score in the goal. - The through pass should ideally be played along the ground and to the side not being covered by the defender. The attacker should indicate exactly where he wants the ball to be passed. - From time to time both front runners as well as their defenders should switch positions and functions with any of the midfield players.
LEARNING OBJECTIVES	- Improve the understanding between the passer and the receiver. - Learning to play a well timed through pass at the right moment to the area indicated by the receiver and with the right pace on the ball. - The attacker receiving the ball should learn how to communicate with the passer and also try to get behind his defender into a better position to play the oncoming ball than the defender.

Variation 2: Through-pass with support from the midfield

PITCH	Mini-Soccer with 2 goals at each end
PLAYERS	10 (3v3 in the midfield area plus two other pairs, one in each penalty area)
EXPLANATION	- This variation helps players learn to attack from the midfield or second line. - The play in the midfield area is the same as in the main game with the exception that just as the pass is made to the tightly marked attacker in the shooting zone, one or even two of the midfield players may join the attack, running into his zone to support the receiver. The defending midfield players have the same right and may support their only defender. The aim of the support of both teams is to establish by surprise a numerical superiority of players in this zone of the pitch and score or clear the ball. - A goal is worth 1 point and if a midfield player scores his team earns 3 points.

6. Keeping possession (3v2) with through passes

PITCH	Divide the playing area (15x18 m) into 3 equal zones (15x6 m)
PLAYERS	6 (3v2, with an attacker in each of the three zones, and two defenders who can play where they like). The sixth player is the third defender who substitutes one of the defenders after they win the ball.
EXPLANATION	- The three attackers try to keep possession of the ball without leaving their respective zones, despite the pressure being exerted by the two defenders all over the playing area. - The best way to make life difficult for the defense is to always pass the ball to the less marked teammate, which frequently is the player furthest away from the ball. None of the attackers can leave the area assigned to him. The ball carrier should avoid going into a 1v1-situation. It is advisable for him to look for a 2v1-situation with the teammate in the adjacent zone or a through pass to his teammate in the end zone. While keeping the ball in possession, which is also possible through running with the ball, a triangle formation should be adopted. This allows the players to have more passing options. - If the two defenders win the ball or it runs out of the practice area, the third defender interchanges position and functions with one of the former defenders. The latter, being outside of the practice area, now counts the seconds the attackers are able to keep possession of the ball, After six attempts by the attackers to establish their record for how long they can keep the ball, the defenders (including the third defender) become the offensive team and one of the ex-attackers becomes the substitute defender. - The team that keeps the ball the longest or plays the highest number of through passes with one ball possession wins.

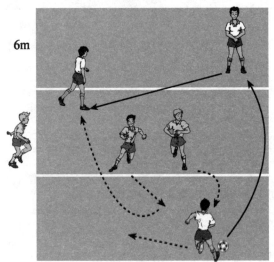

15m

6m

"In soccer, the road to success is covered with many obstacles, defeats and disappointments"

7. 4v4 with a through-pass played through one of the two cone goals

PITCH	A 7-a-side pitch. A playing area of 40x20 meters is marked with cones in the center of the pitch. Outside of this area two cone goals (3m wide) each are positioned on both penalty area lines 11 meters from the end line.
PLAYERS	8 (4v4)
EXPLANATION	- A 4v4-game is played in the midfield playing area with the aim of passing the ball from anywhere inside the midfield through one of the two opposing cone goals. - If the defending team manages to win the ball they become the attacking team with the aim of passing the ball through one of the two goals at the other end of the pitch. - Players learn to transition quickly from defense to attack and play a through pass immediately after the ball recovery.

Variation: 4v4 with through a pass through the cone goal being least defended by a fifth player

See the game before. There is now one additional defender in each team located outside the central playing area in front of the 2 cone goals . His job is to read the intentions of the attacker and intercept their passes through either of the two goals behind him.

"The soccer coach should know that most of his players learn about 10% of what they read, about 20% of what they hear, about 50 % from what they see and hear and about 90 % of what they do"

8. 4v4(5v5) with a through pass to the front-line attacker

PITCH	A full size pitch or 7-a-side pitch
PLAYERS	10 (4v4 plus a front-line attacker, or 5v5). As an option a goalkeeper can be included
EXPLANATION	- A game of 4v4 (5v5) is played in the midfield area of the pitch. After five consecutive passes a through pass can be played into the upper zone where the front-line striker makes himself available to receive the ball and score. - An attack ends with a goal, the ball going out of play or an infringement of the rules. - The game will be restarted with a throw in.

Variation 1: Through pass to an attacker being tightly marked and supported by a midfield player

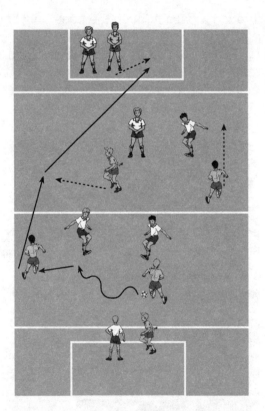

Variation 2: Through pass with the attacker being marked by two defenders
The same as described in the original game but now the attacker is faced by two defenders in the upper zone. To further develop the game one or two midfield players from each team should be encouraged to support their attack or their defense once the through pass was made.

"The strategies of chess are applicable to soccer. Every move must be made with future moves in mind."

9. Through or square pass?

PITCH	A 7-a-side pitch is divided into 3 zones, two on the outside measuring 20 meters and one in the center 15 meters deep
PLAYERS	9 (three teams of three players)
EXPLANATION	- One team of 6 players, split into two groups of 3 attackers, have to pass the ball below shoulder-height from their zone across the central zone to one of their teammates on the other side. Three opponents do everything to intercept these through passes. - To play with success, the attackers, apart from good passing and receiving techniques, have to disguise their through passes, give them sufficient speed and demonstrate game understanding in their play without the ball. After a successful pass the receiver should return the ball as quickly as possible to catch the defenders out of position as they had no time to re-organize their defense. - Furthermore, the attackers should: ♦ Only pass the ball horizontally a maximum of three times before a through pass is executed. ♦ Only pass to the player next to them when they have no possibility of playing a through pass (the risk of losing the ball is too great). ♦ Receive and control the ball in the first five meters of the attacking zone. - For any interception of a through pass by the defenders or any bad control by the attackers within the first 5 meters outside the central zone, the defenders earn one point. - Successful passes between the teams on the outside pitches are worth 1 point.

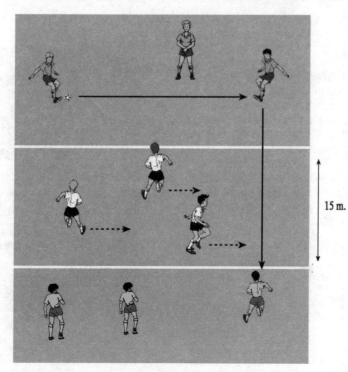

15 m.

Variation 1: Through pass with only two defenders

Younger or less experienced players can practice the former simplified game with only two defenders in the central zone. This makes the execution of through passes easier.

Variation 2: Through pass practice for more advanced players

Five defenders cover the whole width of a full size pitch and try to intercept the through passes of the two teams of 5 players who are again located outside the midfield, 20 or more meters "deep", depending on the level of the 15 participating players.

Variation 3: Through passes in a game of 11 against 11

PITCH	A central zone of 30 x 55 meters is marked on the full size pitch, extending 15 meters to either side of the center line. Therefore, the pitch is divided into three zones, the central zone and the end zones.
PLAYERS	22 (the attacking team has 5 players in the zones up-field and down-field, while the defending team has 4 players in the central zone and 3 up- and three down-field, without counting the goalkeepers of each team)
EXPLANATION	- After the goalkeeper initiates the positional attack, his five teammmates keep the ball (despite the aggressive presence of 3 opponents) until the opportunity arises to play a long through pass from the first playing area through the midfield (despite the 4 opponents) into the third playing area to one of the 5 frontrunners. - Once the 5 attackers control the ball they try to get the better of the 3 defenders and score. - As soon as the through pass is played, the defenders in the central zone may leave the area assigned to them and help their 3 fellow defenders in the third area. - Every successful through pass from one area to the opposite one scores a point while a goal being scored after the long through pass earns another 3 points for the attackers. - After ten attacks the teams switch positions and functions. In the second half of this specific competition both teams are awarded another 10 attacks.

SUMMARY:

A SERIES OF PROGRESSIVE EXERCISES/SIMPLIFIED GAMES FOR IMPROVING THE CAPACITY TO PLAY THROUGH PASSES

1. 3v1 with a through pass to one of the three attackers
Variation: 2v1 with a through pass to one of the attackers in the opposite area

2. 2v2 with a through pass to one of the two attackers
Variation 1: 2v2 with a through pass one attacker
Variation 2: 3v3 with a long forward pass to one of the two attackers
Variation 3: Same as variation 2 but with only 1 attacker in each end zone.

3. 2v2 with a through pass to a marked attacker
Variation 1: 3v3 with a through pass to one of the two attackers being marked
Variation 2: 3v3 with a through pass to the only attacker being closely marked

4. Through pass to an attacker being tightly marked

5. 2v2 with a through-pass to the attacker being tightly marked
Variation 1: 3v3 with a through-pass to the attacker being tightly marked
Variation 2: Through-pass with support from the midfield

6. Keeping possession (3v2) with through passes

7. 4v4 with a through-pass played through one of the two cone goals
Variation: 4v4 with through a pass through the cone goal being least defended by a fifth player.

8. 4v4(5v5) with a through pass to the front-line attacker
Variation 1: Through pass to an attacker being tightly marked and supported by a midfield player
Variation 2: Through pass with the attacker being marked by two defenders

9. Through or square pass?
Variation 1: Through pass with only two defenders
Variation 2: Through pass practice for more advanced players
Variation 3: Through passes in a game of 11 against 11

IMPROVING GOALSCORING

"A goal makes one player happy, an assist, two"

INTRODUCTION

Scoring a goal depends on many factors
In soccer a variety of factors often have an impact on whether an attack ends successfully or not.

The attitude and behavior of the coach
- The coach's character and personality influences the way his players attack and face goal scoring opportunities.
- The socio-cultural environment in which he was brought up determines his philosophy of play. Whether he is conservative or prepared to take risks, inevitably he transmits this attitude to his players. Coaches who have a different mentality than their players generally will have a difficult job.
- Encouraging and supporting players in the important task of goal scoring is a lot more beneficial for them than being critical. For fear of critical comments from the coach, there are attackers who don't dare a shot at goal and instead prefer to pass the ball and give the responsibility and the criticism to somebody else.
- Before fielding a team, a coach should know exactly how many players he has available with offensive and finishing capacities and how many he would like to line up. Are there too many defenders and midfield players with only one frontrunner?
- The coach should encourage both the defenders and the midfield players to have an attacking philosophy whenever the occasion arises. They should systematically join the attack without ignoring their defensive duties.

The attitude and behavior of the players
- The character and personality of the players reflects in the way they approach the attack. Are they carefree and eager to use their creativity as kids or tense and afraid to take risks as is often the case with adults. The education and the environment in which the players were brought up plays an important role. Despite considering all these aspects, the coach should always look for a balance in his team between conservative players and aggressive players who like to take risks.
- Fielding more than one brave, risk-taking player with a goal instinct is a must as otherwise the few goal opportunities likely won't result in a goal. Do we have such players and how many should play the match?
- Can the coach count on attackers who don't mind running systematically free from their markers without receiving the ball?
- Lastly, it is a determining factor to have some aggressive competitive and creative players who manage to win most of their one-to-one confrontations, are capable of getting past their opponent with certain ease and thus creating a numerical superiority in attack and often great goal opportunities.

"A good way to foster enthusiasm in the players is to use a positive vocabulary"

The quality of the final passes, especially the assists

♦ The quality of the final pass (the assist), its execution as well as its reception, determines to a high degree whether the final touch ends with a goal or not.

♦ A simple pass (back or horizontal) secures possession in the attack but slows it down and eliminates any surprise factor; on the other hand, when the players risk a little more with diagonal and through passes, which are often preceded by a feint or a dummy, they are able to unsettle the opponent's defense and often create clear goal-scoring opportunities. Taking more or less risks depends especially on the part of the pitch in which the ball is played. Close to the goal, attackers should take risks.

♦ When no passes arrive up-front, many attackers become impatient and drop back to the midfield in order to get back into the game. This attitude may help the player for a while but doesn't help the team in creating dangerous situations or problems to the opponent's defense. A front-line striker is at his most dangerous in and around the penalty area.

♦ The quality of the pass is very much linked with the quality of the reception and the control of the ball. Receiving and controlling the ball in a side-on position and not head-on with the back towards the goal creates more goal scoring opportunities. The receiver has a better perception of what is happening in the penalty area (where the defenders are, what the goalkeeper is doing, if support is coming down the wings, etc.) giving him far more possibility of finishing the attack successfully.

♦ Top strikers often attract more than one defender. This should allow their teammates to have a little more space. That is why well-timed passes to these teammates, especially when they come from behind, will force the defense to shift their attention to the new danger. In this case, a pass to the striker, who now has more space, may create an excellent goal opportunity.

Shots on goal
Things to take into account when shooting:
- Distance between the ball and the goal.
- Angle of the shot.
- Position of the goalkeeper.
- The number of players between the shooter and the goal.
- The trajectory of the pass to the shooter.

All these variables have to be analyzed quickly in order to decide which part of the foot to use for the shot (inside, outside, instep...), whether to take the ball directly first-time or settle and shoot, if a shot along the ground or a powerful blast into the top corner will offer the best chance of beating the goalkeeper, etc. The more the players practice all these variables, the more quickly they will learn to read the situation correctly, make a good decision and execute different shooting techniques with accuracy.

The need to simulate real-match situations in training:
- All players like to shoot at goal, and often do, and normally a shot is the end product of all the hard work carried out by the rest of the players in the team. Many of the deficiencies with this facet of play are a direct result of inadequate training. For example, shots are usually practiced only by attackers playing against a goalkeeper and often without any active defenders involved at all, which almost never happens in a real game. With this kind pf practice it becomes difficult to improve goal scoring.
- Progress is best made by simulating complex real-match situations during training, which helps an attacker to get a 'feel' for and understand the opportunities that can arise. Furthermore, he gets used to different defensive pressures that require quick perception, thinking and precise technical execution.
- The shooting exercises/games during training should be designed in such a way that the attacker has to think creatively, using his intuition, taking risks, adapting to the situation and at the same time not letting the defenders guess and anticipate what he is going to do.
- Another factor affecting the quality of the shot at goal is that often the ball is not in an ideal position for being catapulted at goal. That is why all players, except the goalkeeper, should practice shooting under pressure from any attacking position, from different distances, with the ball coming from different heights and angles, fast or slow, along the ground or in the air, being in a static or moving position, marked or unmarked. All this will require the scorer to use a wide range of techniques for the shot at goal. The presence of active defenders is a must for advanced players.
- Amongst all the different types of shot, the first-time shot on goal, in other words a shot that is not controlled first, is worth particular attention. This is the most common type of shooting technique used by players at the highest level, as it is more effective due to the power and speed of the ball and the surprise factor.

- It is also worth giving a special mention to headers. Here is some useful information about heading at goal:

- The player should run to the oncoming ball, anticipating his marker's play.
- The player should jump with one or both feet, heading it at the exact moment when the ball in its parabolic curve starts to dip. A good optic-motor assessment helps the player to calculate the speed, height and effect of the oncoming ball and relate these characteristics with the precise moment of the jump and its height. A well trained player knows to suspend himself in the air for a split second when he reaches the peak of his jump, which allows him to put control and power into the header.
- Heading technique should be practiced and learned from an early age so that the players reach adolescence with good technical ability in this important facet of the game.

Essential pre-requisites for making strikes at goal:
- Using the **correct technique** (look for body position, supporting leg position in relation to the ball, the area making contact with the ball at the moment of impact...).
- Choosing the most **effective technique** for the shot.
- Making **decisions** quickly.
- Giving the ball the **adequate speed** depending on how far away the goal is.
- **Accuracy**.
- **Speed of execution** of the shot.
- A high level of **concentration** and good **perception skills** for reading the game situation.
- **Courage and confidence** before making the strike.

Conclusions:
- Generally, it is preferable to shoot along the ground and first time (with no prior control) as goalkeepers have difficulties dealing with these kinds of shots.
- When the ball comes to the attacker he should choose the nearest foot (so, if the ball comes from the left, shoot with the left foot and vice versa), which makes the shot quicker and more powerful.

"Missing the target is a mistake but a bigger problem is not taking the responsibility to shoot at goal at all as attackers must accept the risk of failure "

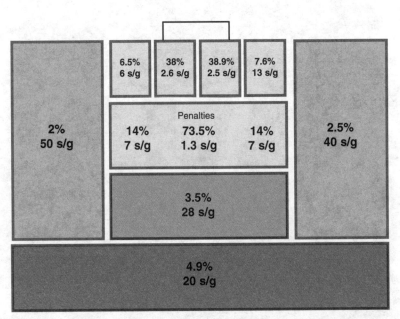

**Effectiveness of shots at goal from different areas of the pitch
(s/g = number of shots taken for every 1 goal scored)**

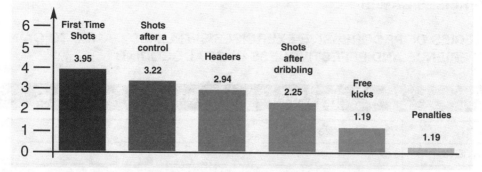

Percentage of different goal-scoring techniques used in the average 14 shots taken in a match

A note related to the following simplified games:

- The following series of progressive exercises and simplified games should allow the players to quickly develop more experience, in theory as well as in practice, in goal scoring, with the aim to become more efficient in these crucial situations of any soccer match.

- The exercises/games follow a natural progression, becoming from a simple start more and more complex. According to the progress of the players, greater difficulties are introduced each time. For example: reducing time and space, adding more players, reducing the numerical superiority of the attackers until goal-scoring is practiced in numerical inferiority as happens generally in the real game.

- Needless to say, all possible analytical shooting exercises, in which beginners and young players hit a stationary and then a moving ball from all angles at goal, are not mentioned here and could be taken from the author's book "Developing Youth Soccer Players", published by Human Kinetics (Illinois-USA) in September 2000.

EXERCISES/GAMES

A SERIES OF PROGRESSIVE EXERCISES/SIMPLIFIED GAMES TO GAIN EXPERIENCE AND EFFECTIVENESS IN GOAL SCORING

1. Running with the ball and shooting at speed

PITCH	1/3 of a full size pitch
PLAYERS	3 (5)
EXPLANATION	- Three (five) players position themselves 30 meters in front of the goal, one on the inside left, one in the middle and one on the inside right. The aim is to run as quickly as possible with the ball to the 16.5 meter-line and shoot at goal from any location inside the penalty area. - A point is earned by the player whose ball touches the net first. After each shot players should rotate their playing positions. - The coach should make sure that some shots are taken with the less skilful foot. - A stopwatch can be used to clock how long it takes each player to complete the task from the first touch until the ball is in the net or touched by a goal keeper.

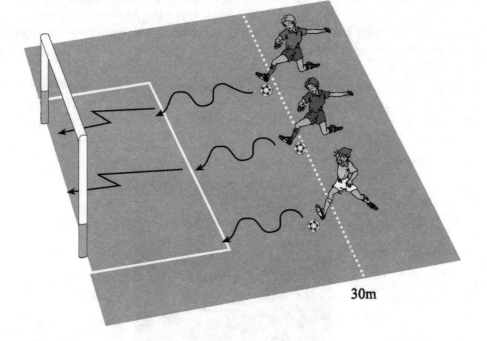

30m

Variation 1: Race between a pair of wings, inside forwards or center forwards from different distances and different starting positions

Variation 2: Instead of individual attacks, now pairs or teams of three compete in a wide range of combinations (as stipulated by the coach), finishing as quickly as possible with a shot from the edge of the penalty box. Each attacker must touch the ball at least once.

2. Shooting with or without controlling the ball first

PITCH	In and around the penalty area
PLAYERS	10 (8 passers, a shooter and a goalkeeper)
EXPLANATION	- Eight players, each with a ball, situated in different positions outside and around the penalty area and one attacker inside (near the penalty spot) with a goalkeeper. - The 8 players with the ball could score directly to surprise the goalkeeper, but mainly pass it in the order and manner as indicated by the coach (accurate, inaccurate, along the ground, at medium height, putting different speeds on the ball) to the attacker inside the penalty area. The attacker must score with a maximum of two touches and as quickly as possible (with or without controlling the ball first). - The attacker should use different techniques for scoring. The choice of the most effective technique to score depends on how the ball arrives. - After having scored ten goals, the attacker swaps with one of the passers. - Each goal scored first-time is worth 2 points. A goal with a maximum of two touches is worth 1 point.

Variation: Shooting with a defender

A defender is now positioned close to the attacker to prevent him from scoring. The inclusion of the defender is to force the striker to 'attack' the ball and when playing it with two touches shield it with his body.

"The coach should strive to make sure that his players are free to 'unlock' their inventive potential when they are on the soccer field"
Marcelo Bielsa

3. Shooting at goal when fatigued

PITCH	1/3 of the full size pitch with a penalty area
PLAYERS	7 (1 attacker, 5 static defenders and 1 goalkeeper) or 2 (1 attacker, 5 cones, and 1goalkeeper)
EXPLANATION	- The attacker sets off from the 30-meter line with the first of the five balls spread across the width of the pitch. He runs with the ball and dribbles around the first static defender or cone and shoots from the edge of the penalty box. After the shot he looks for any possibility of taking a rebound from the goalkeeper. If there is no rebound, he returns to pick up the second ball and so on until he has completed the run with all five balls. - A stopwatch is used to check how long the player takes to complete the shot at goal with the five balls, including the rebounds off the goalkeeper. For a goal scored with the first shot a 10-second bonus is given which is reduced from his clocked time for all 5 shots. For each goal scored with a rebound the bonus will be increased to 30 seconds. - The winner is the attacker who needed less time to shoot 5 times under fatigue.

"Mastering a skill doesn't mean that the player knows to use it in a precise moment in a game and to the benefit of his team"

4. Practicing the first time shot with a wall

PITCH	Played in a racquetball/squash court, with a goal marked with tape on the wall
PLAYERS	2
EXPLANATION	The two players stand 10 meters away from the wall. While one of them kicks the ball as hard as he can against the wall, the other, standing next to him, should kick the rebounding ball first-time with either foot against the part of the wall where the goal is drawn.

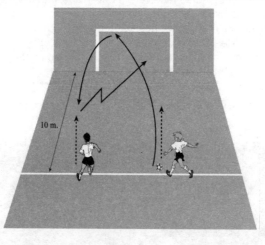

Variation: Practicing shooting under pressure between three players

PITCH	1/3 of the full size pitch with a penalty area and goal
PLAYERS	4
EXPLANATION	A neutral goalkeeper clears the ball towards 3 players at a distance of about 20 meters from the goal. They are separated from each other by 5 meters. All three run towards the oncoming ball and try to gain the best position to touch the ball first and then score with any foot and any technique despite the pressure exerted by the other two.

5. Crossing and heading

PITCH	7-a-side pitch
PLAYERS	6 (two teams of three players)
EXPLANATION	- Both teams attack with a center forward and a right and left wing. Each attacker has to remain in the cone channel assigned to him. - Both teams start their attack simultaneously from about 30 meters from the goal, but in opposite directions. The center forward passes to one of the wingers, who should receive the ball in line with the penalty area, from where he plays a well-timed cross either to his center forward (who occupies the zone in front of the near post), or to the far post for the other winger who is allowed to leave his channel the moment the cross is taken. The target attacker should score with a header in an open goal. - The team that scores first wins.

Variation: Cross and heading with a goalkeeper (and an additional defender)
A goalkeeper is placed in each goal. First he has to remain on his line, then he may rush out and finally he will be assisted by a defender who plays without any restrictions.

6. Scoring when under pressure from two defenders

PITCH	Played in and around a penalty area
PLAYERS	Various passers, 3 attackers and a goalkeeper
EXPLANATION	Various players pass the ball from anywhere outside the penalty area to one of the three attackers, who are near the edge of the penalty box, but each 8 meters apart from the others. The player who touches the ball first becomes the attacker and tries to score a goal before the other two, now defenders, can stop him.

7. Scoring in the 1v1-situation

PITCH	In and around the penalty area
PLAYERS	3 (a defender, an attacker and a goalkeeper)
EXPLANATION	- The defender, from either of the goalposts, clears the ball towards a cone goal (3 meters wide) in front of the penalty area, defended by an attacker. The latter should score in the full size goal despite the aggressive pressure imposed on him by the passer (defender). Depending on the speed and line of his approach, the attacker either takes a first-time shot, receives and controls the ball and shoots or beats the defender before shooting. - Players swap roles after five attacks. The player who scores the most goals wins. - The game should start from both goal posts with pairs alternating their turn.

8. Shooting in a game of 2v1

PITCH	In and around the penalty area.
PLAYERS	4 (2 attackers, one defender and a goalkeeper).
EXPLANATION	- One attacker passes the ball after a visual agreement from outside the penalty area to his teammate on the end line who is marked by an opponent positioned close to one goal post. The teammate runs towards the ball and either returns it first-time to the passer who offers himself for a 2v1 or keeps the ball until he can shoot from close range. He generally returns the ball to the former passer who has a better shooting angle. - A goal is only valid when scored within 5 seconds after the initial pass. - The offside rule is in force - Each player should have 10 attacks (5 in each position) and 5 as a defender.

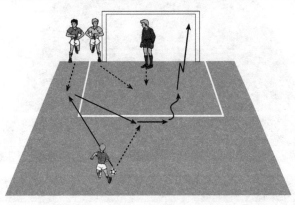

9. Scoring in a 2v1 -situation (variation)

PITCH	1/3 of a full size pitch with a penalty area
PLAYERS	4 (2 attackers, one defender and a goalkeeper)
EXPLANATION	The two attackers start the move 30 meters away from goal. They try to get the better of the defender, without running offside, and score with a shot or rebound within 6 (5) seconds.

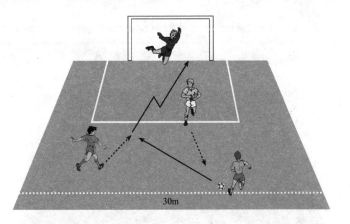

30m

Variation 1:
- A goal is only valid if one of the attackers touches the ball in the penalty area before it is scored.
- A competition can be organized between pairs. The winner is the pair that needs less time to score.

Variation 2:
- When an attacker makes a mistake or loses the ball, he swaps roles with the defender; but if a goal is scored in the allotted time, the attacking pair continues and starts another attack. For a goal, one point is awarded for both attackers.
- The first player to six points wins.

10. Scoring in the 4v2-situation

PITCH	7-a-side pitch or full size pitch
PLAYERS	14 (3 teams -A, B and C- of 4 players and 2 neutral goalkeepers)
EXPLANATION	- On the coach's signal, two teams start a quick attack from the half way line, each heading in opposite directions. In both cases on their way to the goal they are confronted by two defenders who belong to the third team. The defenders try to prevent the four attackers from scoring. - In each attack the team that scores first wins 1 point. After 5 attacks the three teams swap roles until each has had 10 attacks. - The attackers should avoid playing in a horizontal line. Instead they should look to form a rhomboid formation, avoiding the offside rule, and finish the attack with an effective shot before the defenders can stop them.

11. Scoring in a 3v2-situation

PITCH	Played in and around the penalty area from a distance of 30 meters from the goal
PLAYERS	6 (3 attackers, 2 defenders and a goalkeeper)
EXPLANATION	- Setting off from a position 30 meters from goal the attacking team should mount a swift attack, getting the better of the two defenders and shooting at goal. - A competition can be organized establishing the quickest attack or the number of consecutive successful attacks achieved by one team.

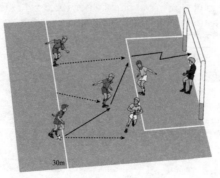

30m

12. Scoring in a 4v3-situation (3v4-situation)

PITCH	Played in and around the penalty area to a maximum distance of 30 meters.
PLAYERS	8 (3v3 plus a neutral attacker and a goalkeeper)
EXPLANATION	- Two teams of three attackers try to win the ball cleared by the neutral goalkeeper. - One neutral player always joins the team that wins possession of the ball to help his three team members to mount a quick attack that must end with a shot at goal in less than 10 seconds. - If this time limit is exceeded, the ball is lost or runs out of play or any infringement was committed by the attackers, the ball is returned to the neutral goalkeeper. - After one team manages to score the game starts again the same way.

Variation: The neutral player always joins the team which lost possession of the ball after it is kicked out by the goalkeeper. This situation simulates a real game situation where attacking generally takes place in numerical inferiority.

30m

13. Scoring in the 2v2 or 3v3 situation

PITCH	The game is played in the penalty box (16.5 x 40 meters) or double the size of the penalty area (33 x 40 meters) with the second goal placed on the 16.5m-line or a 33m-line.
PLAYERS	6 (2v2 plus a goalkeeper in each team) or 8 (3v3 plus a goalkeeper in each team)
EXPLANATION	- One goalkeeper initiates the game of 3v3 in which the 6 players gain important experiences in scoring while under pressure. - The game is played for three periods of 5 minutes. - It is recommended to have several reserve balls available close to the goal posts.

Variation 1: At both flanks channels of 10 meters wide are marked with cones. Both teams position one wing in each channel. Before a goal can be scored, the ball has to be passed to one of the two wingers who, without any defenders nearby, runs down the channel to cross the ball to one of his 3 teammates to score with a header, a deflection or with any acrobatic action despite the pressure from the three defenders and the goalkeeper.

Variation 2: See game 6 from the chapter "The rebound: the second opportunity"

"In the past, game play was delayed until enabling skills were competently performed and tactics were ignored until "mastery" of prescribed skills was achieved"

R. Thorne/D. Bunker

14. Scoring in a 2v3 situation

PITCH	1/4 of a full size pitch with a penalty area
PLAYERS	6 (2v2 plus a neutral player and a goalkeeper).
EXPLANATION	Starting from a position 25 meters away from goal, the attacking pair has 10 attacks to score as many goals as possible. The neutral player always plays as a defender. After ten attack defenders and attackers switch positions and functions.

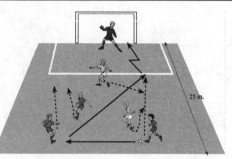

15. 7-a-side Soccer with two balls

PITCH	7-a-side pitch
PLAYERS	14 (two teams of 7 players)
EXPLANATION	- During the first 10 minutes the 7-a-side game is played with one ball and then a second is introduced. This increases the number of shots at both goals which is beneficial for improving the shooting techniques - To focus on long distance shots, goals scored from inside the penalty box are disallowed.

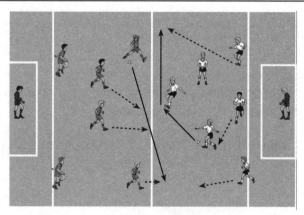

Variation: Scoring is only allowed with headers.

"Luck is the capacity to recognize an opportunity and then, immediately, make the best out of it"

THE REBOUND:
A SECOND CHANCE TO SCORE

"It is easy to miss the target, hitting it is difficult."
Aristotle

INTRODUCTION

The more aware the players are of the necessity to go for rebounds, the more likely they are going to score with this second opportunity. The more rebounds a team produces in attack, the more likely it is that the team will win the match.

Generally spoken, it is more difficult for attackers to take advantage of a rebound than it is for defenders, as at the moment the ball rebounds off the post or off the goalkeeper the defenders are usually closer to the goal superior in number to the attackers.

In order to take advantage of rebounds in attack, a striker needs to have certain abilities, the most important of which is speed (speed of reaction, capacity of acceleration and mental speed, and especially speed in decision making), an aggressive attitude and tenacity to get to the ball before the defenders. Furthermore, an excellent level in agility, flexibility in the tendons and muscles (and also in the mind) and mobility in the joints is of much help to reach the ball first in a struggle between various players in a very restricted area where there is little space and time.

Finally, the capacity to anticipate the possible outcomes of this goal opportunity could make the difference between getting to the rebound first or not. It is best developed with an exposure to a great variety of simplified games in which real game situations appear again and again, and of course during matches.

To achieve a good percentage of success in taking rebounds, it is best that at least two attackers, from different angles, approach or press the goalkeeper after a shot is made on his goal. The attacker should try to cover as much angle as possible and not come too close to the goalkeeper because rebounding is easier when the ball falls in front rather than behind the attacker.

The defenders, on the other hand, should avoid clearing the ball across the front of the goal, as any mistake will become a gift for the opposition.

As far as the goalkeepers are concerned, one of the main errors they make is diving unnecessarily. When forced to go on the ground, they are in a vulnerable position, as for the opposition's attackers it is relatively easy to kick the rebounded ball over the goalkeeper's prostrate body into the goal.

Both the defenders and the goalkeeper should clear the balls wide towards areas uncovered or less controlled by the opposition, and if at all possible towards the wings and never towards the central areas.

"Anticipation is the best way to take advantage of your opponent's mistakes"

EXERCISES/GAMES

A SERIES OF PROGRESSIVE EXERCISES/GAMES TO PRACTICE AND IMPROVE TAKING REBOUNDS

1. Training the rebound with a wall

PITCH	A squash or racquetball court, with a goal drawn on the wall; and two lines marked 5 or 6 meters and 12(16) meters away from the wall
PLAYERS	4 (3 attackers and 1 feeder)
EXPLANATION	- Three players stand 6 meters from the wall. A fourth player kicks a ball from a distance of 16 meters against the wall. The three attackers try to touch the rebounded ball first and score with a first-time shot as quickly as possible in the goal drawn on the wall. - After every fifth rebound from the wall the shooters should change positions. This way neither player has an advantage over the other. - The first player to score three goals wins.

Variation 1: Working together to take the rebound
Three attackers work together to try to score 8 goals in 10 attempts. Once the ball rebounds from the wall they should read the situation correctly so that one of the three is positioned to go for the rebound.

Variation 2: Working together to take the rebound against a goalkeeper
This game can also be played with a goalkeeper who systematically lets all oncoming balls rebound from his body or from the wall without collecting the ball. Now the 3 attackers position themselves at a distance of 12 meters from the wall (goalkeeper). The attackers have only two touches at first and finally only one.

Variation 3: Working together to take the rebound against a defender
The practice develops like in variation 1, but this time a defender is introduced into the game. He stands next to one of the goalposts and runs out to take the defensive rebound and clear it wide or at least put some pressure on the attackers as they try to score with an offensive rebound.

2. Taking the rebound after an individual attack

PITCH	1/4 of a full size pitch with a goal
PLAYERS	4 (3 attackers and 1 goalkeeper)
EXPLANATION	- Three attackers with one ball set off from the 25-meter line and run with it as quickly as possible to the edge of the penalty area, where one of them shoots at goal, preferably at the center of the goal. The goalkeeper must parry the ball in such a way that he lets the ball rebound intentionally into an area in front of the goal so that the attackers have the opportunity to practice the rebound. The goal has to be scored within 3 seconds after the goalkeeper touches the ball. - Every third attack the three attackers swap positions.

Variation: The same with one defender who tries to get the defensive rebound before the attackers can score with an offensive rebound.

3. Taking rebounds amongst three players after a slalom run

PITCH	1/3 of a full size or a 7-a-side pitch
PLAYERS	5 (4 attackers and 1 goalkeeper)
EXPLANATION	- An attacker runs with the ball in a speedy slalom around three of his team-mates who have lined up 3 meters apart in front of the goal outside the penalty area, and shoots at goal without trying to score with this first shot. - Each time one of the players has been passed, he turns around and follows the ball carrier, looking out for an ideal position to be able take the rebound from the goalkeeper after the shot is made. - The three teammates of the attacker should learn to position themselves to either side of the striker in such a way that they cover all positions or angles, forming a semi-circular shape in front of the goalkeeper.

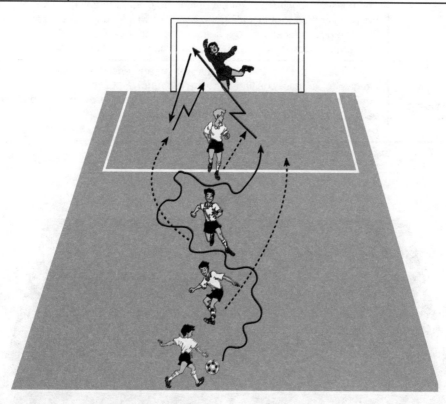

Variation: Taking the rebound in the 4v2-situation

Like the original game but with two defenders, one at each goal post. Once the shot is taken the two defenders intervene, trying to claim the ball from the obligatory rebound made by the goalkeeper and clear it out of the reach of the attackers before they can score with an offensive rebound.

"The aim of education is not only the acquisition of knowledge, it is the capacity to undertake actions at an appropriate moment"

4. Taking rebounds amongst five

PITCH	A penalty area
PLAYERS	6 (5 attackers and 1 goalkeeper)
EXPLANATION	- Four attackers form a semi-circle near the penalty spot, leaving a central channel clear for the fifth attacker to shoot on the run from outside the penalty area towards the center of the goal. - The goalkeeper must save and clear the ball out of the penalty area but never catch it while the four attackers pressure him from all possible angles looking to take the rebound. - Once the striker misses the goal with his shot from just outside the box, he has to swap with one of the other four teammates until all five have had their turn. - The goalkeeper wins a point every time he clears the ball first-time beyond the penalty area (not including the end line) while the attackers earn a point for each goal they score from a first or second rebound. - The game ends when all 5 players have had their turn to shoot.
LEARNING OBJECTIVES	- Players learn to take their chances with an aggressive attitude and, after having gained an ideal position, take the rebound. - Look for a position not too close to the goalkeeper because if the ball falls behind you, taking the rebound is not possible. - Decide quickly which attacker is best positioned for the rebound.

Variation: Taking the rebound in a 5v2 situation

After the first shot, 2 defenders from either side of the goal enter the pitch and help the goalkeeper clear the ball out of the penalty area while 4 attackers and the striker press them.

"The expectation of the coach must be appropriate to the age and experience of his players"

5. Taking rebounds during corners

PITCH	1/4 of a full size pitch
PLAYERS	13 (two teams of 6 players plus a goalkeeper)
EXPLANATION	- Each team has 10 corners (five from each side) to score a goal with the first shot or with a rebound, despite the pressure from 7 defenders. - A goal scored with the first shot is worth 1 point and a goal scored from a rebound is worth 3 points. - To help produce rebounds, the goalkeeper, as in all exercises and games before, is not allowed to catch the ball. Instead he should deflect it or clear it badly to allow the training of the rebound. The 7 defenders try to clear the ball outside the penalty area.

6. Scoring 6v6 in a game with 2 goals

PITCH	A penalty area with two goals
PLAYERS	12 (3v3 plus two support players for each team (one on each post of the opposing team's goal) and a goalkeeper for each team)
EXPLANATION	- After a thrown ball in the center of the pitch, each team tries to score a goal with or without the help of their two support players on the posts who are not allowed to enter the field and can play the ball only with one touch, practicing return passes from the end line. - While a direct goal is worth 1 point, a goal from a rebound is worth 3 points - Duration of the game: 3 periods of 5 minutes each. Each player has to play one period as outlet player. - It is recommended to have reserve balls available close to each goal.

ATTACKING UNDER PRESSURE

*"There is no greater asset on a soccer pitch
than intelligence."*

Cesar Luis Menotti

INTRODUCTION

What does 'playing the ball when under pressure' mean?
A team, or various members of a team, are said to be playing under pressure when the following circumstances take place on a soccer field:

Internal pressure:
- When the players in possession of the ball are desperately 'hanging on' to a result in an attempt to keep the score the same despite the pressure from the opposing team, who take risks and don't give them time to think or space to play the ball with accuracy and security. This situation usually occurs during the final few minutes of a match or during the last couple of minutes of the first half when the ball is disputed much more than in the less critical moments of the game.
- When a team in possession of the ball starts to show signs of physical and mental fatigue, leading to worry and concern in the players.

External pressure:
- When the player in possession of the ball finds himself being outnumbered (1v2, 1v3, 2v3, 2v4).
- Whenever a player in possession of the ball thinks that he is unable to match the high expectations of his officials, of his family, of the spectators or the mass media.

How can a player keep his performance levels from decreasing during these critical moments and how can he cope with the internal and external pressure?
- He must have a lot of **self-confidence**.
- He must make full use of his **experience** (being in the right place at the right time) and not panic even though his teammates are losing their composure as they are only thinking of the score and not of their task at hand.
- He has to make good use of the confidence in his own ability, which should not suddenly disappear under the suffocating pressure being applied by the opposition.
- Instead of worrying about these moments of stress, he should look forward to them and try to overcome them, proving to the rest of the team and the coach that he has been prepared adequately during training to deal with these important moments in the game.
- He has to keep **concentration and awareness** levels high and carry out his responsibilities.
- He must be aware of the factors that are under the attacker's control and that condition the game situation.

"If you want to win, it is important to forget about victory. A little naivete will help you perform better."

EXERCISES/GAMES

A SERIES OF PROGRESSIVE EXERCISES/GAMES TO LEARN HOW TO PLAY THE BALL WHEN UNDER PRESSURE FROM THE OPPOSITION

1. Use your abilities and capacities in 1v1 and 1v2 situations

PITCH	A square of 8x8 meters
PLAYERS	2 (1v1)
EXPLANATION	After a thrown ball in the center of the square, both players set off from opposite corners. A stopwatch is used to time how long the winner of the ball can keep possession against his opponent without leaving the square.
COMMENTS	- Many players find it very difficult to keep possession under these circumstances and so the opposition frequently wins the ball. - The player in possession of the ball learns to make use of the unmarked space behind him, putting his foot on the ball or using his heel to go backwards may give him the time necessary to successfully execute the next action. Furthermore he learns to shield the ball with his body in a side-on position using his arm to not allow the opponent to come too close to the ball, which he protects with the outside of his foot furthest away from the defender. Playing in a side-on position allows him to perceive all movements of his opponent. Selling feints and dummies with and without the ball and suddenly changing the speed and direction and always putting his body between the ball and the defender are other weapons to gain time.

Variation 1: Putting the receiver of the ball under pressure
An attacker, positioned in a corner, receives a short pass from a defender who immediately puts him under pressure. The attacker learns to consider the line of approach of the defender while he is receiving the ball. He tries to get as quickly as possible out of the corner where his options to play the ball are limited.

Variation 2: Keeping possession of the ball in a 1v2 situation
The exercise is similar to variation 1, only now the attacker has to study the
defensive play from 2 defenders who press him. Using the space created
behind him is often a good solution. Top attackers should be put under pressure
after an aerial ball or an inaccurate pass.

2. Control and pass when under pressure

PITCH	A square of 6x6 meters is established with cones in front of the penalty area. On both sides of the square and in front of it, three cone goals (4 meters wide) are put at various distances (between 10 and 15 meters).
PLAYERS	6 (2 attacking passers, 1 central defender receiving and 3 defenders)
EXPLANATION	- The central defender (inside the square) receives back passes from different angles played by his two teammates. He then is put immediately under pressure by 3 opponents who approach him from three sides but can only enter the square once the ball is inside of it. - The ball receiver, despite the intense pressure exerted by the 3 opponents, should manage to keep his self-confidence and calmness and pass the ball through one of the three cone goals. - If the 3 pressing opponents win the ball they have to score against a goal-keeper.

3. Playing in defense under pressure

PITCH	One half of a full size pitch with a line marked at a distance of 28 meters in front of the goal
PLAYERS	13 (5 attacking defenders against 7 defending attackers split 4-3 on the two playing areas and 1 goalkeeper)
EXPLANATION	- When the goalkeeper initiates the positional attack with a pass towards one of the 5 attacking defenders, 3 opponents playing in front of a halfway line (28 meters) start their pressure assisted by another 4 teammates who start their defense from beyond the halfway line. The defending attackers should not allow the attacking defenders to progress on the pitch and achieve their objective to control the ball on the center line of the full size pitch. They form a packed defensive unit to put the opponent's defense under heavy pressure until they are able to take the ball away from the attacking defenders. - After winning the ball, a quick turnover will allow them to attack successfully with a counterattack. - The first objective of the 5 attacking defenders is to avoid the pressure of 7 opponents for as long as possible, making use of their knowledge to play without the ball, using the goalkeeper or a teammate which has made himself available. - The second aim is to progress in the field and control the ball on the 28 meter-line (1 point). - If the "pressing" team scores a goal it earns 1 point. - After each goal or control on the center line, the game is restarted with a throw-in from the goalkeeper.

28m

Variation: 4(6) defenders (not including the goalkeeper) learn to keep possession for one minute or more, despite the full press exerted by 6 (8) opponents (4+4). The time of ball possession is taken with a stop watch. After the ball is lost, the respective players and the coach analyze the mistakes and look for an improvement during the next ball possession.

> *"If any Soccer institution or organization or coach in charge of developing youth soccer sets an unreasonable high level of performance as a standard, they have constructed a formula for failure. The best performance and learning comes from an objective analysis of the real playing capacity of young players, and an adjustment of expectations to reality."*

PART TWO

DEVELOPING
GAME INTELLIGENCE IN
DEFENSE

REASONS FOR A COLLECTIVE
APPROACH TO DEFENSE

"The major obstacle for the progress in soccer is the force of habits. Because of stubbornness many coaches continue with their old coaching patterns without questioning what they are actually coaching"

INTRODUCTION

Coaching defense is underestimated by many coaches in youth as well as in professional soccer. Surveys of physical education students at the "National Institute of Physical Education" in Lleida (Spain) tell us that the practice of individual and collective defense is generally occupying **less than 15%** of all training sessions.

Taking into consideration that in a match two teams of equal level are in a defending role for approximately 50% of the 90 minutes (and a weaker team even more), more coaches must be aware of the importance of coaching how to defend **individually as well as in a unit**.

The reasons for underestimating the coaching of defense are manifold. Players feel that training defensive skills is boring and not as much fun as, for instance, practicing shots at goal. Coaches argue that teaching collective defense is more difficult and that there is generally a lack of knowledge about it due to a lack of literature.

There is still a long way to go until a necessary balance between practicing offensive and defensive plays is achieved. The time dedicated to improving the defense in training has to be increased and more attractive and motivating exercises and simplified games should be offered to defenders, midfield players and front attackers to improve their skills in dispossessing an opponent. The capacity to know which player has to use which technique in a precise moment at a determined place on the pitch demands **game intelligence as well as skill**. This intelligence can be improved with a stimulating coaching program in which player and coach should constantly look to broaden their knowledge and experience.

Coaches should be aware that if the defense performs well in a match but the attack plays poorly there is a good chance to not lose the match, but if the attack plays well and the defense doesn't, then it is very unlikely that the team will win.

Reasons for practicing defense on a collective basis:

1. **Defense is the task of more than one player**. The player who tackles forms part of a defensive unit in which everybody should know his defensive duty in any possible defensive game situation. For instance, when an opponent penetrates with the ball into the opponent's defense, everybody should know who has to approach him, close him down and channel him, why it has to be done, when and how, who should cover the tackler and who is responsible for marking the teammates of the ball carrier closest to the ball.

2. A basic objective when coaching defense on a collective basis is to achieve a **high level of communication** and a perfect mutual understanding between all the players involved in defense. All defenders should learn to interpret the game situation in a similar, or better in the same, way so that they are able to perform as a defensive unit in which each player takes up his specific role or obligation.

3. The coach is the responsible person who imposes on the defenders their **responsibilities and obligations** (which depend on their particular characteristics). He has to make sure that his philosophy of how, when, and where to defend is understood without limiting with his imposed obligations the potential and possibilities of his defenders.

4. Once the young player has been exposed in his early soccer years to a great variety of stimuli for the individual defense (see "Developing Youth Soccer players" by Horst Wein, Human Kinetics,Illinois (USA),2000, page 60-66), it is necessary to learn to defend in a unit. To achieve the necessary knowledge and experience he and his teammates have to be exposed to many hours of practice for the synchronized application of the following 4 defensive principles:

- The principle of **approaching an attacker in possession of the ball** and closing him down.
- The principle of **covering**.
- The principle of **pressing defense**.
- The principle of **anticipation**.

BASIC RULES FOR DEFENDING ON A COLLECTIVE BASIS

10 basic rules which help to improve collective defense

1. Shared responsibility. Defending is always a task for more than one player.

2. Previous analysis. Before starting the defensive duty, the player should:
- Perceive and read the game situation in order to appreciate the options his personal opponent with his fellow attackers may have to resolve the situation to his advantage. At the same time he has to take into account his position in relation to his supporting teammates in defense.
- Process all this information quickly and come to a correct decision on how to defend.

3. Reduce time and space. Whenever possible, more defenders than attackers should quickly position themselves in the zone where the ball is played to give the opposition as little time and space as possible, thus forcing them into mistakes or imprecise play.

4. Condition the attacker. The initiative of the attacking team must be stifled through an **optimal positioning of the defensive unit**, thus conditioning the opponent's play, forcing them to do what the defense wants them to do. Nowadays a defender is not reacting as in the old days, he is acting! He imposes his stamp and initiative and knows to condition or channel the attacker to where he wants him to go. There are various ways to achieve this:

- **Position the whole defense in a certain way**. For example, intentionally leave one or two attackers in any wing position completely unmarked (generally the opponents furthest away from the ball) to entice the opposition to pass the ball to that area which is less of a threat on goal, and give the defense time to reorganize.
  Generally it is a good idea to **channel the opponent's attacks towards the wings** where they have less space and less passing options than in the center of the pitch: Furthermore, it gives the defense more time to think and to apply the principles of pressure.
- **Don't run into the attacker who controls the ball**.
- Select the correct line of approach, taking into account the covering player, and place yourself always closer to the goal and farther inside than the attacker.
- **Don't give your opponent a space**, force him to play in a confined area.
- Force the opponent to play the ball towards your **stronger side**.
- **Reduce his time to observe, to think and to pass or dribble** by putting pressure on him while he runs with or receives the ball. Force him into mistakes.
- Commit or condition the opponent to play in a way that is **uncomfortable for him**. This can be achieved through dummy tackles or by assuming a side-on position to the opponent in order to channel or oblige him to do what you want him to do.
- Make the opponent pass the ball frequently to a less dangerous opponent.

5. Use anticipation skills. Before the opponent gets the ball under control, he should be put under pressure. This can be achieved best by coming close to him with the intention of intercepting the pass before the receiver can reach it. This kind of defense is more successful, economic and constructive than waiting for a tackle until the cover is available.

6. An intelligent defender watches the ball, the positions of his teammates and the rest of the attackers involved in the situation at the same time. **A good defender is not a ball watcher**. While he observes the ball, he also keeps an eye on his personal opponent, the other attackers involved in the play and also his own teammates. This way he knows to position himself correctly in relation to his attacker and to his fellow defenders with whom he always should form a defensive unit. Unfortunately many defenders are very good ball watchers. The ball seems to be a "magnet' for them, as often they forget about the rest of their defensive duties and responsibilities, something which is very common not only in children and adolescents but in adults as well.

7. **Defense should be constructive and not destructive**. Successful defending does not only involve bringing an offensive action to a halt by any means of getting the ball away from an opponent. Soccer is best played when it starts well from behind, from the defense. It is an important objective to win the ball and, without any time lost, be able to mount a new attack. But when defending destructively by committing fouls or kicking the ball wide, the opponent will continue to attack.

   Constructive collective defense allows an immediate turn-over from defense to attack that could be dangerous for the opponent (see the chapter:" The counterattack"). While switching after a constructive defense to attack, care should be taken that the defensive block moves up with the ball to maintain the unit and the readiness for a new recovery in case of a loss of possession.

8. **Turn-over quickly from attack to defense**. After having lost the ball, the defense has to start immediately, without committing the common mistake of leaving a short pause between the attacking move and the defense, thus allowing the opponent to mount a successful attack.

   The defense should **maintain its basic shape** when the team goes in the attack, and in case of a loss of possession, the same player responsible for its loss is generally the first to tackle back. Once the ball has been won by the opponent it is best to use zonal marking that allows the defenders time to take up their best defensive positions and concentrate on their responsibilities.

9. **Communication is a must**. The defenders should communicate frequently, encouraging one another and letting each other know what to do next. Communication is a very important aspect of good defensive teamwork and leads to a more coordinated, synchronized and efficient action against the opposition.

10. **Aggressive attitude is desirable**. Being aggressive is as important for a defender as his awareness of many details of the game situation, such as being balanced or being always at the right place at the right time. The defender should not only confront his personal opponent physically but also with an adequate mental attitude.

"You learn best by doing rather than just listening"

D. Millmann

HOW TO COACH APPROACHING AND CLOSING DOWN AN ATTACKER IN POSSESSION OF THE BALL

"In soccer a lot of things happen simultaneously on the pitch in the same second, what makes the observation and evaluation of the game situation difficult and complex"
Juan Más Rubio

INTRODUCTION

In today's game of soccer defenders are all players in the team without the ball who have to perform different defensive duties for achieving their objective: to win the ball. Their defensive pattern depends very much on how the defender nearest to the ball carrier approaches the attacker in possession because this not only conditions the attacker but also dictates the defensive task of the rest of his fellow defenders.

A special comment should be given here to the most important defender in the team whose performance often decides whether a team wins or loses, and more importantly inspires confidence and security to his teammates: It is the goalkeeper.

THE THREE PHASES OF THE PROCESS OF DISPOSSESSING AN ATTACKER

Approaching the attacker with the ball is only the **first phase** of dispossessing him. In the **second phase** the defender is **shadowing** him to dictate his movements by clever body positioning which also depends on the positioning of the rest of the defense. Generally the defender encourages the opponent to go to his strong side as this is easier for him to defend. But if the defender faces him frontally, the opponent with the ball has two choices to slip away (left or right) as the defender doesn't know where he is dribbling the ball to. Blocking one side while assuming a side-on position would force the opponent to dribble the ball into the direction the defender is prepared for.

Once the attacker moves into the space offered by the defender the **channeling (the third phase)** starts. Channeling in a side-on position is the maneuver used to force the attacker to run into the area desired by the defender, towards the sideline or into areas of the field which are well controlled by the defense. This means channeling is a collective action.

To sum up, successful challenging is the result of clever positioning by defenders to restrict the actions of the attackers and direct them into areas that are:
* less dangerous for the defense (for instance, away from the goal),
* more congested with defenders,
* more easily defended (for instance, close to the sidelines).

Analysis to go through before approaching an attacker with the ball
Before approaching an opponent with the ball, the defender (and also the goalkeeper) should collect as much information as possible through a quick:
* Analysis of his own psycho-physical capabilities and those of his opponent.
* Technical-tactical analysis of the ball carrier.
* Analysis of his own position and that of his teammates.
* Analysis of the position and the runs being made by the opposition.

Once all the relevant information has been processed quickly, the defender, according to the actual game situation in which he is involved (1v1, 2v1, 1v2, 2v2, 3v2, 2v3), should approach the attacker, channel him and retreat alongside the attacker until the best moment arises for tackling.

Analysis of your own psycho-physical capabilities and those of the attacker
An intelligent defender only tackles when he is almost sure of winning the ball. If the defender is slower than his opponent he should surprise him as often as possible by rushing in front of him (anticipation) at the moment of receiving the ball or tackle him before he can pick up speed in his dribbling.

Generally, the defender facing the attacker in front of him tries to slow him down by selling him a dummy while assuming a side-on position. A delay of his tackle, especially when the opponent is skilful, gives the rest of his teammates enough time to get into a correct position to cover and help.

Analysis of his own body position and that of his teammates
It is important to assume at the end of the approach, before and during the tackle a correct body stance with the legs well bent and the feet not flatfooted. Too often the defender makes the mistake of positioning himself in front of the attacker flatfooted and with his feet on the same level, pointing in the direction of the ball. In this position the defender is vulnerable and has no opportunity to slow down the attacker.

A side-on position, a perfect balance, being on the toes and one foot slightly in front of the other to allow excellent footwork are basic requirements for being able to channel the forward or tackle him in retreat. First, the defender steps out of the path of the forward dribbling the ball. Secondly, he places himself slightly to one side of the opponent, thus offering him an open space for penetration. He is now channeling, running side by side or shoulder on shoulder. The defender follows the forward back by means of dummy movements. By these means he forces his opponent into making involuntary moves, so that his chances of success in the duel between the two increases. The defender, without losing his balance, continues to accompany him until he sees a favorable opportunity for dispossessing him.

The great advantage of tackling in retreat or channeling is that the defender has more than two opportunities to dispossess the opponent. On the contrary, after a mistake in a frontal tackle there is no time for the defender to transfer his weight backwards to the supporting leg and then turn around to accompany him. The attacker will be gone already.

Technical-tactical analysis of the attacker on the ball

When approaching an attacker in possession of the ball a defender should evaluate, apart from his own capabilities, the technical-tactical ability of the opponent, which will allow him to make a correct decision about the approximation and challenge. He should take into consideration such characteristics as:

- The attacker's skill and speed.
- The direction in which he runs with the ball.
- If he uses body feints.
- If he prefers a certain technique for beating a defender, for instance going first in one direction and then suddenly moving in the opposite direction.
- If he usually runs with the ball straight to the defender without entering in his range of action or if he tends to run diagonally away from the defender to make him follow.

Analysis of the defender's own position and that of his teammates

This analysis is also very important because if the defender knows that somebody covers him in the 1v1-situation, he will tackle with far more confidence and authority.

That is why it is important to keep the defense compact with short distances between all defenders. Short distances facilitate communication, collaboration and teamwork in defense as long as the players are positioned in a staggered formation and not playing 'flat' or in a horizontal line.

"Building awareness and responsibility is the essence of good coaching"

John Whitmore

If the team is not well positioned, as often happens when a counterattack is mounted, the defender nearest to the opponent with the ball should close him down with good footwork and body composure but with a cool head for not committing the common mistake to rush into the duel. This will give the rest of the defense sufficient time to get back into their basic positions and cover.

Analysis of the positions and runs made by the attackers and his teammates
The defender about to tackle should not focus all of his attention on the attacker in possession of the ball but should perceive the game situation as a whole and monitor also the positions and movements of the rest of the opposition.

"I'm able to control only that which I'm aware of. That which I am unaware of controls me. Awareness empowers me"

John Whitmore

EXERCISES/GAMES

A SERIES OF PROGRESSIVE EXERCISES/GAMES TO TRAIN THE PRINCIPLE OF HOW TO APPROACH AN ATTACKER IN POSSESSION OF THE BALL

1. Tag game 1v1	
PITCH	Half of a penalty area
PLAYERS	2 (1v1)
EXPLANATION	- The attacker sets off from a 25 yard-line in front of the goal. At the same time a defender reacts and sets off from the end line of the pitch opposite the 25 yard-line. The attacker has the objective to cross the end line without being tagged by the defender. - At first the attacker should run at half speed, increasing speed gradually as the defender gains more experience. Finally he should run at full speed. - The defender should approach the attacker as fast as he can in order to get close to him. This way he creates for himself sufficient space to go backwards when trying to slow him down. The slow-down starts when he is approximately 3 yards away from the attacker. Then he assumes a side-on position (never directly head-on-head) in which he is well balanced and on his toes with his legs slightly bent. - No attention is paid to where the goal is located. This happens later. - This practice should be repeated frequently for correcting technical mistakes as well as misjudging in timing and covering the space. - The take-off from both contenders should take place also with both being side-on-side on the 25meter-line or with the defender approaching him from one side line as shown in the illustrations.

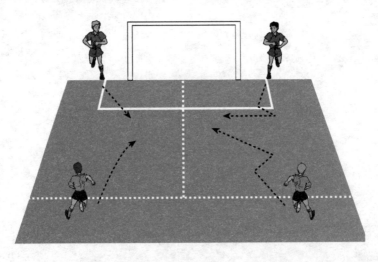

"In soccer all playing actions are made up of a complex combination of perception skills, decision making and execution of technical skills. They all contribute to the success or ball loss. Coaching therefore has to focus on their improvement"

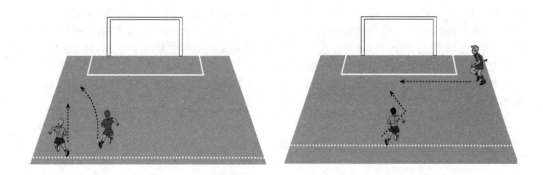

Variation 1: 'get the one dollar bill' game
Both players are positioned on their respective take off- lines at equal distance. A third stands in a side-on position between them in the middle, holding in his hand a one dollar bill. On a visual signal both players set off towards the player in the middle and try to grab the one dollar bill and take it to the opposite start line without getting tagged.

Variation 2: 'conquer the ball' game
This variation is like the original game but with the attacker in possession of a ball. The latter has to take it across the opposing end line with the defender approaching him as early as possible, demonstrating to the coach in each moment that he is capable of assuming in his defensive play an optimal body and feet position in relation to the attacker. The more the attacker is changing the direction of his dribble, the more difficult the task of the defender to adapt becomes. For practice reasons he is not yet permitted to tackle him, nor should he bother about the location of the full size goal.

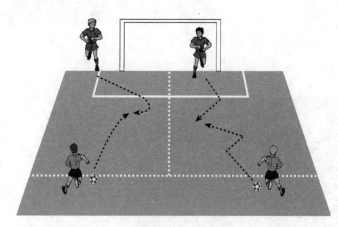

Variation 3: The defender has to learn to approach an attacker also when he is on his left or right side, level with him or also in front on the right and left side as shown in the illustrations. Now for the first time the defender, during his approach, has to take into consideration also the location of the goal so that he can take up a position between the ball and the goal, but always closer to the goal than the attacker.

2. Approach in a correct line, channel and defend in a 1v1-situation

PITCH	Any part of the training pitch with a cone goal 8-10 meters wide.
PLAYERS	2.
EXPLANATION	- Positioned close to a goal post a defender passes the ball with speed from the end line to an opponent standing about 12 meters in front of him. The latter has to control the ball and set off with the intention of dribbling it across the goal line, while the defender, immediately after his pass, approaches him in a correct line for preventing him from running with the ball across the goal line. - The coach or, better, the other players involved should point out any mistake made by both players in their practice.

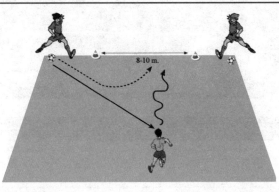

Variation: Approach in a correct line, channel and defend with a supporting player.
- Another defender joins the game and at the moment the ball is passed to the attacker (25 meters away), he approaches him starting from the goalkeeper's area. Then he channels the attacker towards the space which the passer covers behind him. The defender should stop the attacker from entering the goalkeeper's area and score a goal which is defended by the passer.
- The approaching defender soon learns that his way of defense (line of approach, channel and tackling) depends very much on how well the attacker controls the ball .

3. Approach and channel an attacker into the desired direction

PITCH	In a square of 15 x 15 meters with 2 cone goals, each 4 meters wide, put side by side.
PLAYERS	3.
EXPLANATION	- Immediately after his pass from the end line to the attacker at 12-15 meters, the defender approaches the opponent, closes him down and tries to dispossess him from the ball. On the other hand the attacker carries out an orientated control and controls the ball when possible in the cone goal where a score counts 3 points. Only one point is awarded for controlling the ball on the other goal line. - The defender learns to position himself in such a way that the attacker is obliged to go towards the 1 point goal, closing the space in front of the 3 points goal. - The player passing the ball should make sure that this is done from different positions, with different speeds and heights and a little towards the left or right in order to create different problems for the defender who has to adapt not only his line of approach but also his speed of approach to the quality of the ball reception of the attacker.

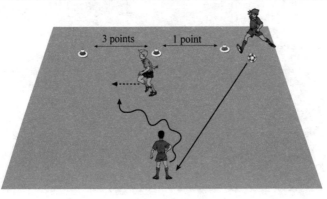

4. Approach and channel an attacker in the desired direction (Variation)

PITCH	15x15 meters, with two goals 6 meters wide next to each other, marked by cones.
PLAYERS	2 attackers and 1 defender
EXPLANATION	An attacker positioned 25 meters from the goals passes to a teammate, who is being tightly marked. The latter should control the pass, get past the defender and walk the ball into one of the two goals, preferably the one that gives more points.
LEARNING OBJECTIVES	When practicing this exercise, the defender tries to resolve various problems, for example... • How should I mark the attacker? • What happens when I mark him from in front? • What happens when an attacker makes a run towards his teammate on the ball? • Is it better to mark the attacker from the side or from behind? • How can I force the attacker to make a certain pass instead of the one he wants to make? • How does the accuracy of a pass impact on defending? • How does the quality of control impact on defending? • How can I force the attacker to attack the goal that is only worth 1 point?

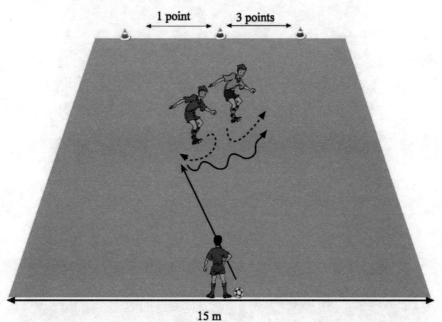

"The success is composed by a series of small daily victories"

197

5. 1v1 on a Mini-Soccer pitch

PITCH	One quarter of a full size pitch
PLAYERS	Mini-Soccer with two cone goals on each end line.
EXPLANATION	A ball is thrown in the center of the pitch and a 1v1 game is played .Every player has to score with a dribble in either of the 2 opposing goals, preferably in the goal that is worth more points for the attacker. For the left (right) footed defender his goal on the right (left) side is more difficult for him to defend. That is why he loses three points when a goal is scored in that goal and only 1 point for a goal scored on his strong side.
LEARNING OBJECTIVES	To use more and more of his intelligence, the defender should ask himself the following questions... • How should I position myself in relation to the attacker? • How can I slow down the attacker in possession of the ball? • How can I limit the space the attacker has to play in? • When is the best time to make a challenge? • When should I challenge from the front and when from the side? How does the attacker's speed influence the way I defend? • What can a slow defender do when up against a quick and skilful attacker?, etc.

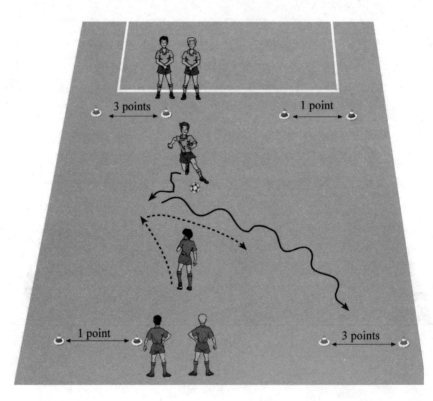

"All coaches have the same objectives, but choose different roads to achieve them"

---

6. Approach one of two attackers from an unfavorable position

PITCH	One quarter of a full size pitch
PLAYERS	3 (two attackers and one defender).
EXPLANATION	The two attackers, 10 meters apart, set off at the same time from the halfway line of the regulation size pitch, each with a ball and running towards the goal opposite. A defender waits at the halfway stage (the 25 meter line). When they are approximately 6 meters from him, the coach calls out the name of one of the attackers, which is the signal for him to stop, while the other continues running with the ball in an attempt to get the better of the defender and score a goal. The defender switches all of his attention to this attacker and tries to stop him from scoring.

Variation: approach one of three attackers from an unfavorable position
Now played with three attackers instead of two.

"I insist in the importance of the details. It's necessary to perfect each small basic aspect of a business (of the game) when you intend that things function well"

Ray Kroc

DEVELOPING GAME INTELLIGENCE IN SOCCER

7. From a 3v3 to a 3v2 situation

PITCH	One half of the full size pitch.
PLAYERS	6 (3 attackers v 3 defenders).
EXPLANATION	- The three attackers start their combined attack from the center line with the objective of scoring in the full size goal. - Three defenders wait to meet them halfway. - When the attackers get close to the defenders the coach calls out one of their names. The called defender abandons the game and sits down, while his two teammates try to overcome the difficulties of being outnumbered by the attackers. One approaches the attacker and the other covers him. - It is a good idea to often call out the name of the defender who tends to pressure the attacker on the ball as this gives his teammates a chance to gain experience in approaching, covering and intercepting passes.

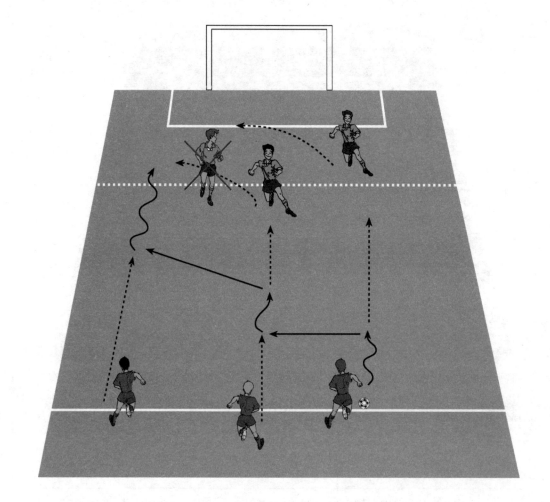

"Before criticizing what has been done, a clear opinion should be formed on what should have been done"

Variation: From a 3v4 to a 3v2 situation

The same as the original game but now from the 4 defenders two will be called off by the coach when the three attackers come closer than 8 meters to the defenders. It is recommended to ask either the two inside or both wing defenders to sit down. This depends mainly on which attacker controls the ball.

The 14 most common mistakes made by a defender approaching an attacker:

1. Approaching too slowly, giving the attacker time and space to take the initiative.
2. Not getting close enough to the attacker.
3. Not approaching in a direct line, irrespective of the position on the pitch.
4. Not slowing down when only a few meters away from his opponent.
5. Running head-on during the last 5-6 meters of the approach, instead of in a curve slightly to the side to the left or right of the attacker. In this way the attacker is forced to play where the defender wants him to play.
6. Choosing to stand in front of the attacker, thus not conditioning his play.
7. Not shortening stride a few meters before reaching and putting pressure on the opponent, or lowering the center of gravity.
8. Not standing on toes, with knees slightly bent, or not being correctly balanced before making the challenge.
9. Making a hasty challenge without waiting and standing close to the attacker (1.5 to 2 meters). At the precise moment of the challenge you must also bear in mind the speed of the attacker and the position of the ball in relation to his feet.
10. Not being able to keep up with the attacker as the defender wasn't able to change direction quickly enough (first going towards the attacker and then moving with him) and/or because of the speed of the approach, or simply because the attacker is faster.
11. Giving the attacker the initiative (not playing feints and dummy challenges).
12. Not maintaining the appropriate distance while running alongside an attacker in possession of the ball, in order to pressure him and force him to go where the defender wants him to go.
13. It is a mistake when defending to be level with the ball or even ahead of it, offering the attacker an escape route backwards.
14. Not channeling the attacker towards a wing away from the danger zone or towards a teammate in defense. Don't forget that "Closing down" an opponent also means that he loses speed and that the threat lessens.

"Awareness is the beginning of all learning. If awareness is obstructed or weak, learning or progress doesn't take place ,or if it does take place, it is random"

D. Millmann

**The 7 most common mistakes made by a defender
when channeling an attacker:**

1. The defender is too far away from the attacker and he is unable to put pressure on him.
2. He looks to the attacker's feet instead of watching mainly the ball, which makes him vulnerable to a feint.
3. He lacks patience and doesn't wait until the ball is further away from the attacker's feet.
4. He is not able to keep up with the quick changes of direction of the attacker because of deficiencies in coordination and dexterity or simply because the attacker is faster.
5. He is not using the permitted body contact when running side by side close to the attacker to gain some time and to force him to lose balance.
6. He allows the attacker the initiative by not selling him any dummy move.
7. He is not channeling the attacker towards fellow defenders or away from the danger zone.

*"The quality of the individual tactical behavior in defense determines
the level of our collective defense"*

HOW TO COACH
COVER DEFENSE

"If you don't know where you have to go, it doesn't really matter which way you choose "

INTRODUCTION

Winning a game cannot be achieved by improving only the attack. In addition to the development of individual defensive skills, the necessity of coaching the collective defense in order to prevent goals being scored becomes obvious.
In the collective defense a player independent of the instructions he has received should always attempt to position himself in such a way that he can fulfill the two most important but conflicting tasks: marking an opponent and at the same time covering the space behind or beside him.

A successful defense is made up of individual players who cooperate well and know how to lend mutual support quickly and efficiently. Changing positions is an extremely important weapon in defense and it takes place whenever a forward breaks through and is taken on by the player nearest to the outplayed defender. Switching positions must be carried out carefully and prudently. A few examples show how it should be carried out:

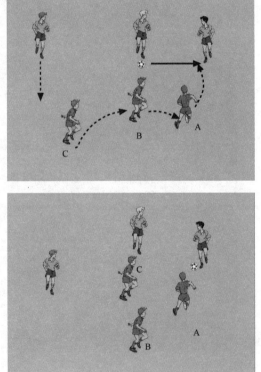

- As the illustration shows, after an attacker has passed the ball to a teammate on his left side, the defenders (A and C) get closer to their teammate (B) who approaches the ball carrier in order to support him in his defensive duties.
- If the defender 'B' is beaten, his nearest teammate (A) approaches him and closes down the attacker, while the outplayed defender (B) quickly switches positions to back up (A), and the third defender (C) controls the attacker down the middle.
- If the attacker decides not to head for goal and passes back instead then the defender 'A' goes back to close down this player, while the others, 'B' and 'C', back up by positioning themselves to form a triangle.

A collective defense which has practiced the art of covering in many hours of training always face their tasks with confidence and never panic, not even when being exposed to situations in which they face numerical inferiority. They are aware that their fellow defenders know to read and interpret the particular game situation and are able to slow down any dangerous attack in order to give them sufficient time to reorganize their defensive unit with good cover.

EXERCISES/GAMES

A SERIES OF PROGRESSIVE EXERCISES/GAMES TO COACH THE PRINCIPLE OF COVERING

1. One attacker against two defenders

PITCH	12 x 12 meters.
PLAYERS	4 (an attacker with the ball, 1 substitute attacker and 2 defenders).
EXPLANATION	- **Problem A:** An attacker tries to run through the cone goal (12 meters wide) in front of him, defended by two opponents who initially stand side by side. Depending on which direction the attacker goes, the nearest defender approaches him or closes him down while the other takes up a covering position to back him up - **Problem B:** The same as above but the two defenders position themselves differently, one in the cone goal and the other one halfway between the attacker and the goal but drawn towards one sideline. Depending on the distance to the attacker and between themselves, they have to decide who has to approach and slow down the attacker and who applies the principle of covering. If the defender at one side feels that he is too far away from the attacker with the ball, the defender in the cone goal approaches him and closes him down while his teammate runs around to cover him. In the illustration the other way of cooperation is shown. - **Problem C:** See problem 'A'. Now a defender is situated at one side of the ball carrier, level with the opposite cone goal, while the second defender starts his quick approach from his goal. Depending on the speed of the attacker the two defenders have to decide who will pressure and slow him down (usually the one who faces him) and who will apply the cover. Care should be taken that the defender closing down the attacker channels him to the side from where his support is coming. - **Problem D:** See problem 'A'. Now both defenders are situated at different sides of the practice area and also at different distances from the ball carrier as shown in the illustration D. Again depending on the speed and direction of the attacker, one of the two defenders, generally the closest to the ball carrier, approaches him, closes him down by running back and channeling him towards the covering defender who has to get into a position behind the first defender.

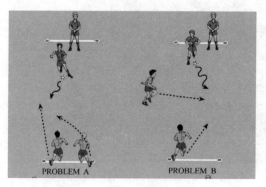

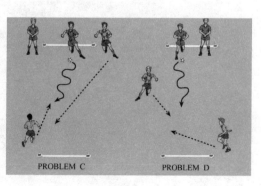

PROBLEM A   PROBLEM B   PROBLEM C   PROBLEM D

2. Two defenders against an attacker who receives a pass

PITCH	Problem 'A' is practiced in a 12x15 meter zone in front of the penalty area.
PLAYERS	4 (2 defenders, and 2 attackers one of whom passes the ball).
EXPLANATION	- The attacker, being closely watched by two defenders, tries to get away with horizontal runs from his marker. Depending on where he runs, one of the two defenders takes care of him while the other one, now without an opponent, covers the space. - When the coach sees that both defenders understood what do to do in each situation (marking or covering), the second attacker at a distance of 15 meters passes the ball to his teammate in front of him. The latter tries to receive and control the ball despite being closely marked by one defender and run with the ball across the goal line, outplaying also the defender who covers.
COMMENTS	Just as with the other exercises the coach reflects with his players on their experience and asks them questions such as: - 'When should a defender mark and when should he cover?' - 'When is the best moment to play a through pass to the marked front runner who faces two defenders?' - 'What is the ideal distance between the defender who is going to challenge and his teammate covering him?' He could put questions to the attackers such as: - 'Is it better to make a run into space towards the middle of the pitch or make yourself available near the goal.' - 'Why?'

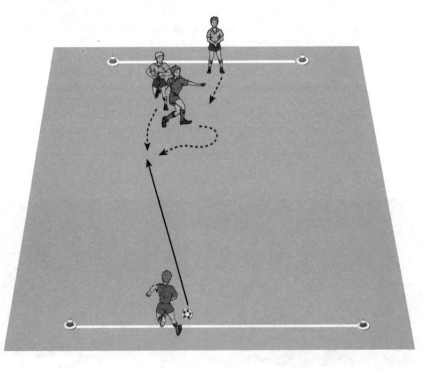

3. 2v2 with two wide goals

PITCH	This is played in a zone on the pitch with two wide goals (12-15m) marked by cones.
PLAYERS	4 (2 defenders and 2 attackers).
EXPLANATION	- Two attackers attack 10 times against one defender in front of them and a second defender rushing into the square from outside (either from the left or from the right side and always from different distances) to assist his fellow defender in the defense. As each situation is different to the one before, both defenders have to read carefully the game situation and decide accordingly what to do in which moment: tackling or covering (see also the "problems" A-D in game 1). - The attack ends with a goal, a clearance by the defenders through the attackers' goal or when the ball goes out of play. - After every attack players and coach have to analyze the outcome.

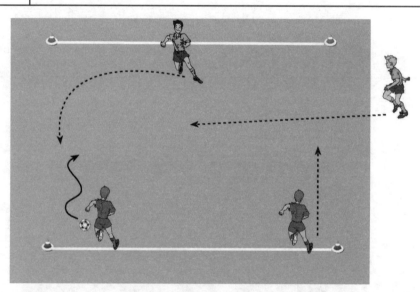

4. 2v3 with a 7-a-side goal

PITCH	One half of the 7-a-side soccer pitch
PLAYERS	5 (3 defenders and 2 attackers).
EXPLANATION	- The problems B, C and D are practiced. The two attackers set off from the center line trying to score from inside the penalty area. Three defenders try to stop this from happening. - One is positioned between the attackers on the center line, the second in front of the ball carrier and the third comes in from one sideline to be able to cover the central defender in front of the penalty box while he is closing down the ball carrier. - For practice reasons the three attackers are obliged to take up different positions after each series of three attacks. - As soon as one of the first attackers touches the ball the two supporting defenders, after having carefully analyzed the actual game situation before the start of the simplified game, intervene by helping the central defender by channeling or tightly marking an attacker while the central defender tries to slow down the ball carrier. - If the attackers do not score after 5 attempts the initial distance between them and the defenders is lengthened. The off side rule is in force in this game.

"The way in which the players communicate among themselves and with themselves, ultimately determines the success of their play"

---

5. 2v2 plus a free defender in each team

PITCH	A Futsal pitch or a playing area of 20x40 meters with a goal at each end.
PLAYERS	6 (2v2 plus a free defender in each team).
EXPLANATION	- The attacking team's objective is to dribble the ball under control across the opposition's goal line (20 meters wide). Each of the 3 defenders needs to decide what to do in which game situation: to approach and slow down the attacker with the ball, to cover or to mark an opponent. His task depends on the development of the game. - The free defender of both teams is not allowed to go across the halfway line but can receive back passes and feed the frontrunners with accurate passes. But his main job is to get experience in applying the principle of covering. - After each goal players and coach analyze together the play in defense.

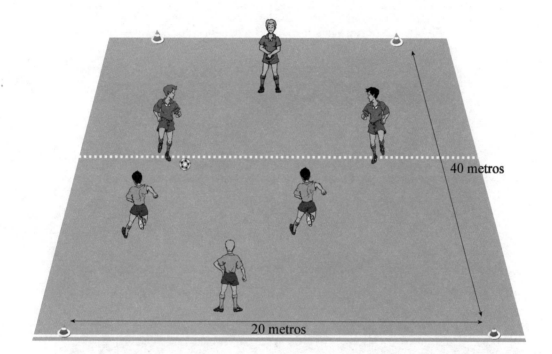

40 metros

20 metros

"A coach should not impose his authority to his players, he should earn it through his superior knowledge"

6. 3v3 plus a free defender in each team

PITCH	The area between the two offside lines of the 7-a-side Soccer pitch with the goals established on the 13meter-offside line.
PLAYERS	10 (3v3 plus a free defender and a goalkeeper in both teams).
EXPLANATION	- The free defender is not allowed to cross the halfway line. His main role is to cover, when necessary, any of his three defenders, although situations may arise where he has to approach and close down the attacker with the ball. He is then substituted in his role by a covering teammate whose job he took over. - The game starts with the free defender playing a pass to one of the three attackers, who try to score in the opponent's goal by controlling the ball on their end line. - An attack ends with a goal (1 point) or with the defense clearing the ball to the opponent who has to remain in the other half of the playing area (1 point). - Each team has 10 attacks and the team who scores the most points wins. - After each goal players and coach comment on the mistakes made by the 3 defenders, especially in covering.

Variation: 3v3 without restrictions

As there are no restrictions for attackers and defenders, every player should know after the loss of the ball what his specific task is. A new experience appears for the defense when the third opponent penetrates with the ball deep into the defenders' half. The following questions may arise:

◆ Whose responsibility is it to pick him up, the nearest defender or the free defender?

◆ How does this decision in the game affect the rest of the team?

◆ What should the wingbacks do when the free defender moves up to confront an advancing attacker?

◆ When should the right-sided wingback cover for the free defender and when is it the responsibility of the left-sided wingback?

"It is the intelligence which really makes the difference between one player and another"

7. 6v6 on one half of the full size pitch

PITCH	One half of the full size pitch with one full size goal and two cone goals (6 meters wide) in the wing positions on the center line.
PLAYERS	12 (6v6, including a goalkeeper in each team).
EXPLANATION	- One team tries to score in the full size goal (3 points) and the other team tries to win the ball and mount a counterattack, trying to pass the ball from any distance through either of the two cone goals (1 point), established in the wing positions on the center line and defended by one goalkeeper. - The game lasts 4 periods of 3 minutes each, with a 2 minute interval after each quarter. - The intervals are used to comment on and correct mistakes in the collective defense with a specific emphasis on covering. - The coach should also look at the individual defensive performances of the six players of the defending team, especially the defenders who are not close to the ball as they have completely different responsibilities than those who are close to the ball carrier. It is formative to analyze with all players who has to apply which of the four principles of the collective defense in the same game situation. That is why it is recommended to freeze the game from time to time to make players aware of which function to accomplish as the best techniques don't serve when the defenders don't understand what is going on in each phase of the game.

The most common mistakes made by defenders:

1. All defenders are positioned horizontally on the same line with no depth.
2. The defense isn't a unit or not compact enough because the distances between the players are too great. This makes their communication and cooperation difficult.
3. The covering defender gets too close (less than 3 m.) to the defender on the ball.
4. The defender who is supposed to close down the attacker does not slow him down.
5. The defender who is going to confront the ball carrier does not know how to approach him correctly, i.e. no acceleration at the start, wrong line of approach, no reduction of speed before reaching the attacker, mistakes in the basic stance before tackling, tackling too slow and without surprise and too often in a frontal position.
6. The defender on the ball doesn't give enough information to the player covering.
7. There is lack of understanding. Two defenders analyze the situation differently and as a consequence make wrong decisions (for example, instead of covering they should put the attacker under pressure or vice versa).

"Traditional coaching had been entirely teacher-directed and largely technique orientated whilst today emphasis is directed on tactical problem solving through games play"

Lynne Spackmann

THE PRINCIPLE OF THE PRESSING DEFENSE

"Pressing is a way of attacking when you don't have the ball"

Arsene Wenger

INTRODUCTION

As opposed to the passive attitude of most defenders (wait and react) years ago, today defensive play has evolved and changed dramatically (go and act). Defense starts immediately after a ball loss and whenever possible the ball carrier is put under aggressive pressure and all possible receivers of the ball are tightly marked. That means more defenders are rushing into the zone where the ball is played than attackers. This way the defense allows the opposition less time and space to think and play which often results in more mistakes. This concept, called pressing, came into fashion during the mid 70's after a period in which soccer was interpreted very much as an attacking game with almost no defensive functions for the attackers.

As often happens with trends, the concept of pressing, which originated 10 years previously in basketball, didn't suddenly appear overnight but evolved gradually and constantly until reaching today's very high level.
Despite a lack of knowledge about pressing defense, this principle has been experienced and adopted since then by almost all teams with more or less success, conditioned of course by the knowledge of how to train it, when to apply it or not, where on the pitch put it in practice, against which team to use it and finally why to apply it.

Playing pressing defense is identified by a series of factors, such as attitude, the characteristic positioning of all defenders in relation to the ball and the opponents and the simultaneous application of the principles of defense, like approaching, covering, triangulation and playing the offside trap which reduces the space available to the opposition's attackers.

How various well-known coaches define the pressing defense.
Pressing is *"A way of attacking when you don't have the ball"*. (Arsene Wenger)

"The pressing defense consists of hassling the opposition incessantly, without respite, in an attempt to regain possession of the ball, and not let the opposition take the initiative in attack under any circumstances. It requires two basic prerequisites: an unshakable fighting spirit and perfect physical fitness, without which the system breaks down totally". (Rinus Michels)

"Pressing can be defined as a series of actions designed to reduce the available space to limit the opposition's possibilities, closing them down quickly, hounding them in all areas, not letting them build an attack no matter where they are on the pitch, with the aim of winning the ball off them and, at the same time, not letting them play 'their' game". (Jose D'Amancio)

"Pressing is putting pressure on all the areas where the opposition is playing or where it is likely to play the ball. What differentiates this system from others is that we don't drop back near our goal to defend when we lose the ball". (Walter Dimattia)

"Through the press the defending team pretends to control the game without being in ball possession." (the author)

How zonal defense and the offside rule facilitate the application of the pressing defense
When playing zonal defense, it is easy to create anywhere on the pitch a numerical superiority of players, a condition necessary to play successful pressing defense. So it is strange to see that most of the teams which play zonal defense don't use the press. For instance, during a throw-in what better tactic than pressing to make it more difficult for the opposition to progress on the pitch?

Another technical-tactical ploy that facilitates the application of the press is the offside rule, or better said, the use of the offside trap. It reduces the space available for the opposition (which makes the play more difficult for the attackers and easier for the defense). It further favors the defense because due to the congestion of players in a reduced space the regrouping of the defense is easier due to the shorter distances. The defense has the facilities to play as a defensive unit with easy communication and collaboration. Luis Aragonés, a well-know experienced Spanish coach said: "The opponent without the ball is not so important, what is important is to put pressure on the player in possession and if it is done well the others will be caught in offside" ("Marca", 1st. August 1977).

Where on the pitch is it a good idea to play a press?
Depending on the characteristics of the proper team, the opposition, whether the match is played at home or away or on the current score, a pressing defense can be played in different ways. It can be applied when the opposition starts to built up their attack from behind with the initial pass from the goalkeeper (full press) or when the defense expects the attackers in a well organized formation close to the halfway line (delay press or half court press).

The advantages of the full press are manifold, one is to take direct initiative of the game and destroy the plans and the pattern of play used by the opposition. Another one is that any mistake of an opponent close to his penalty area might cause a serious setback for his team as the distance of the counterattack for the pressing team is very short and the few defenders around hardly have time to recover after a surprising ball loss. An ideal moment of setting up the full press is a set-play (as for instance the building up from the positional attack which often starts with a wing back who receives the first pass from the goalkeeper) because it is easy to determine and there is time for communicating and for taking over the pre-studied positions. The full press is an ideal weapon to play against weaker teams, especially when it is applied with surprise.

"All behavior of a player on the pitch is the consequence of his actual feelings"

Generally, the press (full press or delay or half court press) is most effective when performed near the wings and especially near the corners of the pitch. It is advisable, by means of good positioning by the frontrunners, to encourage the opposition to pass the ball to these areas of the pitch. Once the pass has been made, immediate pressure is to be put on the player who is going to receive the ball. He should be restricted to play in a confined area with few possibilities of escape. Being on the edge of the pitch he finds himself left with two options: play the ball inside or backwards, because making progress up the field is not possible as the opposition is playing the press. So if the back pass is cut off by positioning a defending forward next to the ball carrier, the only passing option is a long clearance in case he is given the time to do it. But when the ball carrier tries to break free of the press, he takes high risks.

Only quick passing and especially playing one-touch or first-time with good running off the ball creates opportunity for the team in possession to break free.

In case the defensive concept of the pressing team proves ineffective, the whole team adapts to it and decides to drop back to re-organize the defense.

That is why knowing your opponent well allows the defense to choose between pressing the opponent up-field or expecting him close to the half way line, close to the right sideline or better on the left side, or of course not pressing at all.

It is especially important under these circumstances that the defensive line is compact and not spread across the whole width of the pitch. The team should be prepared, in case the pressing defense does not work in this zone, to commit intentional fouls in order to stop a possible attack or counterattack.

When is it a good idea to play a pressing defense?

There are certain situations in which a pressing defense is recommended. Here are some examples:

* When the result is not favorable for one team, it tries to take initiative through a press.
* Immediately after a goal is scored the application of a press could surprise the momentarily demoralized and consequently vulnerable opposition which after conceding a goal against is generally more prepared to take risks.
* At throw-ins.
* During the first 5 minutes of the first and second half (when the opposition tries to follow its game plan) a well executed press may destroy the plans of the opposition.
* When the ball is played close to one side line where the attacking options are more limited and a pressing defense is easier to put in practice.
* Immediately after the initial pass of the goalkeeper or a defender in a built up of the positional attack. Even before this first pass is made the press has started already with an adequate positioning of the frontrunners who leave one opponent intentionally unmarked. This will encourage the goalkeeper or defender to pass the ball in the direction the defenders have looked for.

THE PRINCIPLE OF THE PRESSING DEFENSE

Tactical reasons for playing a pressing defense

1 To surprise your opponent. The element of surprise is very important for success, and this is why it is not advisable to play the press for too long. It is generally the captain or a midfielder who decides when and where to press because his experience tells him when and where a high percentage of success is possible.

2 To not allow the opposition to play their planned game and stifle their offensive possibilities.

3 To break the rhythm of their play, hurrying them and forcing them into more mistakes. This will cause a loss of confidence and could result in surprising counterattacks from the pressing team.

4 When losing in a match.

5 When playing against a slower and technically inferior opponent they are forced to commit even more mistakes.

To make things difficult for the opposition, making them hurry and forcing them to make mistakes often which causes a loss of confidence and more chance of surprise counterattacks from the defenders.

The four stages in the application of the pressing defense

1 **Approach and force the attacker.**
>> For more information see also the chapter: "How to coach approaching and closing down am attacker in possession of the ball"

Approaching the ball carrier starts even before he receives the ball. It is imperative to decide as quickly as possible which defender has to intervene first. This is generally the closest to the ball receiver. These are his problems to solve while approaching the ball carrier:

- Know how far away from his opponent he should stop his approach (this depends on how well the attacker controls the ball).
- Slow down the ball carrier to give teammates time to cover and mark up the other attackers.
- Immediately reduce his passing options by taking up a correct position in relation to the opponent and to the rest of his teammates playing the pressing defense.
- Force the opponent to make a mistake by giving him no time or space, or force him to pass or dribble into a congested area of the pitch.

2 **Channel.** Channel. The ability to channel or maneuver the ball carrier in such a way that he is forced to run into the tackling area of another defender or into less dangerous zones of the pitch (see more about channeling in the chapter "How to coach approaching and closing down an attacker in possession of the ball").

3 **Double teaming.** The application of double teaming is a main characteristic of the pressing defense. An aggressive double team always involves two defenders who put the attacker on the ball under pressure and limit his play. When double teaming, the two defenders outnumber the attacker in this zone. With one player extra they show an aggressive attitude without letting the ball carrier time to observe, think or execute any skill.

4 **A staggered formation.** While the two defenders are pressing the player in possession of the ball, their teammates behind look to anticipate any pass to their opponents, marking them tightly and from in front. The rest of the defenders, especially those on the opposite side to where the ball is, momentarily leave the players they are marking and move further inside towards the ball. They should position themselves in a more central area of the pitch and closer to their goal, ready to intervene at any moment if required to intercept a long pass, cover a defender who has been beaten or to apply a double team.

In a pressing defense not all players tightly mark their opposite number as this would greatly hinder the possibilities of helping out their teammates, due to the distance between the players.

All players need to be fully aware of their role and responsibility for this defensive concept to work. If only one or two players lose concentration then the whole team loses its defensive balance and fails to achieve its objective.

The way to keep the pressing defense working is to adopt a staggered formation around the ball. The player or players who pressure the attacker as he receives the ball need to be aware that behind him there is usually another supporting attacker, who also needs to be monitored, because if he receives the ball he can play it to a teammate on the opposite side of the pitch.

Putting more emphasis on practicing the pressing defense during training
Today's modern game requires attackers to be far more knowledgeable and have the ability to defend both on an individual basis and also in a unit on a collaborative basis.

Every day more pressing attackers and midfield players can be seen who are able to harass and commit an opponent on the ball, who know how to defend when outnumbered, how to approach an opponent, how to shadow and channel him, how to cover or play the pressing defense. This type of offensive player is a concern for any defense who is worried and tense in their build-up because of the opponent's defensive qualities.

Coaches should get their players to practice all types of problem resolving situations when not in possession of the ball with the aim of gaining rich experiences in how to dispossess the opposition with well studied and prepared collective defensive actions as is the pressing defense. Improvement in this aspect of the defense is crucial for the success of any team.

"If it is our desire to triumph in soccer we have to look out for new highways of success instead of always using the same bumpy roads of past victories"

EXERCISES/GAMES

A SERIES OF PROGRESSIVE EXERCISES/GAMES TO TRAIN THE PRINCIPLE OF THE PRESSING DEFENSE

1. Press after a through pass (2v3 and 3v2)	
PITCH	Two playing areas of 12 x 12 meters (20 x 20 meters) side-by-side.
PLAYERS	10 (3v2 on one area and 2v3 on the other)
EXPLANATION	- Three attackers, despite two active defenders, try to pass the ball across the dividing line between the two playing areas to one of their two teammates on the other side. Once the ball has been received despite the aggressive press of three defenders, it needs to be passed further up across the end line and out of the area. - Then the three defenders pick up the ball and become attackers with the same functions as the former attackers. - If the through pass is inaccurate or the two forwards lose the ball to the defense, the three defenders become attackers and feed their teammates in the other area with a pass. - No player is allowed to leave his square. - After an infringement of the rules a free kick is awarded to the opposition. - Any ball control (at least two touches) in the opposing area counts 1 point and for an additional pass by the two attackers across the end line (which means that the pressing defense of the 3 defenders didn't work) another 2 points are awarded to the attackers.
LEARNING OBJECTIVES	- The 2 defenders in the first playing area have to constantly hassle the three attackers to make their passing difficult. - In the second playing area the optimal positioning of all three defenders is a pre-requisite to start with the collective defense, each of the three using the kind of defense which prevents the two forwards from achieving their aim: controlling and passing the ball across their end line.

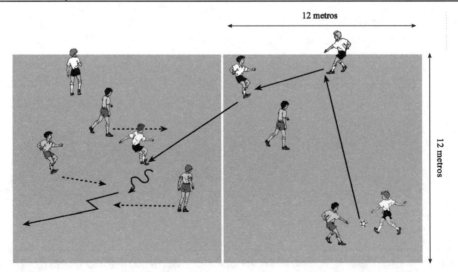

Variation: 4v3 on the first and 3v4 on the second area. Dimension of each area 30 x 30m.

2. Quick turnover from attack to pressing defense (5v3)

PITCH	One half of a full size pitch with two cone goals established in the wing positions on the half way line and a full size goal on one end line
PLAYERS	10 (5 attackers against 4 defenders and a goalkeeper).
EXPLANATION	Five attackers start the game from the halfway line trying to score in the full size goal defended by a goalkeeper. On their way to score they face 4 defenders. If the defenders win the ball they attack and try to score by passing the ball from less than 10 meters through either of the two cone goals on the halfway line. If they lose possession, the five attackers turnover immediately to defend, drop back quickly and adopt the concept of pressing defense in order to channel the four opponents to play in a confined area where they have more players than the attacking opposition.

3. Practice the pressing defense in a game of 11v11

PITCH	Full size pitch.
PLAYERS	Two teams of 11 players.
EXPLANATION	- During the practice game both teams are obliged to play the full press when the opposition starts a new attack from behind. - Later on the coach and then one player announce when a team should use the delayed or half court press. - Furthermore the application of the pressing defense should be considered and put in practice during the throw-ins and when the ball is very close to one side line. - After each press coach and players analyze the outcome critically, discuss the mistakes and show solutions for improving the press. That is why the game has to be frozen, for making all players aware of their obligations and responsibilities.

Advantages and disadvantages of the pressing defense*

Some advantages are:
- It allows the team to quickly regain possession of the ball, or at least stops the opposition from attacking at their leisure, as their space and time to think and play has been very much reduced.
- It forces the opposition in numerical inferiority to play with more risks, to precipitate their actions and therefore become less precise or accurate.
- It is effective against inferior teams and players who are mentally slow.
- The physically superior team can make the game a lot faster, more intense and this way fatigue the opposition in the long run (second half).
- It facilitates counterattacking.
- It fosters a good team spirit.

*According to José Mª Yagüe Cabezón, 1999.

Some disadvantages are:
- It requires a lot of energy (mental and physical) and demands perfect synchronization of the different defensive moves carried out by all players of a team at the same time.
- The players need to have an excellent fitness level.
- It is absolutely imperative that all the passing options are cut off. If one is left open, the concept runs the risk of being totally useless and ineffective.
- It requires total concentration, excellent organization and good teamwork.
- If a full press is played, it generally creates plenty of space between the last line of defense and the goalkeeper. This space could get exploited by quick opponents in counterattacks.
- If one of the pressing defenders has been beaten the defenders have to adjust adequately, as they are no longer playing with numerical superiority.
- When playing too aggressive the defenders may commit a high number of fouls.

The players as well as the coach need to weigh up in few seconds all these advantages and disadvantages with the strengths and weaknesses of their team and the virtues of the opposition to decide whether to use a pressing defense or if it is better not to play it.

"It's a widely accepted fact that improvement in performance is partially related to the quality of the feedback given to the players after having completed a determined play."

D. Millmann

THE PRINCIPLE OF
ANTICIPATION

"An intelligent defender looks at the passes from the passer's point of view"

INTRODUCTION

Another important defensive concept in soccer is anticipation which has to be considered one of the key elements of good defending, especially on an individual basis.

Having anticipation means more or less knowing what is going to happen next in the game. This includes anticipation of one's own movements and those of the rest of the players (teammates and opponents) with or without the ball.

Knowing how to anticipate...
* The trajectory, speed, height and spin of a pass or shot (including penalties)
* The moment a pass or challenge is about to be made
* The technique an attacker will choose to try to beat a defender in a specific situation
* Set plays such as, for example, a free kick, a throw-in or a corner kick
* A poor ball control by an opponent due to the quality of the pass (too strong or too weak or very high or inaccurate)
* A run into space by the opponent
* A close marking of an opponent
* A tackle
* The use of the offside trap
* The use of a full press or a delay or half court press by the opposition

The ability to anticipate requires a series of characteristics which will help the player to perform more effectively. These are:
* Ability to anticipate what is about to happen
* Ability to correctly perceive and analyze the game situation and (by implication) react to the circumstances after having made a quick decision
* Total concentration when reading what is happening on the pitch
* Ability to execute technical skills quickly once the decision has been made
* Belief in oneself

All the above assumes that the player is able to put himself in the position of his opponent in order to find out what he would do in the same situation. When an intelligent defender looks at the passes from the passers point of view he is able to lift his defensive game to a much higher level. The more information the player is able to collect before the real action happens, the better his anticipation becomes. For instance:
* The location of the ball in relation to the opponent's feet
* The position of the opponent and his teammates in relation to where he actually is on the field
* When collecting information from the opponent, particular attention should be paid to his stance and the movements he is making with his eyes and head.

When is it appropriate to anticipate?
- When a long pass is played and the marker is close to the potential ball receiver.
- When the ball doesn't have sufficient speed and there is time to anticipate.
- During corner kicks, throw-ins and long clearances.
- When the opponents play a one-two, especially close to the penalty area.

When is it not appropriate to anticipate?
- When the anticipating player is too far away from his opponent.
- When there is no cover at all behind him which would result in a dangerous situation if the anticipation is executed poorly.
- When the attacker is fully aware of the anticipation qualities of his opponent.
- When the pass is very powerful.

Needless to say, frequent practice of anticipation skills during training sessions, together with a video analysis of his own performances, will help the player to improve his anticipation skills. Critically observing his habits, strengths and weaknesses, both in defense and in attack, will give him self-confidence and a better chance to win most of the duels in the match to come. As a result he is not only improving his own effectiveness but also that of his team.

When teaching anticipation skills the coach first introduces isolated situations or problems with relatively simple solutions, moving later on to more and more complicated ones to which the defender or attacker has to respond adequately.

Many top players are able to correctly anticipate what their opponent is going to do because during their formative years they played other ball games with more than 2 players involved. In these games they learned not to telegraph what they were about to do (conceal their intentions) but instead sold intentionally erroneous information to the opponents, causing them to anticipate incorrectly. They did so because they were fully aware that the opponent is likely to use his anticipation skills in defense. This way they managed to lift their game to a higher level in which intelligence plays an important role.

HOW TO PRACTICE ANTICIPATION SKILLS

In order to anticipate a move a player must look at the situation from his rival's point of view as if he was the player receiving and in control of the ball.

Types of Marking

Anticipation Marking:

a) Long anticipation - While his fellow defender approaches the ball carrier the defender (D) positions himself between his two opponents (passer and receiver), ready to intercept the ball in case the foreseen pass is going to be executed. While positioning himself in such a way that he is able to cover all possible passes to B, he concentrates mainly on the head and eye movements (visual connection) of the ball carrier which indicate with whom he is going to play. **(Fig 1)**

b) Short anticipation - The defender (D) positions himself close to the opponent who may receive a pass but he can also use a long anticipation if another attacker further away is more likely to receive a pass. In this case, the defender has time to run diagonally backward and re-position himself to face the wing. **(Fig 2)**

Fig. 1

Fig. 2

Man-for-Man Marking:
c) As the pass is being made the defender positions himself closer to the ball than his opponent, which means between him and the passer and always closer to the goal than the possible receiver. It is fundamental for a defender to watch at all times not only the ball but also his personal opponent in order to play with anticipation. **(Fig 3)**

Fig. 3

What criteria determine the type of anticipation marking to use?
Firstly, the distance between the attacker in possession of the ball and the player who is about to receive it. The greater the distance between passer and receiver, the easier it is to mark.

Secondly, the area of the pitch where the ball is played is also a factor to consider when deciding which type of marking to use. The closer the play gets to our goal the tighter the marking becomes, until the defense decides for man-to-man marking.

"When you see a good player, intend to imitate him, but when you see a rather poor one, examine yourself"

Confucios

EXERCISES/GAMES

A SERIES OF PROGRESSIVE EXERCISES/GAMES TO TRAIN THE PRINCIPLE OF ANTICIPATION

1. Get experience in using anticipation skills in intercepting passes

PITCH	An area anywhere on the pitch.
PLAYERS	3 (two attackers and one defender).
EXPLANATION	- The defender positions closer or further away from the trajectory of the ball and his opponent in order to experiment with how the distance between him and his opponent and between him and the trajectory of the passed ball are conditioning his success in anticipation as much as the speed of the ball do. - The anticipating player is becoming aware of most of the key elements which he has to master to use anticipation as a defensive weapon: assuming an optimal basic stance to be able to move quickly, being mentally alert, processing cues shown by the ball carrier (head and eye movements as well as body orientation), having an over-all view of the game situation which finally allows him to choose an optimal position in relation to his opponent etc. Once these basic elements have been completed the optical-motor assessment of the player allows him to make a decision on when to anticipate and in which direction to move. - The coach should help the anticipating player with questions to thoroughly understand and later on put these elements into practice.

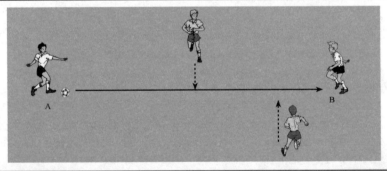

2. Anticipating feinted passes

PITCH	Two cone goals (each 2 meters wide and 4 meters apart from each other) are positioned on the same line.
PLAYERS	2
EXPLANATION	- From a distance of 15 (20) meters one player kicks five balls one after another with a pause of 30 seconds between each pass towards either of the two goals. A defender does his best to cover both goals at the same time. He has to position himself close to both goals a little bit in front of them and without being allowed to approach the attacker in order to narrow the angle of his shots or passes. - After each attempt to anticipate (intercept) the pass, the coach and the anticipating player may have a dialogue about the experience made, led by concrete questions put forward by the coach to allow the defender to understand what to do best in intercepting passes.

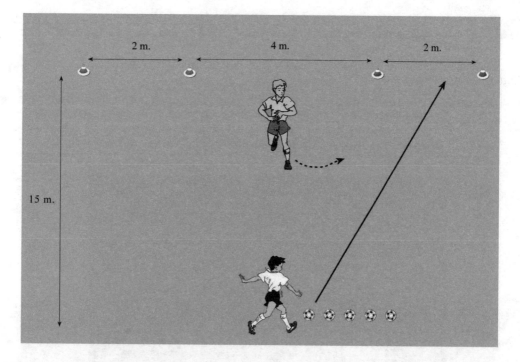

Variation: intercepting passes between 2 attackers with three cone goals
- Two defenders placed in front of three cone goals try to anticipate the direction of the pass of an attacker to his teammate 10 meters behind the three goals. To score, the ball has to be directed to the less defended goal and picked up by the teammate of the passer.
- Each of the 4 players has 10 free kicks and each has to anticipate 10 times.

"When many coaches still coach as they were coached as players, progress in soccer doesn't take place"

3. Game with anticipating passes

PITCH	A playing area 10-12m wide and 20m long
PLAYERS	4 (3 attackers and a defender).
EXPLANATION	A player situated at one end of the paying area passes the ball to one of his two teammates expecting it at the other end, one on each side. A defender between and slightly in front of them tries to anticipate the pass. None of the three players on the far end can move before the pass has been made.

"The soccer of the past we have to respect,
the soccer of today we have to study,
and the soccer of tomorrow we have to anticipate"
Bora Milotinuvic

4. Short and long anticipation marking in a game of 5v5

PITCH	One half of a full size pitch between the halfway line and 16.5 meter -line, using the whole width of the pitch. One wing channel is marked with cones as a "help zone"
PLAYERS	10 (5v5).
EXPLANATION	- Each team tries to score a goal by dribbling the ball across the opposition's end line (either the 16.5-meter line or for the halfway line on the regulation size pitch). - The two attackers nearest to the one on the ball should be marked closely, while the fourth and fifth players who are further away from the ball are "attended" with long or short anticipation marking, depending on the distance between them and the ball. - In this game, the defenders experience what is known as the active zone and the help zone. The latter, as seen in the illustration, corresponds to a lateral zone in one wing position where no defenders are positioned. They orientate themselves more to the zone in which the ball is played in order to create a numerical superiority which facilitates ball recovery. If a long pass is played into this area, there is sufficient time to regroup and form a defensive unit in which each player is fulfilling the task which he assigned to himself due to the development of the game situation.

"The daily work of a man (a coach) without revising it constantly,
is not worth living"
Johan Wolfgang von Goethe

5. 8v8, 9v9 or 10v10 across the width of a full size pitch

PITCH	A full size pitch
PLAYERS	16 (8v8), 18 (9v9) or 20 (10v10)
EXPLANATION	- The game is played from one sideline to the other across the width of the full pitch. The objective for each team is to control the ball on any spot of the opposition's sideline (more than 100 meters long). - Depending on the location of the ball, the defenders close to it or very far away from it use different kinds of marking which the coach has to check during the development of the game. He has to freeze it from time to time to ask the players in defense about their mistakes committed in positioning themselves as part of the whole defensive unit.

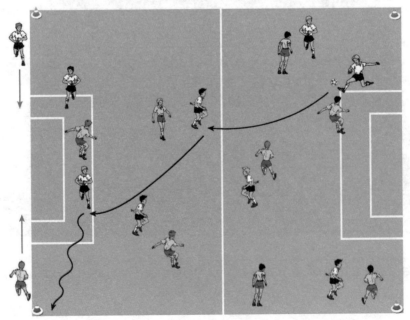

Depending where on the pitch the action is taking place the type of marking is as follows:

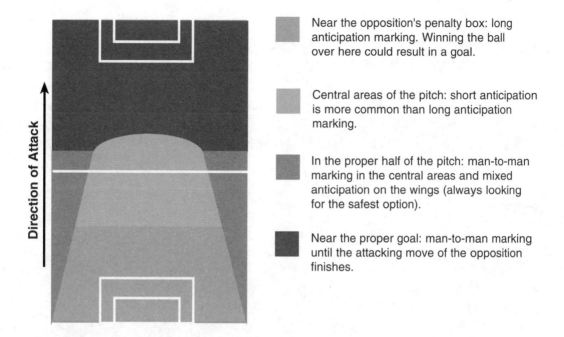

Near the opposition's penalty box: long anticipation marking. Winning the ball over here could result in a goal.

Central areas of the pitch: short anticipation is more common than long anticipation marking.

In the proper half of the pitch: man-to-man marking in the central areas and mixed anticipation on the wings (always looking for the safest option).

Near the proper goal: man-to-man marking until the attacking move of the opposition finishes.

How to mark on different parts of the full size pitch

For a better understanding of the principle of anticipation the two illustrations show different defensive interpretations of the same game situation.

In the first illustration the defense acts on an individual basis with man-to-man marking, while in the second illustration the defense plays as a unit, using anticipation marking which creates a numerical superiority for the defenders around the ball.

As one defender confronts the player on the ball another covers him and the rest of the defenders head towards this active zone of the pitch already thinking of mounting a counterattack immediately after the success of their collective defense.

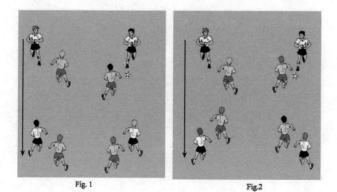

Fig. 1   Fig.2

DEFENDING UNDER PRESSURE

"To have a good game and develop to your full potential, you should forget about the result and concentrate on your task and enjoy the game"

INTRODUCTION

Frequently in the last minutes of a match the losing team puts the opposition's defense under an unrelenting pressure. With their mind focusing on the result rather than concentrating on their task on the field, some defenders "lose their head" and, in the high tempered atmosphere created by a fanatic crowd, make many mistakes. These are not only a result of their technical-tactical deficiencies but also the internal and external pressure they are unable to manage.

Therefore coaches should prepare their players to learn to cope with internal (mental) and also with external (physical) pressure, both on an individual and collective basis. This can be achieved not only through a specific mental preparation of the players but also with an adequate training program where defenders learn to cope with stress factors such as a lack of time and space and playing in numerical inferiority or equality.

The internal pressures that arise when defending

Any negative thoughts or stress have a negative affect on the quality of the perception and analysis of the actual game situation, on the decision making and also on the accuracy of the execution of technical-tactical moves. A defender under stress is often hot tempered or paralyzed, tends to rush, is more than ever aware on the referee's decisions and instead of keeping a cool head and trying to play as constructive as possible is clearing the ball wide.

This internal pressure may appear in other critical moments of the match, such as at the start of each half and in the last minutes of the first half of the match as well as after a goal has been scored. The more the defenders lack self-confidence, the less they are able to overcome the internal pressures which limit them.

High expectations for a favorable result expressed by the spectators, the press, the coaching staff, the family or the presence of a national selector put the players under additional pressure.

External pressures that arise when defending

Generally, external pressure arises as a result of:

- Systematic pressure from the opposition on the defense immediately after the ball is lost.
- Situations of numerical inferiority (especially if there is little time to adjust, as is often the case in transition).
- A technically superior opposition.
- A tactically superior opposition.
- An opposition with superior physical fitness (especially in speed and stamina) and coordination

The best way to learn not to panic and cope with both types of pressure (but especially with the external pressure) without losing performance levels is to expose the players in training to real match situations in which this type of external pressure is simulated. Doing so with sufficient repetitions, the players will learn to deal with these stress factors without negatively affecting their decision making.

Training under these conditions makes the players realize that defending is not merely knowing how to approach an opponent or channel him towards a less dangerous area of the pitch, mark him, tackle with a variety of techniques, cover a defender who faces a 1v1-situation or intercept passes. Before a defender pretends to dominate his opponent, the defender has to dominate himself.

Defending when under pressure requires a perfectly coordinated team effort in which each player has an important role to accomplish.

The 1v2-situation
The situation where one defender is faced by two attackers is the most common situation in a match. It is non-stop. In order to deal with this situation successfully the defender should:
• Read the development of the game situation so that he can anticipate what is likely to happen.
• Be alert all the time, be always in balance, mobile, ready to tackle at any second but generally retreating in order to gain time for support . Don't rush and only tackle in case there is no risk.
• Position his feet correctly and assume a side-on position a little bit closer to the goal than both attackers and between them (but closer to the ball carrier) which makes it difficult for them to pass to each other.
• Encourage the ball carrier through positioning to forget about his teammate and oblige him to run with the ball into the gap offered to him in order to channel him and slow down his individual attack.

- While closing him down, make body feints and movements with the head to get an advantage.
- Know that passes from right to left are generally more difficult to intercept than passes from the left to the right (seen from the defender's position).

Note: For more information and a series of progressive exercises and games consult the chapter in part I "The 2v1-situation- A basic element of the collective game")

The 1v3-situation

This situation occurs sporadically during the final stages of a counterattack and it puts the defender under incredible pressure as he has very few possibilities of resolving the situation to his advantage. But what should the defender do?

- He should keep believing in himself.
- He should keep calm and avoid rushing into a tackle.
- He should slow down the attack by running backwards to gain time.
- He should read the game, seeing things from the point of view of the attacker in possession of the ball in order to anticipate what he might do (a pass to one of his two teammates or a solo run). This is why it is so important to not only take into account the position of the player on the ball, but also where his teammates are located.
- He should try to catch one of them in offside, depending on the position of the attackers without the ball.
- He should, through adequate positioning, force the attacker to pass the ball to a teammate in a less dangerous position or to a weaker one.

"A player who is afraid to suffer is already suffering"

Cesar Luis Menotti

The 2v3 -situation

There are many questions and problems to be answered or resolved by the two defenders. For example:

• Who should approach the attacker on the ball and how should he do this?
• Which defender should cover and how should he do this?
• How to slow down an attack when in numerical inferiority?
• How to force the attackers to pass sideways to avoid a successful through pass?

Note: Please consult a great variety of games for learning to defend situations when being in numerical inferiority in the author's book: "Developing Youth Soccer Players", Human Kinetics Inc., Illinois, 2000.

Statistics demonstrate time after time that the score in many games changes, or even the result is decided, in the last few minutes of each half or after having scored or conceded a goal. These are the critical minutes or moments of a match. So it is advisable to coach youngsters in how to cope during these minutes of the game, especially when the result is unfavorable. For this reason the coach should stress the vital importance of the following:

- Remain calm and have confidence in our possibilities.
- Keep concentration levels at 100%.
- Keep possession of the ball in order to dictate the pace of the game.
- Have confidence and keep the team shape, not falling into the trap of dropping too far back.
- Don't waste energy, control your physical effort.

When keeping in mind these simple guidelines, teams will not continue to clear one ball after another up the pitch with the result that a few seconds later they are again under even more pressure.

DEFENDING COUNTERATTACKS

"When we attack we should be able to switch quickly to defense and when we defend, it should facilitate our attacking moves"

For decades the art of mounting counter-attacks has been an important weapon in the battle for victory, particularly when playing against opponents which are considered the favorites for winning the match.

As mastering the counter-attacking game has become a necessity for every good soccer team, so too should every defense be prepared and organized against fast breaks . Due to the importance that many teams give to counter-attacking and also because of the increase in the number of goals scored with this attacking option, a necessity is born to examine carefully the defense of counter-attacks. Only its future consideration in the training and learning process will assure a necessary balance between the success of fast attacks and their defense.

While the attacking team's aim is to create and then use the space, the defense has to look to reduce the attacker's time and space in order to counter their offensive moves to a maximum, thus reducing their success rate.

A prerequisite for defending counter-attacks successfully is to identify the characteristics which the attackers generally apply during its development and its conclusion (see table in the chapter "The counter-attack"). The defense should do everything possible to not allow the attackers to put into practice most of these components of successful fast breaks such as precise through passes immediately after the ball is won, attacks with a minimum number of passes, receptions of the ball on the quick run, occupying spaces behind the defense etc.

With defenders being aware, trained and capable of carrying out immediately after the ball is lost a quick transition or turn-over from an attacking to a defensive pattern, the opponent who stopped our attack will have difficulties in initiating it quickly with a long precise pass into the depth of the field. Therefore, **killing counter-attacks in the moment of their birth has to be considered the first aim for our defense to win the battle**.

Once the opponent's counter-attack has been started with an initial pass or dribble , the element of mental and physical speed of the defenders is essential in perceiving and analyzing the game situation as well as in the correct decision-making and the motor execution of the response. Intelligent and efficient moves of the defenders, especially of the one closest to the ball carrier, is a key factor for determining the success of our defense, which has to learn to read the game situation and **TO RESPOND TO IT AS A UNIT!** Thinking and acting ahead of time is a must!

That is why our defenders should know that we are vulnerable to counter-attacks when our team attacks against a well organized defense. Everything should be done to:

• assure balance
• assure a correct positioning of our defenders in the depth of the field and
• alert our attackers to anticipate a quick change to take over defensive functions if possession is lost.

Questions like **"Where is the ball located?"**, **"Where are my teammates positioned?"** and **"Where are the opponents positioned?"** have to be immediately answered when the initial pass or dribble of the counter attacker is on the way. Only a quick processing of all the information included in these 3 questions will enable us after the first initial pass (hopefully a short and square one and not a long and vertical pass into the depth of the field) to channel the opponent's attack away from dangerous zones of the field (generally the space in line to the goal and the space behind our defenders) *which is an ideal platform to successfully regain the possession of the ball* through the execution of well synchronized collective defensive tasks such as:

1. The defender closest to the attacker who received the initial pass (now the ball carrier) first has to deny or stop the opponent's forward penetration and give direction to the ball. Through his positioning (always goal side and in a side-on position which allows him to tackle in retreat and an optimal vision of teammates as well as of the opponents in the depth of the field), he shall try not only to reduce the space and time of the ball carrier (delay the continuation of his attack), but also to channel his play to zones further away from our goal, especially to the side lines, avoiding penetrations (better a dribble than a pass) through the center channel of the field. **Any delay in the development of the opponent's attack will allow our defensive unit to drop back and adjust to the situation. It would be a mistake of the first defender nearest to the first counter-attacker to commit himself to an early tackle, because it will accelerate the opponent's attack rather than delay it**. Tackling is only recommended when there is a high percentage of winning the challenge (for instance when the ball is not being fully controlled by the attacker).

2. The defender (or the defenders) who is one penetrating pass away from the ball carrier and nearest to our first channeling defender, has an important role to fulfill in stopping the further development of the opponent's counter-attack. First of all, he must anticipate and read the intentions of the ball carrier through interpreting, thanks to his knowledge and experience, all information which the ball carrier gives with his head movements (visual agreement with the next receiver), his body position (also in relation to the location of the ball) and the position of his feet, especially the supporting foot. He should react accordingly **to not allow the first penetration pass to reach another counterattacker further up the field , who ideally tries to pick up the ball**

on the run. The defender's positioning, besides being always goal side, should allow him to mark the opponent while controlling the space behind him (or them), space in which the opponent tries to penetrate without the ball. Also, his positional play should allow the covering of the most likely passing lanes for the ball carrier, through adapting to the play If an intelligent interception of the penetration pass isn't possible, the defender(s) one pass away from the ball carrier, has more **options to bring the counter-attack to a halt. The first is to slightly infringe the rules and oblige the referee to whistle and the second is to slow down the receiving attacker**. The more the defender is able to keep the attacker from continuing the fast break in a direct line to the goal, the more time his remaining defenders (who are now one pass instead of the former two passes away from the ball carrier) will have to adjust to the new situation, to cover the space or to drop back while keeping the ball and their personal opponent in their field of vision. Ball watching without considering the moves of the opponent (often curving in from behind the defender) is considered a frequent mistake in defense. Once the ball is on one side of the field, the defenders try to keep it there to facilitate a pressing defense.

3. The last defender, furthest away from the ball carrier, generally doesn't mark an opponent but marks the space. Even if an attacker moves into his area (with the ball two passes away), he doesn't mark him in order to encourage the ball carrier to risk a long penetration pass up field which he then anticipates by analyzing the passer's moves. But when the defender(s) in front of him cannot delay or stop the counter-attack, he has to use all his game intelligence in the one-to-one situation to intercept the pass to the front runner or, if that is not possible, to neglect him from shooting from central positions and finally to allow him to take the rebound.
   Finally, in the defense of counter-attacks the goalkeeper must be prepared to cover the space behind the last defender and therefore **shouldn't remain on the goal line but some 5 meters in front of it**.

The defense of counter-attacks requires all players to read and analyze the game situation and then choose one of the following different defensive roles:
* **approaching, on a correct line, the first attacker** who gained the possession of the ball and stopping the penetration of the counter-attack through an optimal positioning in relation to the ball and the first attacker,
* **channeling the attack** to the side lines,
* **denying space and time** through establishing an optimal playing distance,
* **intercepting the pass** through optimal anticipation skills,
* **tackling immediately** after or while the opponent is controlling the ball,
* **tackling in retreat**,
* **sprinting back** (especially from positions opposite from where the ball was lost and the counter-attack was initiated) for blocking passing lines or providing cover, always sliding inward towards the central area of the field while goal sided.

One objective of the counter-attackers is to get behind the defense in order to create scoring opportunities without being obliged to beat a defender in one-on-one situations. That is why **defenders of counter-attacks should always keep the ball AND their opponent in front of them** to deny them any sudden penetration into dangerous areas behind which can be observed frequently when wings cut into the middle of the field behind the defense. Effective communication is the tool to deny the opponents entry into these spaces.

Being aware of the difficulties to defend counter-attacks successfully, most of the time these don't break down because of the capacities of a well prepared defense but due to the opponent's inadequate skills in the execution the techniques of passing, receiving and dribbling at top speed and also because of their poor communication skills.

Since well organized and compact defenses make attacking moves more and more difficult, thus resulting in less goal scoring opportunities, more and more teams have become aware of the necessity to create for themselves sufficient space and then explore it with systematic counter-attacking tactics. As counter-attacking is considered today by many teams a more effective weapon than launching positional attacks, many coaches have to rethink their play in defense in order to recreate a healthy balance between the coaching of defensive and attacking skills within the important aspect of counter-attacking.

* the author appreciates the collaboration from B.Anders

PART THREE
THE INDIVIDUAL GAME

IMPROVING INDIVIDUAL SKILLS, A PREREQUISITE FOR RAISING THE LEVEL OF TEAM PLAY

"Be patient with the most gifted players in your team, even if they spend long periods seemingly contributing few things, because they may turn the match to our advantage in an instant"

In today's game, even a skilful player finds it more and more difficult to get the better of an opponent and create, especially in the opposing half close to the penalty area, a situation of numerical superiority. This is mainly because:

* the defense is generally packed with more and more players,
* defenders are told to commit more and more infringements and fouls in order to stop their penetrating moves,
* coaches are always looking for more efficient tactics to reduce the available space for the opposition.

These days the majority of coaches tend to concentrate on improving team play during their training sessions, practicing communication and collaboration while counterattacking, circulating the ball at speed, defending on a collective basis etc., all concepts in which playing without the ball is crucial for the outcome. However, what should not be forgotten is the fact that the more skilful players the coach has available, the easier it is for him to built an excellent team around them.

It is fundamental for players, especially for children and adolescents, to constantly try to improve their individual technique, which allows them to confront with more confidence many situations and especially the very frequent one that occurs in the game: the 1v1-situation. In this challenge, speed, imagination, flair and technique of dribbling with the ball determine the success.

It is widely believed throughout the world of soccer that the players who really make a difference are born with certain outstanding abilities and that they develop them naturally as they grow up, but reality demonstrate that despite their advantage of heritage they spend hours and hours practicing with the ball. During the first years in soccer the young player should consider the ball like his best friend and give it his full attention. He should treat the ball well, always touching it with care and tenderness until it obeys his master to the fullest and not the other way around. Being as much as possible in contact with the ball, and playing with it anywhere and at any time, as happened years ago in street soccer, is the best and only way to familiarize the young soccer player with the ball. Play and enjoy playing with it in different roles and without any pressure must be the philosophy in the early years of formation of a soccer player. Instead of giving importance to winning, the young players are given the opportunity to explore step by step the fascination of soccer by playing it in all possible roles (also that of the goalkeeper) with small-sided or simplified games. The main objective is not winning at any costs, it is discovering and enjoying the game, without looking for quick results.

"The best talent is wasted without practice"

But when winning becomes the first objective, teachers and coaches concentrate more on tactical and physical aspects than on the acquisition of basic technical-tactical aspects of soccer. Striving more for winning than for developing is a mistake.

Before dominating his opponents, the young player first has to know how to control himself and then the ball and this is mainly achieved by practicing with it as much as possible and not only in the official training sessions.
As in other subjects such as Mathematics, English or History, the young players should be asked to do their homework also in soccer, encouraging them to spend as much time as possible with the ball.

The more young players master the basic ball skills, the more they can allow themselves to direct their attention to other important aspects of the game during a match. This will raise the level of play tremendously. But if their basic technical skills are performed poorly, all the attention of the young player focuses on the execution of the technical skill, which distracts him from other very important aspects of the game.

The teacher and later the coach should include special training sessions devoted to individual ball skills in each training session, particularly between the ages of 8 and 12, in order to cultivate all kind of feints and dummies, different receptions and ball control techniques with one or two opponents nearby, the different techniques to score, to tackle or to beat a defender.

This practice should not be based on analytical exercises only but should also involve simplified games for two and three players in a team in which specific rules will foster the acquisition of the most important technical skills. Technical improvement can be achieved through a frequent repetition of closed skills but additionally also with a practice of a great variety of simplified games especially designed to train and improve a determined technique, not in an isolated way but in the context of the game. When the technique is improved with the help of a simplified real game situation, then the player will have no difficulty in using it correctly in the real game.

"When you don't perform the skill well the first time, you've done better than average"

THE IMPORTANCE OF WINNING THE 1v1 CHALLENGES

"Being able to execute a technique well is only a prerequisite for being able to use the skill later in a match at a precise moment, at an appropriate place and to the benefit of one's own team"

INDIVIDUAL ANALYSIS AND STATISTICS

As result of a statistical survey during the 1990 World Cup, Roland Loy from Germany came to the conclusion that the team that wins more 1v1-situations during a match will win the match 75% of the time.

It is therefore recommended that every player utilize more than ever the video of his matches to learn and improve his performance levels in many aspects. The video will inform him, for instance, about the results of all duels, their frequency and finally also about the reasons why he performed poorly or was successful in the 1v1 situations. The correct use of videos or DVDs is of great help to improve each player's performance (and not only in the 1v1 situations) but also the overall performance of the team as a whole. Often it gives a clear answer about why a match was lost or won, and consequently helps to contribute in preparing the players and the team to resolve many problems before they reoccur in the next game.

But video is also used to analyze the strengths and weaknesses of the opposition, thus allowing the technical team to design an appropriate game plan.

Audio-visual information and statistics are also useful for designing a specific training session or even an individualized program for each player in the team, which as a whole needs to improve on this and other particular aspects of the game in order to win it.

Note: For more information please consult the chapter: "Winning more often thanks to technology"

DIFFERENT 1v1 SITUATIONS

There are several different types of 1v1-situations:
1. 1v1 with the ball on the ground:
   - The ball is controlled by one of the two players involved.
   - The ball is loose, somewhere between the two players.
   - The ball is loose, but closer to one player than the other.

2. 1v1 with the ball in the air (according to Loy these accounted for 40.5% of the 1v1 confrontations in the 1990 World Cup.)

3. An attacker against the goalkeeper
   - With the ball moving along the ground.
   - With the ball moving in the air.
   - With a stationary ball. (penalty or direct free kick).

Every 1v1-situation is different, they are never identical because there are always factors that make them different, such as the position of the ball carrier in relation to the defender, where support is offered or the cover is made etc. The position of the ball carrier could be compared with any of the 12 numbers of

a watch with the player being placed in the center, that means in front of him, behind him, on his left or right, or in mixed positions as shown in the illustration above.

All these possible situations should be simulated in practice until the defenders learn how to position themselves correctly, considering also the position of the goal, the area of the pitch where the 1v1 takes place and what support is available for the attacker as well as for the defender.

Practicing all kinds of 1v1-situation is fundamental for all 11 players of a team, but particularly for:

* Marking defenders
* The sweeper
* The goalkeeper

To win most of his 1v1-confrontations in a match (it doesn't matter whether it is in attack or in defense) is for any player an important objective to achieve as it contributes to the success of his team.

RISK AND SAFETY IN THE 1v1 IN DIFFERENT PARTS OF THE PITCH

The way to face a 1v1-situation depends also on the area of the pitch where the challenge takes place. An attacker should take risks when he is near the opposition's goal, while the defender playing the ball in the same area has to avoid any risk at all and has to play the ball safely, as losing it could become at this part of the pitch a serious threat for his team.

It is extremely difficult to beat a defender in a 1v1-duel in front of the opposition's goal because of the limited space available but it is even more difficult to maintain possession and score due to the covering defenders being nearby.

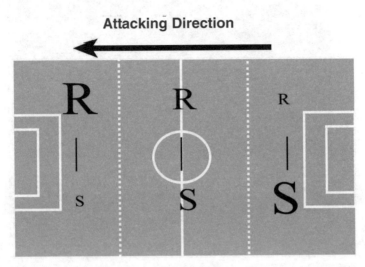

Proportion between security (S) and risk (R) in different parts of the field.

THE BONDING OF TECHNICAL EXECUTION AND TACTICAL APPLICATION AS A BASIS FOR SUCCESS IN 1v1 DUELS

a) The following technical-tactical moves should be performed at high level by the attacker:

An attacker should know how to perform a variety of different individual offensive moves to a high standard, such as, for example:

- Running with the ball and shielding it depending on the position of the defender
- While running with the ball execute a variety of dummies such as:
  - dummy a pass to one side and then run with it to the opposite one using a change of pace.
  - step one or more times laterally over the rolling ball (with a shift of body weight)
  - step in front of the ball and drag the ball behind the advanced standing leg using the sole or inside of the other foot to pass it behind the body to the opposite side.
  - drag with two touches (left-right or inside-outside, or vice versa) and a simultaneous body swerve and then dribble the ball away from the defender
  - pretend to stop the moving ball by almost stepping on it and then with a sudden burst of speed run away from the defender
  - drag the ball backwards with the sole of either foot and then move it with either the inside or outside of the foot to one side out of the reach of the defender.

- shield the ball from the opponent by positioning between the ball and the defender who wants to come in from any side.
- fake a shot and when the defender tries to block the shot, take the ball to either side and shoot from a different position.
- Receive and control the ball with a wide variety of techniques (see chapter *"CORRECT TECHNIQUES AND PROPER TACTICS IN RECEIVING AND CONTROLLING THE BALL"*), using orientated ball controls.
- Various techniques of heading balls to cope with the different trajectories and speeds of oncoming balls.

Once a player has learned, consolidated and mastered these techniques he executes them automatically without having to focus only on the ball as is often the case with beginners. To win the 1v1-situation his focus has to be wider in order to find the convenient solutions to the existing technical-tactical problem.

b) The technical-tactical game of the defender:
Before making a challenge in a 1v1 situation the defender needs to consider:
- ◆ The state of the ball (stationary or on the move).
- ◆ The conditions of the playing surface (wet, long or artificial grass, hard pitch).
- ◆ His position in relation to the lines on the pitch (for example, the 16.5 meter-line because beyond this line there is danger of committing a penalty)
- ◆ His position in relation to ball, the attacker and the rest of the opponents
- ◆ His position in relation to his supporting team members.
- ◆ The speed, coordination and skill level as well as the creativity of the opponent.
- ◆ His technical-tactical ability and coordination level compared to the opponent.
- ◆ The fatigue existing at that particular moment of the match.
- ◆ The outcome of the 1v1-challenges made before.
- ◆ The tactics his team is applying (for example, full press, delay press or half court press).

In order to win the majority of the one against one situations, the defender should:
- ◆ Position himself correctly in relation to the attacker (taking into account the state of the ball, the lines on the pitch, the position of his and the opponent's supporting players).
- ◆ Assume an optimal body and feet position before and during the challenge.
- ◆ Execute the most appropriate defensive technique under the given circumstances.

*For more information, consult the chapter "The Principle of Approaching an Attacker in Possession of the Ball and Closing Him Down"

GENERAL RULES FOR SUCCESSFUL CHALLENGES

An experienced defender will only try to win the ball from his opponent when he is reasonably confident that he can be successful. If in doubt, he waits for a more opportune moment, delaying his challenge by executing dummy moves.

The more he has in mind the following general rules for defending in a 1v1 - situation, the more often he will come out of the duel as the winner.

These are the rules:
1. Always keep goal-side of the attacker.
2. Come close to the ball carrier to limit his time and space, but prepare for a retreat in your desired direction and then wait for the best possible time to execute a quick tackle.
3. Look for the best possible line of approach to close down the attacker.
4. Concentrate on correct positioning before engaging in any defensive duties:
    * Weight evenly distributed between both legs, which are slightly bent, and with the center of gravity not too low and not too high
    * Stand on the toes.
    * The torso slightly leaning forwards.
    * Concentrate on the ball and not on the attacker's legs.
5. Execute dummy moves to create a favorable situation for you and to distract the opponent.
6. Slow the attacker down if he has the ball fully under control.
7. Anticipate what the attacker is going to do
8. When going to tackle make sure that there is the possibility to make another if necessary.
9. Put the attacker under pressure and force him to play a poor pass.
10. Never turn your back towards the ball carrier.
11. Surprise the attacker with a quick tackle. A slow execution of the tackle, even if technically correct, is useless.
12. Vary the type of tackles made.
13. Get ready to mount a possible attack immediately after the duel is won.

A PHYSICAL WELL PREPARED PLAYER HAS MORE CHANCES TO WIN THE DUELS

A soccer player who is able to read and understand the situations quickly, take decisions and act upon them with speed has an advantage in the 1v1-challenges. But, not only are his perception and decision making skills fundamental, but this must also be backed up by the physical fitness which enables him to carry out his mental solution.

The following five physical qualities influence the outcome of the 30-40 1v1-confrontations a player is likely to face throughout a match:

- ◆ Speed of reaction
- ◆ Acceleration
- ◆ Explosive strength
- ◆ Stamina
- ◆ Speed strength

These qualities should be developed and improved during training by exposing the players to a series of exercises such as:

- ◆ Running towards the ball (straight runs up and back, in a triangle, in a square with or without obstacles, with different distances). These runs should be no less than 5 meters long and no more than 30, with an appropriate rest between each one, depending on its length. It is recommended to mix these speed runs with elements which arise during the 1v1-situations such as collecting or touching objects or opponents, selling feints, changing the length of the path, charging the opponent, lowering the point of gravity etc.

DEVELOPING GAME INTELLIGENCE IN SOCCER

* Tag games in which the players, like in their 1v1-confrontations in the match, never know beforehand what is about to take place concerning:
  - The exact direction of the run
  - The exact time when to set off, to accelerate or to stop
  - The feints and dummies which they have to execute

Furthermore it is also important to make sure of an adequate level of stamina, explosive strength and mobility in the joints, for which sufficient specific literature is available.

HINTS FOR TRAINING 1v1-SITUATIONS

* Whenever possible, introduce 1v1-duels in every training session, making sure that the challenges are simulating real-match situations.
* Make sure the 1v1 is different in every training session.
* Make sure that your players are exposed to a great variety of 1v1-situations which should be different in every training session.
* Analyze, evaluate and correct the performance of both players involved, using constructive criticism and discuss with the players the reasons for the outcome and finally work out solutions that can be put into practice immediately. Use a video camera to record these duels and the performance shown in other specific exercises and games in training, so that these can be analyzed afterwards to spot the strengths and weaknesses of the players involved.
Use the same procedure to analyze the last match. Organize video sessions on an individual basis for every player in the team so that they learn under the supervision of the coach to evaluate all the different aspects of their performance (technique, cognition, perception, tactics, coordination and mental state).
* Players benefit from watching in video top players performing in 1v1-duels as this motivates, enriches and encourages them to copy or learn from the mistakes they have noticed in their attacking as well as in their defensive play.
* Design a plan to help each player to progress from month to month, based on the results achieved and observed in the 1v1-duels disputed in the last matches. The objective is always to win more duels than their counterpart.
* Oblige substitutes or injured players to observe determined players in their particular 1v1-duels throughout the match, thus producing interesting statistical information which may improve their performance in this important aspect of the game. This observation not only helps the player concerned but also the substitute to know more about winning duels.

"To play well you have to focus on your "I" interior and not so much on your "I" exterior"

THE PROFILE OF A WINNER IN THE 1v1-DUEL

It takes more than just technique, tactical experience, good physical and coordination capabilities, knowledge and game intelligence to do well in 1v1 situations. It is true that during a shoulder-to-shoulder charge the stronger player will win an advantage, in a race towards the loose ball the faster player will win, and in an aerial battle the better jumper will head the ball. To sum up, for any duel it is always an advantage to be in better physical shape than the opponent. However, being fit and well-coordinated can't compensate for technical errors, poor positioning, poor vision or decision making. But there is an aspect which still has to be mentioned. The aptitude of a player may be excellent but when his attitude, his temperament and his mental state are not that of a warrior a lot of duels will be lost. From the mental point of view coaches expect from any good player:

1. **The ability to impose his personality**, ignoring the fact that he has to face a particularly tough opponent, that he has niggling aches or pains, that the match is not developing to his expectations or his poor success rate in previous duels.
   First the attacker or defender has to dominate himself before he will be able to dominate his opponent, demonstrating his will-power and spirit of a warrior.

2. **Self-confidence, especially in his particular strengths**, often makes the difference. With confidence in one's capabilities, the answers to when, how, where and why to get involved in a 1v1-situation and when to avoid it and better wait for support from a teammate are much clearer as the player just concentrates on his task at hand without being affected by internal factors. Self-confidence allows him to better analyze the situation in order to discover how to overcome or stop his opponent. Simultaneously, and based on what the player has perceived, he should make a decision on what to do and how to do it. And all this has to happen at "the speed of light".

3. **Imagination and creativity**, which allows him to do the unexpected (especially as an attacker) and to take risks at the right time (especially as an attacker).

4. **Aggressiveness**, but not in excess, as this could work against him. The rules of the game stipulate what is and what is not permitted.
   An aggressive defender harasses his opponent when he receives the ball, puts him under pressure when he tries to control it, unsettles him with his physical presence and demonstrates in his duels his willingness to impose himself on his rival and win, when possible, all 1v1-situations.
   An aggressive attacker always looks for the shortest route to goal, goes for any loose balls and shoots from all angles and even presses the goalkeeper after every shot in order to look for a rebound. Once he loses possession of the ball he tries to win it back immediately.

5. **Self-control**, especially when things are going wrong during the match and opponents provoke him intentionally to oblige him to focus away from his tasks on the pitch.

As seen, winning the 1v1-games is a result of technical, physical and intellectual capacities without forgetting to consider the mental and emotional state of the player involved, something to which more attention has to be paid in the future.

THE DUEL BETWEEN GOALKEEPER AND ATTACKER

Usually, good communication and understanding between the goalkeeper and his defenders means that he should rarely be left in a one against one situation with an attacker. It is very unusual for a goalkeeper to run off his line to challenge an attacker on the ball if a defender has the possibility to close him down. Good observation of how the players are positioned in his half and how the match is developing always precedes any decision to quickly come off his line to take up the best possible position to narrow the angle that the attacker has for the shot. Indecision, or delaying his move, or coming off his line too late, always favors the attacker.

When the goalkeeper comes off his line he should stop 3-4 meters away from the attacker in order to adopt a good basic position (legs spread and slightly bent, body leaning forwards and arms extended slightly to the sides). This textbook position gives him the flexibility to be able to react as quickly as possible to any type of shot or if the attacker decides to run to his left or right. He should only dive for the ball in an attempt to claim it in his hands if the attacker tries to dribble past him.

Apart from the aforementioned one against one situations, the goalkeeper also intervenes on a number of occasions during a match in aerial battles. If the ball is crossed into the box from a corner or any other direction the goalkeeper needs to judge the flight of the ball carefully to decide whether to catch it or compete for it with an attacker by punching it clear with his fist or two fists.. The latter is not really a genuine one against one situation as there are more defenders and attackers influencing the outcome near where the ball arrives.

I am not concentrating on standard one against one situations here (free kicks, corners and penalties) and how the performance of one or other of the two parties involved (goalkeeper or attacker) could influence the outcome of the duel. However, for more information on these topics I suggest you consult the appropriate literature which will give you more specific advice.

1v1 games ending with a shot on goal

	1. 1v1 with shot at goal
PITCH	One half of the full soccer pitch with a full size goal
PLAYERS	3 (1v1 plus a goalkeeper). Various pairs compete amongst themselves in 20 meter wide channels marked by cones.
EXPLANATION	- The attackers set off from a line marked at 25 meters from the goal with the intention to score. The respective defenders, at the first touch of the ball, take off from different positions. • The defender confronts the attacker (starting in a head-on position). • The defender confronts him from the left or right side (side position). • The defender is half a meter behind the attacker on his left or right side . - A goal has to be scored in less than 5 seconds after the first ball touch and always from inside the penalty area.

25 metros

Variation: Two 1v1 confrontations
The first defender is allowed to tackle only in front of the 25 meter line while the second defender only enters a 1v1-duel when the attacker manages to cross this 25 meter line. He approaches him from the 16.5 meter line.

2. 1v1-challenge for a loose ball with a shot at goal

PITCH	One half of a full size pitch with three 20 meter wide channels
PLAYERS	3 in each lane (a passer, an attacker, and a defender) + a goalkeeper

EXPLANATION	- An attacker passes the ball along the ground or in the air towards his team-mate, tightly marked by a defender. The latter tries to receive the ball, overcome his counterpart and shoot at goal.
	- The aerial pass or pass along the ground should be made:
	   ◆ From the halfway line.
	   ◆ From in front (from the edge of the penalty box).
	   ◆ From the side (from any point of one of the side lines).
	- As a variation, it is not decided beforehand who is attacker and who is the defender. The player who first manages to touch the ball becomes attacker with the aim to score a goal.

COMMENTS	**Objectives for the attacker:** ◆ When running for the ball the attacker has to try to "gain an ideal position", meaning he assumes the best possible position in relation to the defender which allows him to play the ball first. He achieves this by running into the defender's path, obstructing him and at the same time shielding the ball and/or carrying out a charge (a shoulder-to-shoulder challenge). ◆ Keep possession of the ball after having claimed it by shielding it with his body. ◆ Use feints and dummies while running with the ball and also while executing the shot at goal. **Objectives for the defender:** ◆ Anticipate the first pass and reach the ball first by getting the better of the attacker during the approach. ◆ Carry out a charge at the right moment to outbalance the attacker. ◆ Step into the path of the attacker. ◆ Pressure the attacker and execute dummy moves. ◆ Time the tackle perfectly.

3. 1v1-challenge for a loose ball with additional pass by the defender

PITCH	One half of a full size pitch with three 20 meter wide channels.
PLAYERS	3 in each lane (a passer, an attacker, and a defender) + a goalkeeper

EXPLANATION	- After receiving a pass from his teammate, the attacking defender has to pass the ball across the center line despite the aggressive pressure from the defending attacker.
	- Flat and high passes should be served to the marked defender by his teammate:
	  ♦ From the halfway line (a back pass).
	  ♦ From a position on one of the side lines which is level with or slightly in front of or behind the two contenders.
	  ♦ From the goal.
	- If the defending attacker wins the ball he tries to score in the goal defended by a goalkeeper

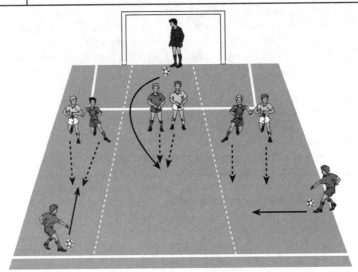

"Each person has his own style of movement, and any change made in the execution of a movement must be undertaken within the individual's style"

L. Mourehouse/L. Gross

4. Two 1v1 confrontations played on a Mini-Soccer pitch

PITCH	Mini-Soccer pitch with two cone goals on each end line
PLAYERS	4 (in each half a 1v1 is played)
EXPLANATION	- Each pair of contenders plays in only one half of the pitch. - After a throw-in from a neutral player in of one half of the pitch, the contenders try to win possession of the ball score in either of the two cone goals with a dribble while the defender's objective is to conquer the ball and pass it to his teammate on the other half of the pitch. Then a new challenge starts until one attacker is able to dribble the ball across either of the two opposing cone goals despite being pressed by the defender.

5. 1v1-situations in the air

PITCH	A penalty area with a second full size goal opposite the regular one
PLAYERS	4 (2 neutral passers, one attacker and one defender)
EXPLANATION	A winger crosses the ball from either side from outside the penalty area. Two contenders vie for the ball in the center of the penalty area, each trying to score in the goal assigned to him. As a variation both goals will be defended by goalkeepers who are not allowed to interfere in the duel between forward and defender.

"A great performance is often not associated with struggle, exhaustion and pains"

EMPHASIZING INDIVIDUALIZED TRAINING SESSIONS

"Soccer does not advance thanks to the number of matches played, but through a systematic development of original ideas and concepts"

INTRODUCTION

In many sports an individualized training program is the only way to prepare (gymnastics, athletics, boxing, judo, swimming, etc.), but up until now it has not been an important coaching method as far as technical-tactical and physical training is concerned for team sports such as, for example soccer.

THE IMPORTANCE OF INDIVIDUALIZED TRAINING

The coach should realize that every team is made up of individuals with particular characteristics. While the collective training sessions with the same exercises and games for everyone improve communication skills, good teamwork and understanding each other and the game of soccer, individualized training seeks to improve and perfect technical-physical deficiencies detected in the performance of an individual player. Furthermore it is often put in practice to recover players after an injury.

For most coaches, the majority of team training time is used to prepare all the players in the same way, regardless of their playing position, characteristics and skill level, with perhaps parts of two training sessions a week dedicated to individualized training sessions. But few are giving individualized training the importance it deserves due to the complexity of its application and also because of the time involved in finding the right medicine to cure the patient and to plan the sessions after having investigated and defined exactly the strengths and weaknesses of each player. An improvement of individual technical and physical aspects can only be achieved with all players when coaches consider the necessity to train individually, and not only for those players who recover after having been injured. The better a player dominates the fundamentals and has no obvious deficiencies in his physical preparation, the more his team as a whole will benefit from his contribution.

THE ROLE OF THE COACH IN THE INDIVIDUALIZED TRAINING

The 5 step approach:

1. First of all the coach and his assistant must have a thorough knowledge of the skills and qualities they expect from a specific player in a specific position on the field and how an injury would affect his performance.

2. Next, the deficiencies of the player concerned have to be identified through a detailed observation of all aspects which influence his performance (especially negatively)

3. The third step is designing a plan for an individualized, personal or specific training program for this particular player which meets his actual needs. When drawing up the individualized training program for a particular player, his particular position in the team has to be taken into account. There are positions in the team like that of the goalkeeper or the sweeper (last defender) where the individualized training seems obvious, but also the wingbacks or wingers may have similar individualized sessions as do the front runners, the midfield players or the marking defenders. Moreover, players who commit similar errors can train together, initially alone, and later on against one or more opponents.

Individualized or specific group training must become a must for all players, regardless of their position on the field.

4. After having selected the exercises intended to correct and improve the weaknesses in one player's performance, the coach should convince the player that by practicing them long enough, he will surely improve in this desired aspect of his game and the team will benefit from his improved contribution. It is important that the player identifies himself with the different exercises and their objectives designed by the coaching staff.

5. Finally, the plan has to be put in practice and evaluated together with the player and modified if necessary. The stop watch and a video camera are two tools which help to measure the achieved performance level. Furthermore both help to motivate the player in the process.

"Techniques will only improve through repetitive practice "

EXERCISES/GAMES

EXAMPLE OF THE EXERCISES/GAMES TO PRACTICE INDIVIDUALIZED TRAINING

1. Individual attack with speed (35 meters)	
PITCH	One half of a full size pitch
PLAYERS	2
EXPLANATION	- A player standing on the center line receives and controls the ball which arrives from behind or from the side, at which point the coach starts the time-clock. The player is timed to determine how long it takes him to dribble across the 16.5 meter line and score from inside the penalty box into the empty goal. At least three ball touches have to be carried out. - After three months, the player should have improved the speed of the run by 0.2 seconds. - Subsequently, the coach might ask for a shot on goal defended by a goal-keeper and in case of a rebound the attacker has to go for it. - **Variation:** On his way towards the goal the player has to overcome various obstacles.

2. Around a square

PITCH	A square with side lines 8-10 meters long.
PLAYERS	2
EXPLANATION	The two players set off at the same time from opposite corners heading in the same direction with the objective of running outside around the square with the ball. The winner is the player who completes two circuits first.

3. Around a triangle

PITCH	A triangle is marked with 5 cones placed in a "slalom" at its base line (8 meters).
PLAYERS	2
EXPLANATION	Setting off from different corners and running in the same direction, the two players run around the triangle with the ball and at its base line do a slalom run (in and out of the cones). **Variation:** Without the ball. **Variation:** One player dribbles the ball and the other chases him without the ball as he runs around the triangle.

"The only valid comparisons are between the player's present, past and future performance. A player shouldn't judge himself by comparison with others as there is always someone better."

L. Mourehouse/L. Gross

4. Zig-zag run

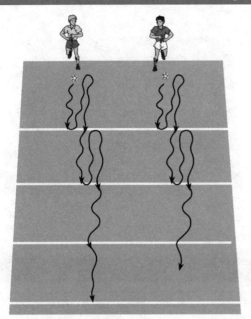

PITCH	A training area of 10m x 20m with horizontal lines at 7m, 11m, 17 m and 20 m
PLAYERS	2-10
EXPLANATION	All the players, each with a ball, should complete the course in the following manner: run to the first line (7 m.), return to the start, run to the second line (11 m) and return to the first line, and so on until each player completes the zig-zag by crossing the 20m-line.

5. Change direction and pace with the ball

a) The L

PITCH	A right angle is formed with 3 cones 3m apart.
PLAYERS	1
EXPLANATION	- A player starts from the center and dribbles the ball as fast as possible along the 3m-line to one exterior cone, returns, turns 90°, runs to the third cone and back to the center cone etc. - The idea is to complete as many sides (3 meters) as possible in 30 seconds.

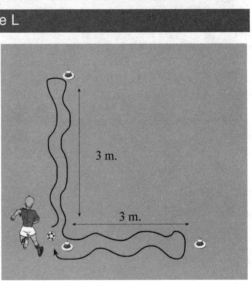

3 m.

3 m.

b) Beating a defender who tackles from a side

PITCH	A cone goal 8 (10) meters wide
PLAYERS	2
EXPLANATION	- An attacker is situated with the ball 9 meters in front of an unoccupied cone of a cone goal with the defender standing at the other cone. The aim of the attacker is to dribble the ball across the goal-line with the defender trying to prevent it. As soon as the attacker touches the ball, the defender sets off from his unfavorable position on the far cone in an attempt to occupy the space in front of the attacker and close him down. - If the attacker isn't quick enough to cross the line before the defender approaches him, he has to create space for himself either by changing the direction of his run at the right moment and/or changing pace until he gets rid of the fast approaching defender. - Throughout his offensive move the attacker should look up in order to observe and analyze the position and speed of the defender, because the way he defends will affect his decision. Moreover, he should practice until he consistently chooses the best moment to change direction and/or pace with out falling into the common mistake of running with the ball into the range of action of the defender. The more he obliges the defender to run with full speed, the easier it is for him to dribble past him on the side from where the defender is approaching.

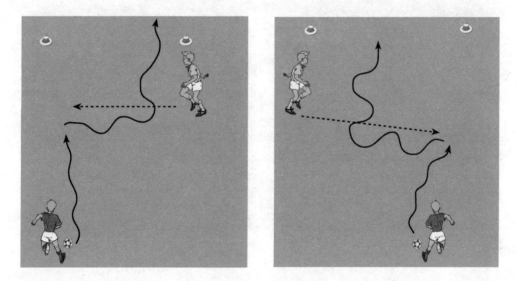

"The genuine coach generates ideas and opens the mind of his players. His far-reaching task is to let the players think instead of thinking for them. This means that the coach grants certain freedom to his players, involving them in the problem solving process and the decision making"

---

c) 1v1 with 4 goals

PITCH	An area of 12x16 meters divided in two halves, each with two cone goals (4 meters wide) positioned as shown in the illustration.
PLAYERS	22 (and another two as substitutes when the first pair rests)
EXPLANATION	- Each player defends two cone goals, one on his end line and the other one on one side line just before the halfway line. - The player with the ball starts his attack from his goal on his end line. His aim is to dribble the ball across one of the two opponent's cone goals. - When the attacker touches the ball, the defender defends his two goals and, if successful, turns over to attack and tries to score with a dribble in one of his opponent's goals. - The attacker should score at least 8 times in 10 individual attacks. - Any mistake in attack or defense has to be identified by the proper player with the help of his coach. - After 5 attacks players switch roles. - It is highly recommended to first practice this game as a tag game without the ball to identify the key points in the physical part of the game.

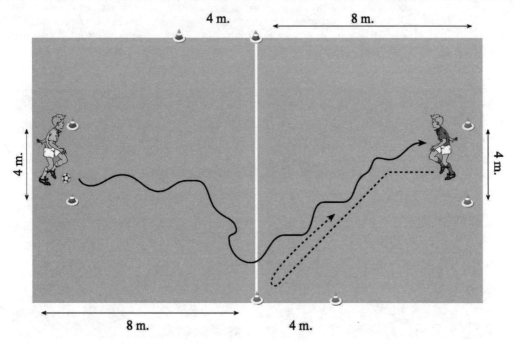

"It is not only the variety of the ingredients of a menu (training session), but also the way it was prepared and presented that will determine its success"

---

6. Heading as a shot or clearance

PITCH	1/3 of a full size soccer pitch with a goal
PLAYERS	10 (4 passers, 2 attackers, 3 defenders and 1 goalkeeper)
EXPLANATION	Various players give aerial passes from a variety of angles into the penalty area. While the attacker tries to score with a header, the defender tries to head the ball clear towards one of his two teammates on the edge of the penalty box, taking into account which is less marked by a second attacker close to the 16.5 meter-line. **Variation:** See exercise 8 in the chapter: "Correct techniques and proper tactics when receiving and controlling the ball"

"To cure a disease, it's not sufficient to undergo a diagnosis. It is imperative to look for the roots of the problem and to apply the pertinent remedies"

7. Heading at goal in a counter attack

PITCH	A 7-a-side soccer pitch
PLAYERS	6
EXPLANATION	- Two teams of 3 attackers start their attack from the center line heading in opposite directions. The center forward of both teams is in possession of a ball. - He passes the ball to one of his wings who must stay in the cone channel close to the side line. The wing dribbles the ball with speed down the channel until he reaches the penalty area and then plays a high centering cross. - The center forward and the winger from the other side move into position to head the ball into the empty goal. The winger from the opposite side is allowed to leave his channel when he sees that the other winger is prepared to cross the ball. - The ball is crossed in from different sides, distances, heights, angles and speeds to force the two attackers to adapt to the changing situations. - **First competition:** There is no time pressure. The team of three that scores more headers in ten attempts wins (1st level of difficulty without a goalkeeper or a defender). - **Second competition:** The team that scores first with a header wins a point. After each series of 5 attacks with crosses from one side, the opposite wing takes 5 crosses. After 30 attacks the winning team is declared. - **Third competition:** The two attackers in the penalty area have a maximum of two touches (with head or feet) to score before their opponents. If the ball touches the ground, the goal will not be allowed. - **Fourth competition:** 2nd level of difficulty with one defender. - **Fifth competition:** 3rd level of difficulty with a goalkeeper who starts on the goal line and later is allowed to come out of his goal. - **Sixth competition:** 4th level of difficulty with a goalkeeper and one defender.

8. Chilena (or Bicycle Kick)

PITCH	Any area of the pitch with a goal.
PLAYERS	Various pairs.
EXPLANATION	One player throws the ball from different angles to his partner who stands with his back towards the goal. He may score directly with a "chilena" or first touch it with any part of the body and then execute the "scissors" kick.

9. Shots at goal

PITCH	1/3 of a full size soccer pitch with penalty area and a goal
PLAYERS	7 (1 center forward, 5 passers and a goalkeeper).
EXPLANATION	- A front striker is situated in the center of the penalty area. Five teammates from different distances outside the penalty area pass the ball with different speeds, heights and spins to him. He has to adjust to the trajectory of the oncoming ball and score: ♦ with either foot first-time ♦ with two touches or three touches without letting the ball touch the ground ♦ with his weaker foot only ♦ with any type of header - Later a defender is added whose job it is to intercept the passes or stop the striker from scoring. - Finally, the striker practices receiving, controlling the ball and shooting, despite the presence of two defenders and a goalkeeper.

"Practice makes perfect only if you are doing it right."
L. Mourehouse/L. Gross

"Practice doesn't make perfect if you are repeating a wrong motion or playing a wrong soccer competition all year around as happens with millions of children around the globe."
Horst Wein

10. Accurate passing with a moving ball

PITCH	1/3 of a full size pitch with 5 cone goals (3 meters wide), established in a semi-circle 20 meters from the passing zone. Make sure you have enough balls available.
PLAYERS	1 (later 2 or 3 defenders are added)
EXPLANATION	- Setting off a few meters in front of a passing zone (3m x 5m), a player has 20 seconds to dribble one ball after another (total of five) into the zone and then score in all 5 cone goals. Despite the time pressure, accuracy in passing in 5 different directions should be expected. - Later, first two and then three defenders are introduced. They have to position themselves close to the 5 goals to prevent the attackers from scoring 5 times in any of the 5 goals.

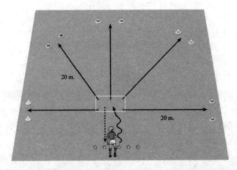

11. Accurate crosses

PITCH	A playing area in and around the penalty area with a full size goal
PLAYERS	5 (4 attackers and a goalkeeper).
EXPLANATION	- After a run along the sideline a winger crosses the ball to one of the three players. The first to touch the ball becomes the attacker and has to score despite the presence of the other two active defenders. - For more exercises see "Developing Youth Soccer Players" by Horst Wein, Human Kinetics, 2000, pages 48-56.

12. Challenge in a 1v1-situation

Examples of two 1v1-games. To score a goal the ball has to be controlled on the opponent's goal line.

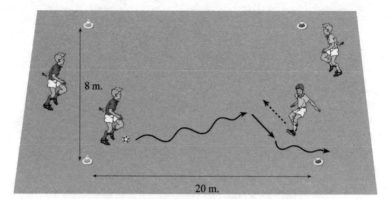

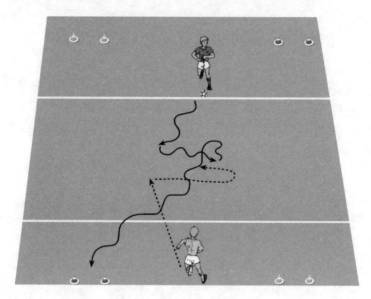

"How you react after having lost the ball or the game will determine how long it takes you to make the next positive play"

PART FOUR

ORGANIZING
THE VICTORY

WINNING MORE OFTEN THANKS TO TECHNOLOGY

"In the next decade technology will change the game more than rule modifications"

Almost unlimited applications

Not only will athletes be equipped with the most technologically advanced equipment and apparel, technology will even get inside their heads to provide them with the most advanced information on their performances - all edited down to reinforce the particular messages their coach is trying to get through to them. And soccer will not be an exception.

The various high-tech digital video analysis software programs which are now on the market will soon play a huge behind-the-scenes role in professional soccer. They have been designed especially for coaches and trainers to accurately measure what really counts in soccer. They gather information on team dynamics and individual performances in training and especially in competition, with the coach deciding precisely what he wants to know. This video analysis system is called SCOUTING. And the coach who controls the system Scouter.

The flexibility of a Video Analysis System allows coaches to go under the skin of a match. There is no spewing out of meaningless data because the system allows us to set up a variety of templates specific to the match-to-match requirements of the coach. The software allows coaches and players to compare the play of both sides and make game-plan adjustments on the spot and also for the long term can track the development of individual players or teams through a database of video and statistical information. The team which has done an analysis of the proper game performance as well as that of their opponents obviously has an advantage going into a match.

While the head coach is watching the game, one coaching staff member records the game in case it is not being televised, and a scouter introduces via voice recognition software all the data of interest during the development of the match onto a lap-top computer, setting up a database of incidents from the game such as:

- All the interventions of a chosen player (with or without the ball) during the game. His clips serve as a useful database for analyzing his defensive and/or offensive performance to be then used to the benefit of the player in the half-time interval ,if considered necessary.

- All specific moves or set pieces from our own team or the opposition during the match. For example:
    - all the free kicks taken no further than 33 meters from the opposition's goal or from our own goal
    - all the goal attempts on our own or the opposition's goal and the build ups that preceded them
    - all the crosses made from both wings or from one particular wing attacker
    - all the 1v1- situations that occur, specified for both teams and also for each individual player

- all the corners, for and against,
- all the challenges made by the different players in one team or all all the 2v1-situations for both teams in attack or for different players in one team those made by one individual player only,
- all the plays in numerical inferiority and their outcomes
- all the positional attacks which started from our own penalty box and where they break down (the same can be done with the opposition's attacks) to compare the results with those from previous matches
- all passes or only all long passes (more than 25 meters) with their outcomes
- ball losses and where they happened on the field. This can be done for the whole team or for any player on the field and compared with the result achieved by other players or by the same player in a previous match, etc.

The computer can edit the collected data at any time of the game or after it. That is why before half-time the coach may have a series of clips available of those plays that interested him most in order to use this information in his half time talk. The software can instantly play back on screen that part of the game for the players. At the same time, statistics are produced outlining the success or failure of each intervention or move made by an individual player or for the whole team.

An important point is how the Coach presents to the players all this information before or after the match. If he has the list of actions ready to analyze the opponent, he must offer a big screen projection (min 80") with a portable projector, this will make the understanding easier, especially if the coach has an optical pointer to draw over the image.

A broad range of uses for the software

1. The software allows the coaching staff to run off a tape, BROWSEABLE CD or DVD. We have to take in consideration the quality of the captured video, because this will affect the capacity of the computer hard disk. If we use maximum digital quality, we could waste about 20Gbs per complete match of 90 minutes. 1hour = 13Gbs. If we decided to capture in compressed quality, then we will have a complete match in about 700Mbs of hard disk space. Actually the software can memorize the data for a maximum of 8 individual players, which is an edited package of every time he is in or near the action during a match. The coaches then review the sequences recorded on a DVD together with the player during the week and talk through what he did right and where he has to improve. For assessing his performance even better, the software can also pull out a videotape from earlier in the season and encode it on the spot.

From the player's perspective he can self-analyze his performance with the data stored in the computer driven system. This will get him thinking about his individual performance and taking on responsibility for his own game rather than being told what to do.

For instance, after the match a player receives a copy of all his 1v1-situations in attack as well as in defense to take home and review it that night.

2. The computer driven video system also looks - if the head coaches wishes it- at what is actually happening with the team during the match. The different data are introduced in the computer at the same time they happen in the match, producing simultaneously statistics which can outline the success or failure of each intervention for either the team or an individual player. The facility for coaches to see instant playbacks during the game can not only hone the half-time team talk of the coach, but helps him to decide which tactical change or substitutions needs to be made, because he will have all statistical information on each player at his fingertips.

3. In exactly the same way, the software allows the coach to "spy" on the opposition. The coaching staff can also compile tapes focusing on the opposition star player (or also on the whole team as a unit) and give them to the specific player who has to watch him in the match to come. The Digital Video Performance Analysis helps to understand how the opponents play their game, thereby allowing for the development of tactics to counter the opponent's strengths and capitalize on their weaknesses. It provides the head coach with sufficient information to develop a tactic to beat them at their own game.

4. The digital video analysis software can also be used for technique analysis. For instance all of a forward's shooting action could be taken, stored and then clips could be produced to be analyzed frame-by-frame by the coaching staff and the player.

In training the software helps to improve the learning of the player. Seconds after the session, any player can refer to the systematically collected data and images independently. Also the coach is able to see and then comment upon all the details from the training session that was filmed and sent to the laptop.

The system also allows the coach and the player to watch the recording at different speeds, so specific moves can be watched in slow motion or using the freeze-frame feature, which is very useful for analysis and consequently for learning.

5. Finally the digital video analysis also serves motivational purposes, highlighting and storing particularly inspirational pieces of team play to show back to the team for positive reinforcement.

Using any of the Digital Video Analysis Systems on the market to record a soccer match can highlight some interesting results. For example:

- **84% of goals scored are produced from moves with three or less com bined actions** (German league 1997/98). In other words, it is not always a good tactic to build up the game with positional attacks with a lot of passes. It seems that it is efficient to attack quickly with less than four passes or dribbles (as with counterattacks), or better still, it is best to conquer the ball near the opposition's area, which could be achieved best through anticipation skills and/or the use of the full press.

- **32% of all goals scored come from standard situations with a stationary ball** (penalties, free kicks, corners) and this trend is increasing.

- On average you need to make **11 goal attempts to score one goal**.

The benefits of using video and computer technology to aid a player's learning and training process or that of a team are, as seen with the above mentioned examples, practically limitless. Once a weakness has been detected in an individual player or with the team as a whole it is the function of the head coach to make maximum use of the accurate and detailed information to better the performance of the individual player or the team for the next match.
It has already been proven that this technology is an ideal supplement to the less efficient method which is prevalent at the moment and based on human experience and human error.

More information and success in the future
The increasing professionalism of all sports means that those who want to get to the top and stay at the top can't afford to be left behind. There is so much scrutiny now in soccer that there is nowhere to hide on the pitch, so players must take this technology on board. Clubs or coaches who continue to accumulate data on a subjective basis and then leave it up to the coach to analyze all this information without using a computer driven video analysis system to increase performance levels (and furthermore are not working regularly with a sports psychologist on the technical staff), will start the season with a definite disadvantage.

When the opponents are probably just as fit, just as skilled, and just as committed as your team is, then maybe a Digital Video Analysis System can deliver the edge.

"Sports and technology are interrelated like never before in a never ending quest to stretch the bounds of human performance"

THE PERCENTAGE GAME

"The road to success has very few travelers because the majority of them got lost along the way looking for short cuts"

Playing the percentage game means knowing how to get the best out of each player by limiting his errors as much as possible. When a player, for example, is not confident in playing through passes, especially deep into the opposition's half, he should refrain from playing them, and instead pass the ball short to a player who feels more comfortable making this type of a pass. A player who is aware of the importance of playing the percentage game only plays risky through passes when he is fully confident that the circumstances on the pitch demand it, when he has the technical ability to do so and when, most important-ly, his success rate in through passes in previous matches was above 66%.

Playing the percentage game means that in every situation of the game a player must think of using the technical-tactical skill that at that particular moment is most likely to be successful. If a marker is particularly adept at anticipating when his opponent is about to receive the ball, then he should use this skill as often as possible during the game, especially against a skilful and quick opponent who may outplay him in a 1v1-situation because of his speed and dribbling abili-ty. But when a player does not have the ability to read and anticipate the inten-tions of the opposition, it is better not to use "anticipating marking" and instead challenge the opponent when he is just receiving the ball.

Playing the percentage game can also be interpreted in other ways: A center forward near the penalty area, who is controlling one of three passes has a suc-cess-rate of 33% in this type of move. But if this important aspect of the game has been practiced enough with lack of space and time, with opposition and several variations, the player would surely improve his success-rate in this par-ticular move in subsequent matches.

Another example: a winger who only manages to successfully cross the ball to his attacking colleagues in 12% of all his cross attempts has a very low suc-cess-rate and consequently is not performing to a high standard. The same is true for a defender who only manages to win the ball in 28% of the 1v1-situa-tions he is involved in.

Collecting all the results for a player in a certain game situation (see the chapter "Winning more often thanks to technology") helps the coach to plan and improve training programs on an individual basis, attempting to improve the weaknesses via continued and frequent practice encompassing all possibilities.
When a team doesn't use a digital video analysis system to perfect an individual player's game during or after the match, it is advisable to collate information and statistics for all the moves of an individual player in one match (complete statis-tical data of his performance).

When the coaching staff uses this information to compare the number of suc-cessful interventions and the number of errors made by a single player during the collective play, they can educate him to have " the percentage game" in his mind for the next match.

The interpretation and use of the complete statistical information and statistics of various players not only increases the rivalry between them, but also is reflected in the improved flow of team play and more efficiency in the moves, which in turn leads to a greater possibility of winning.

The percentage of successfully executed interventions is different for each player because the ability of each player to only do what he truly masters depends largely on the individual's personality and character. The player should never seek to shine on a personal level, but instead try to play his role as part of an effective team.

Knowing how to play the percentage game means also that the players in the team take into account the score and the time until the final whistle. Another example: a player who knows from his statistics that playing a deep aerial pass only has a 38% chance of being controlled by his teammate, won't risk it when his team is winning by a goal with little time left in the match and so will look for a short pass or a long square or horizontal pass.

The same is true for all critical moments in a match (like the three minutes after scoring a goal, the last few minutes at the end of each half, and the first few minutes of each half). During these critical moments, which often decide the outcome of matches, it is important to know how to play the percentage game.

For all of the above reasons, knowing how to play the percentage game is fundamental in order to improve performance both on an individual and team basis.

SEVEN TIPS ON HOW TO IMPROVE YOUR PERCENTAGE GAME

1.Don't make two consecutive mistakes.
The way to build confidence and guarantee a good performance is to carry out a successful intervention in the next move after making a mistake. This could involve your next pass, or the next 1v1-situation. On the other hand, making another error because you complicated things or took too much of a risk, will put a tremendous amount of pressure on you in your next playing action. While you're worrying about what's going to happen in your next contribution to the game, your opponent is growing in confidence.

This is why, under these circumstances, you should always perform the execution you are most comfortable with, without forgetting a bit of variety. It is worth knowing that even a good player is unsuccessful with an average of three passes in every ten he executes. Don't try to fix everything with one 'fantastic' pass. Instead, play the most practical pass given the circumstances. If these practical tips are considered by each player in your team it will improve their percentage of good passes, would make the game more fluid and faster, with more team play, more confidence and ultimately better results.

2. Play high, diagonal passes into the opposition's half in the space behind the defense.

To achieve as many successful long passes as possible into the opposition's half, it is advisable to play the ball high and diagonally into a space not controlled by the defenders. Depending on the starting position, the defender close to the attacker has the same possibilities to claim the possession of the ball. Playing well-timed diagonal passes is a good tactic, as long as your attacker anticipates the moment of the pass and times his run well in order to get to the landing point of the ball before the opposition.

3. Adequate positioning is crucial for good defending.

Many players defend a lot better with their right foot than with their left. If this is true in your case, position yourself slightly to the left of the ball, opposite the right shoulder of your opponent, as in this way you leave more space on your strong (right) side. If you prefer to use your left foot, as is the case with many left-footed wingbacks, do the opposite, position yourself approximately half a meter away from your opponent, slightly to his right, inviting him to attack you down the left. Provoke your adversary into playing down the side which suits you best (taking into account where you are on the pitch, and the position of your covering teammate). Using this tactic to your advantage, your opponent may opt to try to dribble around you down the narrow side, which greatly lowers his chances of success and increases yours considerably.

Moreover, you should try to avoid standing head-on to the ball carrier as this allows you to time your tackle well while running with him on his side. Standing slightly to either side of your opponent allows you to see both goals at the same time, and so the 1v1-situations are more likely to be won by the defender.

4. When in possession of the ball and your teammates are tightly marked, the space behind them covered and no safe pass is available, then run diagonally with the ball away from your defender and you will see how new passing options become available.

5. Give your corner kicks maximum speed and a height of no more than 2.50 meters.

This will give the defenders less time to intervene and the strikers more chance of surprising the goalkeeper with a powerful first-time shot at goal. The end result is a higher success-rate for the attackers, more rebounds and more mistakes by the defenders.

6. It is better to mount counter-attacks than to use positional attacks, as this will give your team a higher success rate.

7. When counterattacking your team should not use more than four plays, as this will increase your scoring percentage.

ANALYZING YOUR OPPONENT'S GAME

"The quality of the observation conditions the correctness of the preceding evaluation. He who knows a lot sees a lot"

One of the most important jobs for the coach is to try to fully prepare his players for the next match, taking into account all the factors affecting each player's performance to a lesser or greater degree, both on an individual and team basis. To achieve an optimal performance the coach or player should, amongst other things:

a) Go to watch his opponent play in several matches or analyze his play with videos, so that he can obtain as much information as possible about the opponent's strengths and weaknesses in attack, midfield and in defense. The more experienced the observer, the better the quality of the information collected, because someone who knows a lot sees a lot. This is why good coaches always have good observational skills.

b) Put himself in the position of the opponent's coach and ask himself what weaknesses and strengths he might have discovered in his team and what his tactics might be to overcome the opponent.

A good coach not only anticipates his opponent's possible tactical plan, on an individual player and team basis, but he also studies and familiarizes himself with their favorite pre-studied moves and set plays. In other words, the coach should think about the game well in advance, using his imagination to capture and process the style and characteristics of the opposition.

The ability to put together a tactical plan for each game, trying to take advantage of the weaknesses and overcome the strengths of the opposition, is a skill every good coach should have.

The well-prepared observation of how the opponent plays and of the habits of each individual player is a fundamental part of any technical, tactical and mental preparation for each match. The team, guided by the coach who gives them specific observational tasks, should be involved in the collation and evaluation of data on each of the players in the opposition. In this way, the players learn to observe their next opponents more like a coach than a mere spectator.

Why is it a good idea to watch and analyze your next opponents well in advance?

Systematic observation of the attributes and habits of your opponent helps the observer (player or coach) to…
a) Learn more about soccer in general and especially about their next opponent.
b) Obtain information about the best way to deal with the opposition in specific situations, looking at the way the team usually plays under these circumstances and if necessary can change the way his team normally plays to counteract the opposition.
c) Prepare mentally for the different alternatives that they may have to face in the match, which in itself is an advantage.

d) Reinforce self-belief and self-confidence.

e) Create the main basis to decide how to approach the majority of the 1v1-situations against your opponent, which will contribute significantly to the likely success in the match.

It is important to know that all players have characteristic moves, typical for their style of play. When having observed them being used in similar circumstances again and again, then we can speak about a habit. All players of the opposition (and even the referees) have characteristic habits and tendencies of which his next opponent has to be aware to counteract them successfully.

Examples of characteristic habits	The best way to counteract these characteristics
Doesn't normally run towards the the ball to control it.	Try getting past the opponent in order to intercept the pass.
Usually controls the ball with his back to his opponent, shields the ball well with his body before turning continues the attack.	Don't anticipate or pressure during the control, it is better to wait for the 1:1 situation.
Usually plays feints and dummies when dribbling.	Don't rush into the challenge, but run with him.
Normally prefers to dribble down one side.	Position yourself well and close the space, inviting him to run down the other side.
Wins the majority of 1:1 situations.	Avoid 1:1 situations and seek cover from your teammates
The goalkeeper has a weaker side.	Direct the ball towards his weaker side.
The goalkeeper often plays outside the goal so that he can act, if necessary, as a 'sweeper' in defense.	While trying to win back possession in the opponent's half, think about taking a shot from distance to surprise the goalkeeper.
The goalkeeper has a very high success-rate in the 1:1 situations.	Don't get too close to the goalkeeper and shoot before he has a chance to narrow the angle.
A specific defender has the habit of running with the ball near his own penalty area before passing it.	When this player has possession of the ball he should be harassed and pressured by two players in an attempt to win the ball before he passes it.
An attacker has very good defensive qualities.	Our defenders shouldn't risk running with the ball at all and pass the ball in time

By looking at these 10 examples it's clear to see that **good observation** of a particular opponent is always a useful guide to help know how best to play against him under specific circumstances. We just have to hope that the opposition doesn't spend even more time and effort in observing and analyzing the players in our team.

"There comes a time in performance when too much knowledge is detrimental. Then you have to decide which you want to be, an analyst or a performer."

L. Mourhouse/L. Gross

IMPROVING TEAM PERFORMANCE BY ESTABLISHING ROLES FOR EACH OF THE PLAYERS

"Success is a ladder which you can't climb up with your hands in your pockets"

American proverb

The main objective for every player in a team is to win. In relation to this fundamental objective, all the others seem to be less important.

On the way to achieving the best possible result in the next match, in addition to a specific game-plan to follow for the whole team, almost all of the players should be assigned a **specific role** before the match or better a day or even two days before. However, the said role or roles should never put pressure on the player. Instead, the expectations of what the coach expects from a single player should help him to contribute in the most efficient way to make sure of victory.

A role requires a player to carry out in a certain way specific tasks as part of the **team plan**, just as each member of the coaching staff fulfills a specific role as part of the coaching team.

Generally speaking, the role of a defensive wingback is very different from that of a 'sweeper' or midfield player, just as the coach performs different tasks than the manager or fitness coach, before, during and after the match.

A soccer team, as an organization, requires different people who carry out different tasks, before, during and after the match, depending on the specific function for which they were hired. The soccer player, although mainly exposed to collective training sessions in which he learns to speak the team's proper soccer language, is also trained individually for his specific role, **tailored to his mental, physical and technical characteristics**. The better he accomplishes the role assigned to him in a match, the more success his team will have. It doesn't matter whether he is a specialist for free-kicks, a goalkeeper, an excellent distributor of the ball, a sweeper or an attacker who makes the difference through his outstanding skills in the 1v1-situations.

Performing his best and contributing his particular piece to the game doesn't prevent him from accomplishing other general functions in attack and in defense for which he was prepared in the collective training sessions.

LOOK FOR CLARITY AND ACCEPTANCE WHEN SETTING UP THE ROLES

Establishing a role, or various roles, for each of the players in the team is the job of the coach, who ideally seeks the cooperation and acceptance from the players, who in turn must understand the importance of their roles in the functioning of the team. The coach should ask each player his opinion and should explain why he was given this particular role or roles and not others for this specific match, considering, apart from the player's qualities, those of his teammates, and also those of his likely direct opponent and the opposition in general. When doing so, it allows the player in question to see his task clearly.

Understanding the role perfectly is as important as accepting it.
Research carried out by Locke and Schweiger (1979) has demonstrated that a player performs his task a lot more willingly and effectively if he is involved in helping to establish his particular duties.

When a coach outlines, apart from the clear definition of the role, a specific target that the player can and must achieve (for example, as central defender concentrate on anticipation marking and don't let your personal opponent touch the ball more than twice in each half of the match), he should look for the player's acceptance. A clear definition of the role, a common establishment of a target and the acceptance facilitate its **successful execution**.

The targets (objectives) set for a player in a match should not be too difficult to achieve, as we do not want to put the player under additional pressure. But neither should they be too easy, requiring little physical or mental effort whatsoever. Experience has shown that achieving easy objectives does not help to get the best out of an individual player or a team. Assuming that the player has accepted the targets set for him by the coach before the game, the effort required to achieve them should be directly proportional to their degree of difficulty.

Accepting the role is always easier when the coach knows how to convince the player that the responsibilities assumed by each individual are imperative to the success of the team as a whole, each player being an important cog in the wheel. So, even if the role involves a tremendous amount of hard work and sacrifice, such as that of the player who has "to mark out of the game" the opposing distributor or "brain", he performs it willingly.

CHECK THE ACCOMPLISHMENT OF THE ROLES

During the game and after having performed the role or roles, the coach has to find out if the players to whom he assigned roles have managed to accomplish them. At half-time and especially after the game the coach and the respective player should evaluate together, with or without video assistance, to what degree the objectives set before the game have been achieved.

Another way of checking the effectiveness is to use during the match a simple point system in which a player is watched exclusively by either an assistant coach or an injured player and is given a positive or negative point for each intervention on the pitch. These are totaled to give a **Total Performance Score**. For example, a player earns a positive or negative point after each 1v1-situation). In this way, the coach is able to monitor how each player is performing his role or his specific tasks at any stage during the match by merely looking at the number of points obtained.

"Hope for the best, but prepare for the worst"
English Proverb

This ability to store information on different aspects of offensive play (for example, the result achieved for passing or ball control) and defensive play (for example, the percentage of successful or poor challenges or covering), helps to highlight the weaknesses of each player so that these can be corrected by practicing specific exercises/games in subsequent individualized training sessions. The Total Performance Score also highlights the strengths of each player, which helps the coach when he is deciding which role to allocate to which player.

Hubie Brown, former coach of the New York Knicks, said once: *"To transform the innate potential of a player into performance you have to establish roles and set targets for him"* (Danish, 1983)*. This is why it is so important to know in which position on the field the player performs best so that his potential is exploited to a maximum for the benefit of his team. Having his roles well defined, understood and accepted will help the player to perform well.

As the game develops a player's motivation depends not only on the result but on the effectiveness of his personal opponent and his ability to accomplish the specific role assigned to him.

If in the team analysis after the match the coach publicly acknowledges a particular player's performance and valuable contribution to the team's success, it is likely that the player will maintain and continue these high standards in the subsequent matches.

TRAINING FOR A SPECIFIC ROLE

The capacity to successfully accomplish a determined role is helped by special training with **specific objectives** that might include technical-tactical considerations or some physical qualities which condition the player's performance (like, for example, a lack of explosive power).

With specific training sessions the coach has to make sure that all different aspects of a player's role are worked out and developed satisfactorily. If a frontrunner is asked to increase his effectiveness in receiving the ball when being tightly marked by an opponent, then he has to be exposed to exercises and games in which he must time his movements into space, establish a visual agreement with the passer, use feints and dummies and a change of pace to get away from the defender etc. Each of the elements that make up the whole technical-tactical move has to be perfected.

"The secret of a good team is order and discipline, especially during the critical moments of a match. One of the most important jobs for a coach is to make sure that each one of his players understands exactly what he has to do in any given situation in the game"
Josep "Pep" Guardiola

Examples of establishing roles for young players between 12 and 16 years

The main role as far as technique and tactics are concerned

1. As a winger, keep an eye on the opposition's wingback. Instead of marking him, force him to be concerned about you all the time .
2. As a winger, move into a more central area of the pitch when your wingback is about to receive the ball close to the side line. This will enable him to pass the ball into the gap created by the winger or to penetrate with the ball in the space vacated.
3. Play the next 6 passes without making a mistake.
4. Play 5 successful through passes, but only when the time is right.
5. All the free-kicks taken from our half should reach a teammate.
6. Always seek a 2v1-situation, avoiding 1v1-situations.
7. Mark your opponent in such a way that you can anticipate and get to the ball before he does. Don't let him receive the ball more than 3 times in each half.
8. Run less with the ball (not more than 5 times in each half).
9. Don't rush into 1v1-situations. Have patience and confidence.
10. Achieve a 100% success-rate with throw-ins.
11. Force the attacker towards your favorite side or where a teammate is covering at that moment.
12. Don't be afraid of missing the target when shooting at goal. Conceal your true intentions.
13. Look for a one-two or triangular combination to introduce yourself into the attack 6 times during the match.
14. Look for at least 5 quick turnovers from defense to attack . You should know before you tackle what you are going to do with the ball before you win it.
15. Hide the moment and direction of your passes on 10 occasions.
16. Put pace on the ball when passing. Also with short passes.
17. Every time there is no teammate available, instead of passing the ball backward, run diagonally with the ball away from your opponent and take advantage of the new spaces.
18. When marking an opponent use your skills in anticipating and "gain the position" in front of him before he can receive and control the ball.
19. As frontrunner in the opposing half, receive 90% of all balls in a side-on position which allows you to see what is going on between you and the opposing goal.
20. Always make yourself available for a pass, giving predefined cues to your teammate in possession of the ball.

Examples of sub-roles in the mental area

1. Don't let yourself be influenced by the comments or actions of others.
2. Believe in your own capabilities and don't have doubts. Give yourself positive reinforcements or orders.
3. If you make a mistake, blame someone else and concentrate on your next intervention.

THE IMPORTANCE OF ESTABLISHING POSITIVE RULES FOR THE GROUP

While the assignment of a role refers mainly to players as individuals, collectively there should be certain rules of conduct which establish a way of doing things that everyone in the team adheres to. Acting passively when you lose possession of the ball, going on greedy runs too often in the match in 1v1-situations, playing too much as an individual to the detriment of team play, commenting or otherwise getting involved in the decisions of the referee, playing frequent aerial passes instead of keeping the ball on the ground… are things that could persist throughout a whole season, unless other guidelines are established.

If this happens, the coach must try to convince all the players (**especially the most gifted and influential players**) of the need to do things differently, explaining the possible consequences if there is any resistance to the change. That is especially important with the leaders or key-players. When they (together with the coach) accept and follow the new behavior patterns, the rest of the players will follow suit.

In the process of formulating positive guidelines for the team, the coach should give his players the opportunity to participate in a workshop to define them clearly and to allow them to familiarize themselves with the guidelines. This will assure that the agreed rules of conduct will be applied later.

Although the main objective in a match is to win, there are exceptions. When, for instance, the development of a game demonstrates clearly that one team is far superior to its opposition, the members of the weaker team, thinking that there is no way to win the match, lose motivation, interest and aggressiveness. To avoid this possible apathy, the coach should set objectives with **a clear performance target** which is not victory but something else which favors the team's spirit and preparation for the next match. The coach can ask his players to completely ignore the result at that moment and start to play a new game with a 0:0 score. Now from this moment onwards the team does everything to not concede another goal, which means that they try to keep the team compact with short distances between the line of forwards, midfielders and defenders. This gives the defenders more possibilities to help one another. Furthermore, the coach tells his team to try to keep the opposition from playing the ball more than 3 times into their penalty area. If these partial objectives have been achieved and if every player has done his very best, the team can leave the pitch after the defeat with their heads up even after having been defeated by a difference of 3 goals.

* See Locke ,Edwin A.,and Gary P.Latham: "Establishing Objectives in Sport", in the Sports Psychology Journal, Vol.7, 1985, 205-222

"While a player shows responsibility to his teammates when accomplishing his role he should know that he achieves his goals not only through hard work but also through the enjoyment of playing"

STIMULATING
GAME INTELLIGENCE AND THE
UNDERSTANDING OF SOCCER

*"Good coaching should take a performer beyond the
limitations of the coach's own knowledge"*
John Whitmore

TOWARDS A CHANGE OF THE COACHING STYLE

Nothing is permanent, with the exception of change. We belong to a society inextricably linked to change, where new knowledge appears daily, opening new possibilities we could have never imagined some decades ago. What is considered valid today could already be out of date tomorrow, due to the frenetic evolution in many aspects of life.

The path to success is always under construction. The construction has to be seen as a process, not as an objective that must be reached in a particular given time. The game of soccer evolves continuously, and every coach should aim to adapt to its ever-changing demands to stay competitive.

One of the principle aims in the formation of soccer coaches is developing people who are able to do new things and inject new ideas into the game, rather than blindly repeating what other generations of coaches did in the past. Striving for excellence demands more creativity, innovation, and mental flexibility. Instead of teaching their players what they experienced during their careers as players and coaches, they must learn to unlock the innate and dormant potential of their players and to guide them finally **beyond their limitations**.

How can coaches achieve this? First of all, the tutors of future coaches (as well as those who already train players on a daily basis) should make sure that:
- **divergent thinking** in their pupils is encouraged,
- every individual feels free to **express his personal opinions**,
- **new technical-tactical movements** are developed and applied,
- being **creative and innovative** is part of the success in the game,
- players generate most of their knowledge and experience **on their own**.

In other words, **they should apply a different style of teaching that is not based on mere instruction**. Instead of acting as instructors or trainers, coaches should become consultants, observers, planners, and organizers of information and skills, trying to stimulate their pupils to advance and to excel until they are able to even surpass the coach's own limitations.

Up until very recently, soccer training was all about the execution of movements, leaving aspects like cognition (knowledge) and motivation to one side.

In recent years the coach has taken on a very different role. Instead of being a technical-tactical coach who tells his players what to do in particular situations in the match, he is more like a teacher who, apart from stimulating the technical, tactical and physical capacities in his players, assures that they understand what they are doing and why they are doing it and not the other way around. Instead of concentrating only on how to execute the skills, now coaches guide their pupils in improving at the same time their capacity to read the game (their perception skills) and also their decision making.

A SHIFT TO LESS INSTRUCTION AND MORE STIMULATION

The traditional way of teaching and learning based on instructions which didn't allow the student or player to contribute actively to the solution of any problem needs to be changed. Instead the coach must give space and time to his students to discover the problems or game situations by themselves to allow them to perceive correctly, to collate data, to evaluate, to judge and to organize the information, to remember solutions, to come to conclusions, to imagine, to invent and create.

Teaching this way we follow the advice from Johan Wolfgang von Goethe some 200 years ago: *"Youth prefer to be stimulated instead of being instructed!"*

According to John Whitmore in *Coaching of Performance**, a pupil only remembers 19 percent of what the teacher taught him some three months ago through instruction or telling, whereas he can recall 32 percent of what was demonstrated and explained. Yet in cases where pupils were given the opportunity to generate the information on their own, but with help of a teacher, fully 65 percent of the information was memorized.

That is why **soccer players should be allowed to actively participate in the coaching and learning process** in order to develop complete athletes who eventually become independent from the frequent instructions of coaches which may limit them. True learning takes place best when the decisions which up to now have been made by the coach are now made by the pupils.

Bloom considers human creativity as the pinnacle of mental activity and human achievement. Unfortunately, few coaches know how to stimulate this ability in their players. The teaching styles and rigid methods seen on most soccer fields tend to strangulate more than stimulate the player's capacity for creativity.

During training, instead of giving their players sufficient opportunity to cultivate these innate capacities present in everyone to a greater or lesser degree, coaches tend to control and dominate everything, fearful of losing control of the situation by giving up any control to the player. **Often the pupil learns even better without the presence of an instructor.** A coach's objective is to open the mind of his players so that they can improve and have the possibility to generate new ideas. **With his questions he should make the players think**, instead of thinking for them and giving them constant instruction, without realizing that this style of coaching is limiting a player's learning potential.
Expert coaches with a wide wealth of technical-tactical knowledge often have a

"Playing soccer without thinking is like shooting at goal without aiming"

hard time withholding their expertise. However, those who know a lot do not necessarily have a lot to give. They are used to imparting their knowledge through constant instructions about what, when and how to do the task instead of encouraging their pupils to discover what's right or wrong, allowing them to generate their own experiences. **Too often, coaches give their players solutions to remember instead of problems to resolve on their own**.

THE SKILL OF POSING QUESTIONS

To develop the players' active involvement in the training and learning process, coaches must master the skill of posing questions. Awareness and responsibility are better raised by asking than by telling. It follows therefore that the primary form of verbal interaction from a good coach is the **interrogative**.

The most effective questions are open ones that require descriptive answers. In contrast, closed questions with "yes" or "no" answers shut the door on the exploration of further detail. That is why coaches should concentrate on **open questions**, ones that begin with words that seek to quantify or gather facts: what, when, how much or how many.

Through systematic questioning by the coach, the pupils are self-generating the information. Thanks to intelligent questions, many players become aware of problems that they have never noticed before. They bring into consciousness those partially obscured factors that later on make the difference between winning and losing.

The questions should pique the interest of the players, oblige them to think, examine, judge and evaluate until they find solutions to the problem presented by the coach. On the contrary, when the coach instructs or just tells the player what to do in certain moments or situations of the game, he does not stimulate any of these active mental processes and the player becomes passive.

Once soccer coaches have been convinced of the need to modify their style of coaching, from beginners up to the national team, they soon discover **the key to unlocking and developing the innate potential and game intelligence of their players** and with their improved performance levels game of soccer will rise to the levels we dreamed of decades ago.

"When a coach instructs he denies or neglects a player's intelligence. When he asks, he honors it"

BIBLIOGRAPHY

Almond, L. 1983 "Teaching games through action research" Pp.185-189 en "Teaching Team Sports"   Roma: Comitato Olimpico Nazionale Italiano/Scuola dello Sport

Blázquez, D. 1986: "Iniciación a los deportes de equipo", Barcelona, Martínez Roca

Blázquez, D.1995: "La iniciación deportiva y el deporte escolar", Barcelona INDE Publicaciones

Coca, S. 1985: "Hombres para el Fútbol"- Una aproximación humana al estudio psicológico del futbolista en competición, Gymnos Editorial (Madrid)

Dietrich, K 1968: "Fussball spielgemäss lernen- spielgemäss -üben" , Karl Hofmann Verlag, Schorndorf (Alemania)

Dietrich, K./Landau.G. 1976: "Beiträge zur Didaktik der Sportspiele" Tel 1: Spiel in der Leibeserziehung - Kkarl Hofmann Verlag, Schorndorf (Alemania)

"Il Nuevo Calcio" , Revista Mensual del "Editoriale Sport Italia S.r.l", Via Masaccio12, 20149 Milano (Italia)

Leitner, S. 1991: "So lernt man lernen" Freiburg (Alemania) Herder Verlag

Mahlo, F. 1981: "La acción táctica en el juego" La Habana :Ed. Pueblo y Educación

Martín, D. 1982: "Grundlagen der Trainingslehre" Schorndorf (Alemania) KarlHofmann Verlag

Millmann, D. 1979: "The Warrior Athlete-Body,Mind and Spirit", Walpole, NH: Stillpoint Publishing

Moorehouse, L./Gross, L. 1977: "Maximum Performance" , New York: Mayflower Granada,Publishing

Mosston,M. 1988: "La enseñanza de la Educación Física", Buenos Aires, Ediciones Paidos

Ostrander, S./ Osrander, N. /Schroeder, L. 1979 "Leichter lernen ohne Stress - Superlearning", Bern, Scherz Verlag

Robbins, A. 1987: " Poder sin limites ", Barcelona, Ediciones Grijalbo

Spackmann, L. 1983: "Orientamenti practici per l'insegnamento dei giochi " en L´ insegnamento dei Giochi Sportivi ", Roma, CONI-Scuola dello Sport

Thorpe, R./Bunker ,D. 1983: "A new approach in teaching of games in physical education curriculum" en"Teaching Team Sports", Roma , CONI -Scuola dello Sport

Thorpe, R./Bunker,D /Almond,L. 1988: "Rethinking games teaching" , Northans, England, Loughborough University

Whitmore, J. 1997: "Coaching for Performance", London, Nicholas Brealey Pub.

Ziglar, Z 1986: "Pasos hacia la cumbre del éxito", Bogotá Editorial Norma,S.A.h"

RESUME OF HORST WEIN

- Masters degree in Physical Education from "Deutsche Sporthochschule Köln with Hennes Weisweiler (Borussia MG, FC Köln, FC Barcelona and NY Cosmos)

- Lecturer for P.E. at "Universität Münster", "Techn. Universität München" and at the "Instituto Nacional de Educación Física" de Barcelona

- Head Coach of the German (2 years) and Spanish Hockey National Team (12 years) with an Olympic Silver Medal and a European Cup Gold Medal

- First coach of the western world to be invited by the Soviet Union to train their top athletes in Moskow and Alma-Ata

- Selector of the Hockey World XI and coach of the European Hockey XI in1974

- Director in the Sports Department of the Organizing Committee of the XX Olympiad in Munich and assisted in the organization of the Asian Games inTeheran

- Regular cooperation with the International Olympic Committee "Olympic Solidarity"

- Lecturer of the "Centre of research and development" (CEDIF) of the Royal Spanish Football Federation and the Andalusian Football Federation

- Assessor in recycling the knowledge of the football (soccer) coaches of Inter Milan,
  Universidad Nacional Autónoma de Mexico ("Pumas"),
  Youth Football Federation of Uruguay (Comisión Nacional de Baby Fútbol)
  Cruz Azul de México and Club de América (México)
  Club Atlético Peñarol de Montevideo and Nacional Montevideo (Uruguay)
  "Universidad de Fútbol "in Pachuca and FC Pachuca (México)
  Club de Fútbol Nacional de Montevideo (Uruguay)
  Universidad Católica de Chile
  Santa Fè de Bogotá
  FC Sunderland, Arsenal and Leeds United (England)
  Necaxa and Rayados de Monterrey (México)
  INAF- Instituto Nacional de Fútbol in Chile
  National Institute of Sports in Colombia
  The English Football Federation
  Northern Ireland Institute of Coaching
  Universitorio de Deportes de Lima, Alianza Lima and Sporting Cristal (Peru)
  Escuela Superior de Entrenadores de Fútbol (Eseful) in Lima (Peru)
  Head Coach of NIKE Football Club (UK),
  Scottish Football Association
  Federacíon Salvadoreña de Fútbol
  Federación Nacional Autonoma de Fútbol de Honduras

- FIH Master Coach with coaching assignments in 5 Olympic sports in 53 countries

- Author of 31 sport text books, two Multimedia Football Coaching Courses, one CD, videos, one DVD and numerous articles in magazines and web pages, some published in Spanish, German, English, Dutch, Italian, Japanese and Russian.

e-mail:horstwein@eresmas.net   Tel./Fax: 34- 93-6746246